Indochina Monographs

Intelligence

by

Col. Hoang Ngoc Lung

U.S. ARMY CENTER OF MILITARY HISTORY

WASHINGTON, D.C.

Library of Congress Cataloging in Publication Data

Lung, Hoang Ngoc.
    Intelligence.

    (Indochina monographs)
    Distributed free to government and academic research
libraries.
    1. Military intelligence--Vietnam. 2. Military
intelligence--United States. I. Title. II. Series.
UB251.V5L86   959.704'38   81-10844
                                      AACR2

Reprinted 1984

CMH PUB 92-14

This book is not copyrighted and may be reproduced in
whole or in part without consulting the publisher

Indochina Monographs

This is one of a series published by the U.S. Army Center of Military History. They were written by officers who held responsible positions in the Cambodian, Laotian, and South Vietnamese armed forces during the war in Indochina. The General Research Corporation provided writing facilities and other necessary support under an Army contract with the Center of Military History. The monographs were not edited or altered and reflect the views of their authors--not necessarily those of the U.S. Army or the Department of Defense. The authors were not attempting to write definitive accounts but to set down how they saw the war in Southeast Asia.

Colonel William E. Le Gro, U.S. Army, retired, has written a monograph (1981) allied with this series, Vietnam: From Cease-Fire to Capitulation. Another book, The Final Collapse by General Cao Van Vien, the last chairman of the South Vietnamese Joint General Staff, will be formally published and sold by the Superintendent of Documents.

Taken together these works should provide useful source materials for serious historians pending publication of the more definitive series, the U.S. Army in Vietnam.

                                                JAMES L. COLLINS, JR.
                                                Brigadier General, USA
                                                Chief of Military History

INDOCHINA MONOGRAPHS

TITLES IN THE SERIES
(title--author/s--LC Catalog Card)

The Cambodian Incursion--Brig. Gen. Tran Dinh Tho--79-21722	CMH PUB 92-4
The Easter Offensive of 1972--Lt. Gen. Ngo Quang Truong--79-20551	CMH PUB 92-13
The General Offensives of 1968-69--Col. Hoang Ngoc Lung--80-607931	CMH PUB 92-6
Intelligence--Col. Hoang Ngoc Lung--81-10844/AACR2	CMH PUB 92-14
The Khmer Republic at War and the Final Collapse--Lt. Gen. Sak Sutsakhan--79-607776	CMH PUB 92-5
Lam Son 719--Maj. Gen. Nguyen Duy Hinh--79-607101	CMH PUB 92-2
Leadership--General Cao Van Vien--80-607941	CMH PUB 92-12
Pacification--Brig. Gen. Tran Dinh Tho--79-607913	CMH PUB 92-11
RLG Military Operations and Activities in the Laotian Panhandle--Brig. Gen. Soutchay Vongsavanh--81-10934/AACR2	CMH PUB 92-19
The RVNAF--Lt. Gen. Dong Van Khuyen--79-607963	CMH PUB 92-7
RVNAF and U.S. Operational Cooperation and Coordination--Lt. Gen. Ngo Quang Truong--79-607170	CMH PUB 92-16
RVNAF Logistics--Lt. Gen. Dong Van Khuyen--80-607117	CMH PUB 92-17
Reflections on the Vietnam War--General Cao Van Vien and Lt. Gen. Dong Van Khuyen--79-607979	CMH PUB 92-8
The Royal Lao Army and U.S. Army Advice and Support--Maj. Gen. Oudone Sananikone--79-607054	CMH PUB 92-10
The South Vietnamese Society--Maj. Gen. Nguyen Duy Hinh and Brig. Gen. Tran Dinh Tho--79-17694	CMH PUB 92-18
Strategy and Tactics--Col. Hoang Ngoc Lung--79-607102	CMH PUB 92-15
Territorial Forces--Lt. Gen. Ngo Quang Truong--80-15131	CMH PUB 92-9
The U.S. Adviser--General Cao Van Vien, Lt. Gen. Ngo Quang Truong, Lt. Gen. Dong Van Khuyen, Maj. Gen. Nguyen Duy Hinh, Brig. Gen. Tran Dinh Tho, Col. Hoang Ngoc Lung, and Lt. Col. Chu Xuan Vien--80-607108	CMH PUB 92-1
Vietnamization and the Cease-Fire--Maj. Gen. Nguyen Duy Hinh--79-607982	CMH PUB 92-3
The Final Collapse--General Cao Van Vien--81-607989	CMH PUB 90-26

Preface

The war in Vietnam was often called an intelligence war. The challenges and responsibilities placed on the South Vietnam—United States—Free World intelligence community were great and constant.

During this long war the entire intelligence program improved each day as our data base expanded, as more was learned about the elusive enemy, personnel were trained, and new procedures and techniques were tested and found effective.

The most rewarding experience in intelligence activities during the Vietnam war was the very close cooperation and coordination between American and Vietnamese military intelligence personnel and systems. It was this cooperation that helped RVNAF military intelligence upgrade and become self-reliant during the post-cease-fire period.

This monograph attempts to record all the facts concerning intelligence activities, its organizations and coordination procedures, its successes and failures during the period from 1965 to the final days of the Republic of Vietnam. In this attempt, one of the difficulties I faced was the lack of documentation to help make my work more accurate and more substantial. To overcome this shortcoming, I have interviewed several former colleagues of mine, American and Vietnamese, all of them highly experienced with intelligence activities in Vietnam. Apart from their invaluable contributions, most of the writing was based on my personal knowledge and experience.

I am indebted to General Cao Van Vien, Chairman of the Joint General Staff, Lieutenant General Dong Van Khuyen, Chief of Staff—under whom I served several years as Assistant Chief of Staff J2, JGS—, and

Brigadier General Tran Dinh Tho, Assistant Chief of Staff J-3, JGS, for their valuable comments. Lieutenant General Ngo Quang Truong, Commanding General of I Corps and Major General Nguyen Duy Hinh, Commander of the 3d Infantry Division, contributed thoughtful remarks and the practical view of field commanders.

Finally, I am particularly indebted to Lieutenant Colonel Chu Xuan Vien and Ms. Pham Thi Bong. Lt. Colonel Vien, the last Army Attache serving at the Vietnamese Embassy in Washington, D.C., has done a highly professional job of translating and editing. Ms. Bong, a former Captain in the Republic of Vietnam Armed Forces and also a former member of the Vietnamese Embassy staff, spent long hours typing, editing and in the administrative preparation of my manuscript in final form.

McLean, Virginia
31 October 1976

Hoang Ngoc Lung
Colonel, ARVN

Contents

Chapter		Page
I.	INTRODUCTION	1
	Nature of The Vietnam War	2
	Role of Intelligence in the Vietnam War	10
II.	INTELLIGENCE, CULTURE, AND LANGUAGE	18
	Characteristics of Vietnamese Culture and Language	18
	Communist Culture and Language	22
	South Vietnamese Culture and Language	26
	Language, Translation and Cultural Interpretation	31
III.	REPUBLIC OF VIETNAM AND UNITED STATES INTELLIGENCE ORGANIZATIONS IN SOUTH VIETNAM	37
	The RVN National and Local Intelligence Coordination Committees	37
	Vietnamese Civilian Intelligence Agencies	46
	Vietnamese Military Intelligence Organizations	54
	United States Intelligence Organizations in Vietnam before the Paris Agreement	76
IV.	INTELLIGENCE COOPERATION AND COORDINATION	79
	Concepts and Problems	79
	Combined Intelligence Activities	81
	Intelligence Cooperation and Coordination at The Field Level	109
	Military Intelligence Detachments (MID)	111
	Cooperation and Coordination in Human Intelligence	112
	Cooperation and Coordination in Aerial Photo Reconnaissance	118
	Signal Intelligence	123
	Intelligence Training	126
V.	MILITARY INTELLIGENCE COOPERATION AND COORDINATION IN VIETNAM FOLLOWING UNITED STATES MILITARY DISENGAGEMENT	129
	Defense Attache Office, Intelligence Branch	129
	Difficulties Encountered	131
	United States-ARVN Intelligence Cooperation and Coordination In the Face of New Difficulties	136
	Conclusions	143

Chapter	Page
VI. SUCCESSES AND FAILURES OF ARVN INTELLIGENCE	145
The 1968 General Offensive	145
The 1972 Easter Offensive	153
The Post-Cease-Fire Period	158
The 1975 General Offensive	180
VII. COMMUNIST INTELLIGENCE	192
North Vietnam's Intelligence Theory and Practice	192
North Vietnam Intelligence Agency	196
COSVN Intelligence Organization	198
Sources and Dispatching Methods	208
Successes and Failures of Enemy Intelligence	216
An Evaluation of Enemy Intelligence	221
VIII. CONCLUSIONS	232
GLOSSARY	241

Table

No.		Page
1.	Interrogation Process	100

Charts

No.		Page
1.	Organization, National Intelligence Coordination Committee	39
2.	Organization, Provincial Intelligence and Operations Coordination Committee	43
3.	Organization, District Intelligence and Operations Coordination Committee	43
4.	Organization, Central Intelligence Office	46
5.	Organization, National Police Command	50
6.	Organization, Military Security Department	56
7.	Organization, Special Technical and Security Branch	58
8.	Organization, Divisional Technical Detachment	60
9.	Organization, RVNAF Military Intelligence	65
10.	Organization, J-2, JGS	67
11.	Coordination and Supervision of Combined Intelligence Centers	68
12.	Organization, G-2/Corps	70
13.	Organization, Sector/Security/Intelligence Platoon	72
14.	Organization, Air Intelligence	73
15.	Organization, Naval Intelligence	75
16.	Organization, Combined Intelligence Center, Vietnam	85
17.	Organization, Combined Document Exploitation Center	92
18.	RVNAF, Document Evacuation Channel	93
19.	Routing of Communist Documents Captured by FWMAF	95
20.	Combined Interrogation Compound Layout	98
21.	US Element, Combined Interrogation Center	97
22.	ARVN Element, Combined Interrogation Center	99
23.	RVNAF, POW Evacuation Channel	102

No.		Page
24.	US Forces, POW Evacuation Channel	102
25.	Organization, Combined Materiel Exploitation Center	106
26.	Organization, Unit 101	114
27.	Organization, DAO Intelligence Branch	129
28.	Organization, Unit 306 — J-2, JGS	132
29.	Enemy Military Command Organization	200

Maps

1.	Location of J-7 Centers and Stations	61
2.	Location of Division Technical Detachments	62
3.	Radar Control System	165
4.	Deployment of Tanks and APC	166
5.	Deployment of Heavy Artillery	167
6.	New Route 14 or Truong Son Corridor	169
7.	Pipeline Systems	170
8.	Enemy Territorial Organization in South Vietnam	199

Illustrations

Aerial View of Dong Ha — Post-Cease-Fire Period	160
Communist Radio Equipment	171
Soviet Portable Flame-Thrower — Model LPO	172
Soviet 23-mm Automatic Anti-Aircraft Gun ZU-23	173
Caliber .30 .50 Anti-Aircraft Machine Guns	174
Soviet 57-mm Anti-Aircraft Guns — Model S-6	175
Soviet Field Guns and Howitzers	176
Soviet Armored Personnel Carriers	177
Chicom T-59 Tank	178
SA-7 Anti-Aircraft Missile and "SAGGER" Anti-Tank Missile AT-3	179
Air Attack on Tan Son Nhut Air Base, April 28, 1975	191
Nha Be Pol Storage Destroyed by Sappers, Dec 2, 1973	218

CHAPTER I

Introduction

During the Vietnam war, there was a constant improvement of intelligence as each day passed. It is usually recognized that during the final years of cooperation between the Republic of Vietnam and United States combat forces, the commanders at most echelons were better informed about the enemy than in any war in the histories of these two nations.

This was made possible because of the close coordination and cooperation between RVN and US Military Intelligence personnel and activities. This cooperation of joint planning, execution and exchange of information was essential because the RVN and the US were faced with an elusive enemy who, justifiably enough, earned such rhetorical qualifications as "unknown" or "mythical". Knowledge about the enemy, as we confronted him in Vietnam, was not an easy proposition. But it was not an unattainable goal, nor did it elude our success altogether.

There is general agreement that the Vietnam war was a complex venture. It was this complexity that heavily influenced intelligence activities and subjected them to unprecedented challenges. As a result, an examination of intelligence, its organizations, its successes and failures must be made in the context of the war and preceded by an insight into its nature, its historical perspective and the opposing views that each side held with regard to its basic goals in this war.

Nature of the Vietnam War

A recent popular Vietnamese folk song about the war laments:

> "A thousand years of domination by the Chinese invaders, A hundred years of domination by the French invaders, Twenty years of internecine fighting, day in day out."[1]

In just a few phrases, the song eloquently sums up the long history of Vietnam, the history of a small nation constantly plagued by wars. Through many invasions from the North, the Chinese repeatedly attempted to annex the tiny Viet nation, and to subjugate and assimilate the Viet people. During the ten centuries of Chinese domination, from 111 B.C. to 938 A.D., numerous Vietnamese heroes rose up against the invaders to wrest back their independence. No Vietnamese can forget the story of Trieu Quang Phuc, the first Vietnamese military leader who employed guerrilla tactics to defeat the invaders of the Liang kingdom (7th century), or Emperor Quang Trung who, by a surprise blitzkrieg, annihilated the Ching corps at the end of the 18th century.[2]

Then came the French who created a colony out of Vietnam for nearly a century from 1858 to 1945. The history of Vietnam under French suzerainty abounds in heroic uprisings and resistance movements, all of them waged with the sole purpose of reclaiming national identity and independence. Not until 1945 was this independence finally restored and precariously maintained before the whole nation was plunged into war against the French who sought again to impose their rule. It was unfortunate that this anti-colonialist war, although fought by the whole people, was led by hard line Communist cadres. This was gradually to

---

[1] "Mother's Legacy", composed by Trinh Cong Son.

[2] The given name of Emperor Quang Trung is Nguyen Hue. The Communists chose Nguyen Hue as code name for their 1972 Easter Offensive because they were greatly impressed by the blitzkrieg tactic used by the Emperor to annihilate 200,000 Ching invaders in 1789.

change the nature of the war when it became apparent that the Viet Minh regime was leaning toward socialism through the "agrarian reform" of 1950.

Up until that time, the Viet Minh had not revealed the future direction of their regime. The people believed they fought a sacrosanct war for national independence, no one anticipated that the cause they were fighting for was to serve the Communist leaders' own purpose.

In 1950, the Viet Minh leaders launched a country-wide "Agrarian Reform" campaign, the first step toward creating an egalitarian society. This proved to be their biggest mistake because the excesses and brutality of zealous cadres completely alienated the land-owners and, by extension, most of the educated "petite bourgeoise."[3] It was a turning point and the seed of ideological difference, heretofore submerged beneath the patriotic fervor, began to take roots.

But the real turnabout came when the Republic of Vietnam became an independent nation south of the 17th parallel. For the first time since 1945, a sense of national identity prevailed — which emboldened the Vietnamese of the South to defy and oppose the Communist regime in the North. Now that they were able to live under a regime of their choice, they were willing to defend it when it came under threat.

It was not the first time though that the Vietnamese fought among themselves. During its long history, Vietnam had been the theater of many fratricidal wars, the longest and hardest of which lasted over a century, from 1627 to 1774. This was the contest between the Trinh dynasty in the North and the Nguyen dynasty in the South. Within a period of forty-five years, large-scale warfare broke out six times in the Dong Hoi area (16th parallel) between the feuding dynasties. In the end, both sides were exhausted and neither was powerful enough to dominate

---

[3] The Agrarian Reform campaign gave rise to many resentments among the Vietnamese population, and even among Communist cadres and troops. Truong Chinh who was responsible for this campaign, was then released from his post as secretary general of the Labor Party in 1956 by order of Ho Chi Minh.

the other. So they reconciled their difference and agreed to coexist on either side of the 16th parallel until 1774 when the Tay Son dynasty defeated both of them and reunified the country.

The remarkable thing about all these civil wars was that no matter which dynasty came to power, the regime remained basically the same and monarchy was maintained. The people by and large hardly felt any difference in their lives.

However, as early as in 1945, when the national purpose focused on reclaiming independence, first from the Japanese and later from the French, a new and most difficult question arose concerning what kind of regime was in store for Vietnam in the immediate future. For although the people would readily accept any government within a definite regime, they would not readily consent to any regime. As a result, a shift in national purpose gradually took hold and the struggle for independence gradually gave way to a conflict whose objective became the search for an appropriate political system. This polarization of political convictions among the Vietnamese turned the conflict into an ideological war fought between the Communists on one side and the Nationalists on the other.

For twenty years, this war dragged on. Its duration was a measure of its complexity because, in contrast with the Trinh-Nguyen contest which was local in nature, the war between the North and the South of Vietnam today was fought under the influence and with the implications of an international conflict.

Communist Viewpoint

To the North Vietnamese, their war aimed at achieving a socialist regime for Vietnam. In their view, the war was a just war led by the Communist Party on behalf of the working class. Their duty lay not only with the national cause but also with the international Communist movement, because the history of international proletarian revolution greatly influenced the way North Vietnam conducted the war. For them, the 1917

Russian Revolution and the Chinese Communist take-over of 1949 had invaluable lessons to be applied to the Vietnam war. As a matter of fact, the North Vietnamese conduct of the war almost exactly duplicated the pattern used by the Chinese Communists. The handbook entitled "Out Enduring Resistance Certainly Wins" by Truong-Chinh who is considered as North Vietnam's foremost theoretician, contains arguments drawn from Mao Tse Tung's work, "Yu Chi Chan" (Protracted War). According to Truong-Chinh, the Vietnam war and the war in China bear remarkable resemblance in that they were both fought against much larger and more powerful enemies. Consequently, success must depend upon the time factor. Time was necessary, Truong-Chinh argued, to create a balance of forces which would increasingly favor the underdog.

Oriental philosophy is at the source of this concept of time. Whereas the Western world thinks of time in the short term (time is money), and favors the military concept of lightning war (blitzkrieg) and speedy victory, the Orientals believe they have all the time they need to achieve their goals. To them, perseverance is the key to success. As a result, the guiding principle in China as well as in Vietnam is to "give up space in order to gain time". Hence, the fundamental approach to conflict is the conduct of protracted war. The Communists theorized that a protracted war of resistance would progress through three military phases:[4]

   First stage: Strategy — defensive; tactics — attack
   Second stage: Strategy — stiff resistance (preparing for offensive); tactics — attack
   Third stage: Strategy and tactics — counter-offensive

In more descriptive terms, Phase 1 aims at organizing, consolidating and preserving forces; Phase 2 aims at progressively expanding the forces and Phase 3 is the decisive phase whose aim is the destruction of the enemy. The transition from one phase to the next was discussed by Ho Chi Minh, "It is possible to examine the general situation in order to divide it into big stages, but it is not possible to cut off completely one stage

---

[4]Truong Chinh, *Primer for Revolt* (Praeger, New York, London 1963), p. 154.

from the other like cutting bread. The length of each stage depends on the situation in the home country and in the world, and on the changes between the enemy forces and ours."

Truong-Chinh follows in Mao's steps when he asserts that Phase 3 can be extended because of the possibility of negotiations. The customary concepts of reciprocation, of give and take, are not included in Truong-Chinh's idea of negotiation. The Revolution's goal excludes compromise. Negotiations are conducted with the sole purpose of gaining time, the time necessary to consolidate friendly forces and at the same time to attrite and wear down the enemy. In his work, "People's War, People's Army," Vo Nguyen Giap reasserts that the concept of protracted resistance and the three-phase strategy are the most correct military conduct to confront the enemy's military strategy of lightning attack and lightning success. According to Giap, protracted war will evolve from guerrilla warfare to conventional warfare and a war of movement coordinated with attacks against enemy's strongholds. Guerrilla warfare is the kind of war fought by an armed force which is technically inferior and lesser-equipped, but which prevails because it has the morale and spirit to challenge and overcome advanced weapons and technique. However, as Mao observes, guerrilla warfare cannot achieve victory because it can only be likened to the mud which bogs down an enemy but can never destroy him. Hence, guerrilla warfare ought to be closely coordinated with a war of movement and the relative importance of its role depends on the situation pertaining to each phase.

Protracted war, however, cannot be conducted if all the people, all ages and both sexes, do not participate in it, and the people in the rear of the battlefield must support the front. Lenin wrote, "In order to wage a real war, there must be a solid and well organized rear." The concept of people's war includes the concept of participation and contribution. Truong Chinh emphasized, "Wealthy people should contribute their wealth, strong people should contribute their strength, talented people should contribute their talents to the Resistance," for war is not fought only on the military front, it is also fought in all other areas:

political, economic and cultural. Political warfare seeks to unite the entire people, while diplomatic activities gain the sympathy of all the world and isolate the enemy.

The economic struggle strives to achieve a self-sufficient economy and at the same time to "encircle" the enemy's economy by sabotaging all instruments of production and preventing the enemy from "using the war to feed the war." The cultural struggle must forge thoughts in order to create in the people the spirit and endurance required for a long war. Various forms of traditional propaganda like folk songs, group singing, and plays are used to inflame the people's spirit with new thought and dedication.

The three elements: "protracted," "all people" and "total" are the three principal elements for the conduct of the people's war, as Mao Tse Tung laid them down. However, the Vietnamese Communists have applied this concept of the people's war with creativeness of their own in order to fit the circumstances and exploit the situation in Vietnam. The situation changed radically after the Geneva Agreement in 1954 which created two political regimes, one in the North and one in the South. In 1960, when North Vietnam became seriously intent on conquering the South, its strategy in South Vietnam still bore the specific imprint of the "people's war." Nevertheless, the term "people's war" apparently was no longer deemed expedient by the North because it would imply the aggressive character of the war. As a result, another label was chosen for the war being waged in the South, a "revolutionary war," which implied that it was generated by the people of South Vietnam who revolted to overthrow the government of South Vietnam. The goal of the Revolution was to establish a people's "democratic" regime before crossing over to socialism. But whether "people's war" or "revolutionary war," the strategy still called for a protracted struggle to be conducted in three phases. But the concept of protracted war has undergone some change. While maintaining that their strategy was still a protracted war, the North Vietnamese argued that they could achieve their goal in a relatively short time.[5] It is noteworthy that this change in concept could have taken place at the time when there were strong indications that the United States would soon become

---

[5] North Vietnam Resolution No. 13, 1967.

directly involved in the Vietnam war. The fear that the people and cadre might loose heart at the prospects of a prolonged war against a great power impelled Le Duan, the Party's secretary general, to this argument. He emphasized that North Vietnam, having learned from experiences of the 1945-54 war, could achieve an early victory. In order to achieve this early victory, the Communists launched the general offensive, general uprising of 1968, or in conceptual terms, passed on to Phase 3.

After the offensive failed, there was an animated debate among the Communist cadres over the validity of the three-phase strategy.[6] If the strategy were still valid, it implied that the Communists had admitted to the failure of Phase 3 and a retrogression to Phase 2. In effect, through COSVN Resolution No. 9 issued in July 1969 the Communists directed a reversion to the earlier phase through "small attacks but assured successes." They presented a new argument for it, advocating abandonment of the three-phase strategy and instituting a single phase, the offensive.[7] They insisted that the "revolutionary war" of the South had become a total "people's war" involving all the people of Vietnam, North and South, and all aspects of their lives, and that the North had always been the "great rear area of the great front-line area."

South Vietnam Viewpoint

While the Communists always developed and expounded a clearly defined concept of the conduct of the war, the Republic of Vietnam never had a unified concept. To South Vietnam, the war was a defense against Communist aggression from the North. South Vietnam was an advanced outpost of the anti-Communist front in Southeast Asia. As such, it was entitled to help, to receive substantial aid for as long as it was necessary from the Free World, represented by the United States. Since it was a defensive war, its military strategy was to

---

[6]Captured enemy document, corroborated by POW's and ralliers.
[7]Ibid.

push ahead with the pacification of the territory and the population, to free them from the influence and threat of the Communists. To confront guerrilla warfare, the Army of South Vietnam had been organized and trained along the lines of a conventional army heavily dependent on fire power and mobility. Military tactics were based on conventional techniques and modern weapons. This was the inevitable by-product of the political circumstances prevailing in South Vietnam. The political instability in South Vietnam resulting from skirmishes between the various religious sects, the "revolution" of 1 November 1963, and the subsequent developments compelled total reliance on the US strategy in the conduct of the war from 1965 to 1969. The strategy called for the expansion of the RVN Armed Forces, from 400,000 to 1,100,000 men and their gradual take-over of combat responsibilities.[8] Following the 8 June 1969 Midway Conference a new program was initiated called Vietnamization. The armed forces of the Republic of Vietnam would gradually accept full responsibility for ground combat operations in place of US forces which along with other Allied forces, would be withdrawn from South Vietnam battlefields. After the Paris Agreement of 1973, and faced with the new military situation and the prospect of diminishing aid, a new concept was conceived for the conduct of the war, "fighting a poor man's war." A lesson was learned from this attempt, however. It is easier for an armed force to upgrade from guerrilla warfare to conventional warfare than the other way around.

Comparisons

In the Vietnam war, both North and South Vietnam depended heavily on foreign aid for every rifle, every cartridge, every drop of fuel and even every grain of rice. The major difference between the two sides resided in the fact that while receiving military and economic assistance, North Vietnam consistently conditioned their population and army psychologically to achieve self-sufficiency, relying primarily on their own

---

[8] Lieutenant General John H. Hay, Jr., <u>Tactical and Materiel Innovations</u> (Department of the Army, Washington, D.C.: 1974), p. 172.

resources and regarding aid as simply supplemental. This was not the case with South Vietnam for which foreign aid was a way of life. To the government as well as to the population, it was always expected that this abundant US aid would not terminate for as long as it was needed.

In addition, during the whole course of the war, North Vietnam enjoyed a continuity of leadership. From the start to the end, the same leaders directed the war effort and so there was consistency and continuity in the planning and conduct of the war. Furthermore, the institution had a memory and learned from experience. In contrast, political instability in South Vietnam denied it these advantages of leadership.

The war in Vietnam was an ideological war and also a war of mass psychology. For the North Vietnamese, who knew how to use their ideology to influence and take advantage of mass psychology, their war had proceeded in accordance with the rules they had laid out or projected. In contrast, not only was South Vietnam unable to employ mass psychology to support its ideological purpose, it had let mass psychology act on the rules of its war to the extent that, in the final months, a mere tactical blunder had turned into an uncontrollable event that set in motion the rapid deterioration of the situation. Perhaps this was a peculiarity of the Vietnam war.

Role of Intelligence in the Vietnam War

The importance of intelligence, as it influences political and military activities, is no matter of dispute. But while there exists universal agreement as to its importance, different concepts exist concerning the role of intelligence in decision-making, different subjective biases have influenced objective analysis of intelligence information, and differing technological capabilities have determined, to a large extent, the priorities adopted by nations in the employment of intelligence collection systems. Thus, national ideology and characteristics have greatly influenced the development of concepts and techniques of intelligence collection, analysis and exploitation. So when an examination is made of the intelligence effort of each of the parties involved in the Vietnam war, all the characteristics, strengths, and weaknesses of each participant can be found reflected in the way he organized and employed his intelligence systems.

North Vietnam placed great emphasis on intelligence. Its intelligence was organized and operated to achieve the political and military objectives of the war. Its intelligence structure was unified at the top, but the universal rule of compartmentalization was observed in the operation of human intelligence collection. North Vietnam placed greatest emphasis on human intelligence and included in this category was the institution of people's intelligence, conforming to the "all people" and "total" character of the people's war.

The US intelligence apparatus in Vietnam was part of and within the framework of the total US intelligence establishment. Thus, it relied primarily on advancements in science and technology. It reflected the characteristics of a great power which could afford a multiplicity of big organizations, each having its own collection apparatus and often competing with one another in collection, analysis and production of knowledge about the enemy. The contributions made by US intelligence, particularly in collection, were so effective that they created an abnormal reliance on US intelligence. The reliance was so great that many Vietnamese officials, including some military commanders, took it for granted that every piece of information coming from an American agency was valid regardless of the professional competence of the reporter or the authority of the source. Others even believed that no enemy move or scheme could ever go undetected by US collection networks and that if it did it was only because the US, for political reasons, wanted it to happen that way.

Brief History of RVN Intelligence

This over-reliance on US intelligence stemmed in part from the relative infancy of South Vietnamese intelligence. Small elements of the National Army of Vietnam were created as early as May 1950 but its general staff was not organized until two years later. By this time the army's strength had reached 120,000.[9] The first coherent South Vietnamese military intelligence organization was the J-2 element of the General Staff, with 32 men commanded by a Vietnamese captain. The Military Security Service (counterintelligence) activated at about the same time, was commanded by a Vietnamese major. In early 1953, a counterintelligence element was added to the General Staff as a separate staff component designated J-6. By July 1955, the authorized strength of J-2, General Staff, had been augmented to 46 with the activation of the Imagery Interpretation Center. But up until the day the Geneva Accords were signed in 1954, South Vietnamese military intelligence activities were performed by the French Forces' "Deuxieme Bureau" which functioned as a separate organization and acted on its own initiative. Unfortunately, but characteristically, when the French Forces withdrew from Vietnam they took with them all their experience and systems of collection as well as their intelligence files.

The Vietnamese officers who manned the J-2 section of the General Staff at that time were not career intelligence men. Only a handful of them had taken a basic, battalion-level intelligence course conducted by a French Officer at the Thu Duc Reserve Officer School. As required by the activation of new units, or the upgrading of existing ones, there was an urgent need to train intelligence officers. In September 1955, a number of English-speaking officers were selected to attend a Military Intelligence Course in the Philippines. They became the first instructors of the newly created Intelligence School. The incipient character of Vietnamese military intelligence was reflected by the original training materials prepared for the school. For example, in a training text on the subject "Importance of Intelligence in Combat," there was the following passage: "A newly commissioned Second Lieutenant was assigned to a unit. When he reported to the unit commander, the latter said, I will make you Intelligence Officer of the Battalion." "Consequently,"

---

[9] QLVNCH Trong Giai Doan Hinh Thanh, 1945 - 1954 (The RVNAF During Their Formative Years: 1945 - 1954 (Military History, Vol. 4, J-5/JGS, Saigon: 1972).

the text went on, "intelligence is very important." It is possible
that the instructor may have thought that he was adequately illustrating
the point that intelligence was important enough to be considered on a
par with other staff functions.

Politics and Intelligence

From 1954 to 1963, military intelligence efforts were largely
oriented toward collecting domestic political intelligence. It was the
period of political turmoil during which leaders of the First Republic
were faced with armed rebellions of religious sects in 1955-1956 and
later with the Buddhist opposition movement in 1963. The South Vietnamese
intelligence structure during that time was an agglomeration of separate
agencies each directly or indirectly controlled by the Presidency, but
all serving the same political goal of consolidating the new regime.
Under the Presidency, the Service of Social and Political Studies was
responsible for domestic political intelligence collection while the
Service of Liaison was charged with foreign intelligence, directed
primarily toward North Vietnam, and later on — with security protection
for the President and his closest advisers, Mr. and Mrs. Ngo Dinh Nhu.
When the Buddhist opposition movement reached its climax in 1963 with
the active participation of students, all intelligence agencies, both on
the civilian side and the military side, focused their activities on
gathering domestic political information. The J-2 of the Joint General
Staff thus found himself performing a task that went beyond his intended
mission and authority.

The November Revolution of 1963 brought about a complete reversal
of the process by decentralizing the intelligence structure and making
its constituent organizations separate and responsible to various
authorities. Thus, from a situation of complete centralization in the
office of the Presidency, the national organization for intelligence went
to the opposite extreme. The interplay of politics and competition for
power never permitted intelligence to achieve one of its basic operating
principles, unification of effort. The Service of Liaison found itself

placed under the Commander-in-Chief of the Armed Forces, the 300th Special Group, the strategic intelligence organization, was detached from J-2 and made responsible to the Office of the Chief of Staff, Joint General Staff. The Signal Intelligence Unit was attached to the Central Intelligence Office which reported directly to the Chief of State. Despite this subordination signal intelligence was often fed directly to field units without reference to or coordination with OACS, J-2. In 1964, when the government was turned over to civilians, the signal intelligence organization became an independent agency and was initially placed under the Ministry of Defense. Later, it was formed into a staff division and placed under the control of the Chief of Staff, JGS, with the designation J-7. Next the Military Security Service was transferred. It was placed under the General Directorate of Political Warfare instead of under the Ministry of Defense. This organizational concept was patterned after the Republic of China.

The domestic political situation made its impact on military intelligence. Lacking centralization and unified guidance, intelligence efforts became diffused and of little value. Adding to the problems, during this embryonic stage intelligence facilities were woefully inadequate and intelligence personnel still lacked technical know-how and professional experience. The military intelligence organizations operated independently of each other and the collection effort was limited geographically to South Vietnam. Intelligence pertaining to North Vietnam or Eastern Laos was produced only occasionally and did not constitute a systematic effort under centralized planning and direction. On the civilian side, the Central Intelligence Office was in theory responsible for gathering domestic political intelligence and foreign intelligence, both military and political. In practice, however, due to the political upheavals of the period, it concentrated its efforts on domestic politics, almost totally neglecting foreign intelligence. The General Directorate of National Police, which came under the Office of the Prime Minister, was responsible for public security and order, as well as intelligence concerning Communist infrastructure activities.

Commanders and Intelligence

South Vietnamese military intelligence came of age in 1965 when, as a result of the increased tempo of war, the national leadership began to appreciate its importance. The active participation of United States forces in the war brought about close intelligence coordination with RVN forces, and it was this coordination that gave the greatest impetus to Vietnamese military intelligence. The most remarkable progress was achieved in combat intelligence. A tremendous amount of information was collected about the enemy. However remarkable the progress, the exploitation of new opportunities for collection and the tactical use of the intelligence produced were not developed to their full potential. Because of their lack of intelligence training and experience, most Vietnamese commanders did not understand that intelligence was theirs to direct and use and not the exclusive property and responsibility of their intelligence officer. As a consequence, no effective efforts were made to improve intelligence collection or exploitation. To these commanders, there was but one estimate, that of his intelligence officer. The commander's estimate was something seldom found. Most military operations were conducted for the purpose of destroying the enemy and very rarely indeed were they attempted for the sake of gathering intelligence.

Military intelligence resources were frequently misused or even abused. It became a widespread practice for Intelligence and Security Teams at District level and Intelligence and Security Sections at Province level to be used more often in VIP escort and protection duties than in intelligence gathering. Reconnaissance companies organic to division and regimental units were primarily deployed as shock units or reinforcements. A tragic example of this occurred in the battle of Phuoc Long in December 1974. While Communist forces included two infantry divisions supported by artillery and armor units, the defense of the city was assigned to three reconnaissance companies detached from their respective divisions, the 5th, 18th, and 25th Infantry Divisions. The result was that all three companies were totally destroyed, and the three divisions of MR-3 were without reconnaissance capabilities when serious fighting broke out later.

Some commanders even went so far as to require their intelligence officers to produce estimates that befitted the commander's own view of the situation. If the commander's report on progress of pacification and development had been filled with good results, his intelligence officer was certainly not allowed to divulge any contradictory information, such as the increased activities of the enemy infrastructure, the enemy's success in collecting rice and taxes, etc. As an example, no effort had been made to report information contained in a captured enemy document indicating that during the first three months of 1973, the enemy in Dinh Tuong province had succeeded in collecting 40% of its 586-million piaster tax goal for 1973. Apparently, if such a report had ever been made the province chief's good standing with the central government would have suffered, and he had to make sure this never happened. On the contrary, if friendly losses in any important operation surpassed the normally acceptable figure, reports might list the enemy's capabilities as including a great number of units whose identities were yet to be confirmed. This falsification of facts ostensibly justified the losses incurred and covered up any deficiency which might have caused them. Furthermore, it established the basis for obtaining more operational support.

Besides this widespread practice, there was also a dangerous tendency among commanders to show off the extent of their knowledge about the enemy. Many vital sources of information that should have been kept secret, either because of their origin or importance, were unfortunately made public.

The war in Vietnam, as mentioned earlier, was an ideological conflict in which politics strongly influenced military policies and dictated the conduct of the war. While North Vietnam successfully used its dictatorial regime as a solid basis for the effective organization and operation of its intelligence system, South Vietnam suffered from political instability and from the interference between factional and transitional politics and military intelligence affairs. To become efficient and productive, an intelligence organization must be in effective command of time and space, because these two elements interweave and make up the intelligence coverage network. The larger the loops of the net, the greater the chance for the prey to escape. Time is necessary to provide continuity for intelligence operations. Space is needed to make knowledge thorough and complete. Knowledge about the enemy on the front line must be complemented by knowledge about the situation in his rear. In the case of the war in Vietnam, the enemy rear not only covered North Vietnam, it included by extension the whole Communist bloc, particularly the USSR and Red China.

Denied the capability to collect adequate information about the enemy outside South Vietnam and forced by internal political circumstances to operate a fragmented intelligence apparatus, South Vietnam intelligence agencies were ill equipped to perform their crucial tasks. In fact one might wonder, as in the other aspects of the war, whether internal rather than external factors most influenced the course of the war and brought about its tragic conclusion.

CHAPTER II

Intelligence, Culture, and Language

Characteristics of Vietnamese Culture and Language

Vietnam, because of its position in Southeast Asia, was initially a crossroads of two major civilizations that reacted vigorously with each other: the Chinese civilization and the Hindu civilization. The Chinese civilization finally prevailed and profoundly affected Vietnamese culture mainly because, in addition to the geographical proximity of the two countries, Vietnam had been politically subjugated by China for over a thousand years. During this long period of domination the Chinese attempted to absorb the Vietnamese people into their mass by direct assimilation. They imposed their philosophy, education, customs and manners, but the Vietnamese persistently resisted and endeavored to maintain their own culture and language. Although the Vietnamese borrowed their writing system from the Chinese for over ten centuries, they made a conscious effort to replace it gradually by a system of their own. Not until the 17th century (1627), however, was a romanized writing system created and officially adopted as the national script (Quoc Ngu). Chinese characters, as a result, were used only in traditional rites until recently. During the protracted struggle for survival and national independence, several Vietnamese generals of historical fame made use of cultural actions to win battles against Chinese invaders. General Ly Thuong Kiet of the Ly dynasty (10th century), for example, skillfully took advantage of the popular belief in mythology. In 1077, he planted one of his men in the Truong Hat temple to act as a demigod. To the accompaniment of bell tones, the man incanted a poem written in Chinese characters that aroused the morale of Vietnamese troops and upon which the Chinese invaders recoiled in utter confusion:

> The Emperor of the South rules over the land
> of the Southern Country;
> This destiny has been indelibly registered in
> the Heavenly Book;
> If you dare, rebellious savages, come violate it;
> You shall undoubtedly witness your own and complete defeat.[1]

Confronting the powerful Mongolian army in 1284, the great Vietnamese national hero, Marshal Tran Hung Dao, appealed to his troops through a resounding proclamation that bolstered their confidence and determination to fight. Emboldened by the proclamation, his troops tatooed the words "Sat Dat" on their arms, meaning they were resolved to kill the Mongolians.[2] Then, after defeating the Ming invaders in 1424, General Nguyen Trai issued the famous "Great Proclamation upon the Pacification of Wu", intended as a declaration of independence for the Vietnamese people and as an affirmation of viability of a separate national culture:

> Our nation, Greater Vietnam,
> Is founded on an ancient civilization.
> Its land and boundaries have changed,
> But its customs are always different
> from the North.[3]

---

[1] <u>Kham Dinh Viet Su</u>, 1960, p. 101. The original text reads:

> Nam Quoc Son Ha, Nam De Cu
> Tiet Nhien Dinh Menh Tai Thien Thu
> Nhu Ha Nghich Lo Lai Xam Pham
> Nhu Dang Hanh Khan Thu Bai Hu

[2] This practice was imitated by several ARVN troops after the 1968 general offensive. Instead of "Sat Dat", they tatooed "Sat Cong" (Kill Communists) on their arms.

[3] Excerpt from the original text which is written in Chinese characters. The Vietnamese translation of this passage reads:

> Nuoc Dai Viet ta
> Nen van hien cu
> Non nuoc coi bo da khac
> Bac, Nam, phong tuc van rieng

To the Vietnamese people, national independence was a subject of utmost importance. If the nation came under foreign domination, the Vietnamese believed that this domination would only be short-lived as long as they maintained a separate culture and a separate language. In the beginning of the 20th century when Vietnam had come under French colonial rule, Nguyen Ba Hoc, a famous scholar, commented prophetically:

> "If the Vietnamese language survives,
> Vietnam will survive."

His words are praised and venerated by every living Vietnamese. Vietnamese culture nevertheless bears a profound imprint of Chinese civilization and culture. Until recently, this influence was most conspicuously reflected in politics, economy, culture, and education. The traditional Vietnamese concepts of nationalism, national organization, public administration, laws and regulations were all patterned after Chinese institutions. Divisions of work, production, commerce, and the Vietnamese writing system, textbook, examination, etc. were either Chinese-introduced or borrowed from the Chinese. Before the introduction of Western culture, Confucius had been regarded by the Vietnamese as a saint and sage whose classics and moral teachings were accepted as intellectual criteria and behavioral rules. Among other things, Confucius professed the theory of "true expression" which says that "it's important to use words with accuracy; if words are not accurate, our expressions will be erroneous and our undertakings will fail." While not intended as a linguistic rule, the Confucian theory of true expression is in essence a philosophy which promotes social order, an order based on society's hierarchy and stratification. Confucian philosophy in many respects does not befit the basic tenets of Communism and represents a major challenge to Communist ideology, especially in backward societies like traditional China and Vietnam. Because of its popularity, however, North Vietnam Communists cunningly avoided attacking it publicly and chose instead to take advantage of it for their own purposes. For example, the war they waged in South Vietnam was called a war of liberation, a war of just cause because it was the Confucian "true expression" of the Vietnamese people's aspirations. For all its merits, Chinese culture made its impact felt only among the Vietnamese mandarinate and literates who made up the minority elite. The great majority of the populace, however, displayed and fostered its own kind of culture, a culture purely Vietnamese by nature. Throughout the generations, this culture has been expressed, recorded and propagated in the form of simple, short popular literary pieces such as proverbs, folk songs, lyrical poems and ritual chants. The composition of these songs and poems is simple, the language used plain and pleasant. When sung or incanted, their rhythm and tones create gracious and gay music sounds that express the ingenuous but emotional nature of a people who earnestly cling to their own way of life. This national character still exists today, and during the war both sides, North Vietnam and South Vietnam, made conscious efforts to employ these literary forms with a goal to win over, mobilize, and incite the people into working and fighting for a cause each side claimed as right.

Vietnam began to assimilate Western culture when the French occupied it in the middle of the 19th century. With its appealing novelties, the newly introduced Western civilization considerably altered the traditional Vietnamese way of life, which still had maintained ties with Chinese culture.

By 1945, under French colonial design, Vietnam was administratively divided into three separate regions: North, Center and South (Tonkin, Annam and Cochin-China, respectively). Although they speak the same language, the Vietnamese living in different regions have different phonetic pronunciations, several different terms and expressions, and a few highly localized accents. When two Vietnamese from different regions meet for the first time, they are usually conscious of the difference in their speech habits. This creates interesting difficulties but never prevents them from understanding each other. Apart from the Vietnamese, there also exist about two dozen ethnic groups, each of which speaks a different language.

The 1954 Geneva Accords partitioned Vietnam into two regions: North and South. Over 800,000 northerners chose to migrate South while nearly 80,000 southerners were regrouped to the North.[4] As a result, Vietnamese

---

[4] Latter figure based on Communist documents. RVN official reports estimated the number of southerner regroupees at 100,000.

speech gradually became more unified than ever before. However, with
the new demarcation line holding North and South incommunicado, with
opposing political regimes, and under different foreign cultural influences, there gradually developed profound differences between North
and South Vietnam in terms of culture and language, including military
terminology.

Communist Culture and Language

In North Vietnam, efforts were made by the Communist regime to
eliminate the lingering influence of Chinese classical education and
Confucian — Mencian philosophy, which are considered as expressions of
a feudalistic and backward heritage still deeply ingrained in Vietnamese
culture. Emphasis has equally been placed on the elimination of French
cultural influence which has been criticized as an instrument for in-
vasion, and the genesis of a romantic, "petit bourgeois" literature.
North Vietnam wanted to find a way toward a new culture consistent with
its regime and having the effect of popular attraction. This, the
Communists found in a complete return to the age-old popular culture
but they had to go through a transitional period. Initially, from
1948 to 1954, North Vietnam seemed to prefer the use of classical Chinese
vocabulary even in daily conversation. The language used by Communist
political cadre sounded especially pedantic and conceited, burdened as
it was by formal, archaic expressions that were no longer of popular
usage. It was the period during which Communist Chinese were taking over
mainland China. Their complete victory in 1949 spurred the North Vietnamese political cadre into a passionate study of Red Chinese revolutionary
methods, from theory to practice. It was also the period during which
North Vietnamese cadre were sent to China for training. Chinese training
materials were subsequently translated into Vietnamese. The use of
classical Chinese vocabulary became therefore widespread and fashionable.
Political slogans during this period used a mixture of Vietnamese and
classical Chinese terms, such as "Solidarity, Solidarity, greater Solidarity."

Ho Chi Minh himself usually quoted Chinese classics. His favorite phrase was "Progress must be made each day, every day, again and again."[5]

After North Vietnam became a separate nation above the 17th parallel in 1954 and after the first Indochina war had ended, it made a deliberate effort to build and restructure the Vietnamese culture and language after its political outlook. The first visible change was the disappearance of classical Chinese in language and terminology. More emphasis was placed on the use of simple, plain Vietnamese language with a view to make it easy to understand and memorize by the populace. For example, "truc thang" (helicopter), a term borrowed from classical Chinese, is now called "may bay len thang" (aircraft which rises vertically); "thuy quan luc chien" (Marines), also a term of Chinese origin, is called "linh thuy danh bo" (naval troops fighting on land). Several other terms, mostly military, went through the same transformation. Foreign geographical names which had heretofore been transcribed into Vietnamese through Chinese pronunciation and accepted in daily usage were discarded in favor of direct transliteration. Thus, "Hoa Thinh Don" (Washington), becomes "Oa-Sinh-Ton"; "Mac Tu Khoa" (Moscow) becomes "Mot-cu", etc. Another new feature of North Vietnamese Communist language was the enrichment of Vietnamese vocabulary by compounding common words. This compounding process is similar to the Communist technique of devising abbreviations. It can be understood only by those Vietnamese familiar with their usage. A common word like "ba" (three) for example, can be the root for over one hundred compounds, such as "ba cung" (three together), "ba khoan" (three postponements), "ba mat" (three aspects), etc.; the list is inexhaustible.[6]

---

[5] Translation of the original Chinese phrase "Nhat Tan, Nhat Nhat Tan, Huu Nhat Tan".

[6] Each compound in fact expresses a political slogan or policy in abbreviated form. "Ba Cung" (Three Together) stands for "Cung An, Cung O, Cung Lam" (Eat Together, Live Together, Work Together). "Ba Khoan" (Three Postponements) stands for "Khoan Yeu, Khoan Cuoi, Khoan De" (Postpone Love, Postpone Marriage, Postpone Babies). "Ba Mat" (Three Aspects or Efforts) stands for "Binh Van, Quan Su, Chinh Tri" (Enemy Troop Proselyting, Military Effort, Political Effort).

In their efforts to broaden a popular culture and language, the North Vietnamese Communists fully exploited the merits of traditionally popular literature such as plainness, simplicity, flexibility, lyricality, and images. Careful studies of rules governing the composition of folk songs, lyrical poems and ritual chants helped sharpen the Communist propaganda technique to the point that every piece of propaganda became easily accepted and widely propagated among the populace. This was the reason why the Communists were so successful in the areas of information and propaganda. Every emulation campaign, every official holiday, every economic or military campaign were accompanied by psychological actions. To stimulate production, for example, the Communists advanced the slogan "Each Person Works Like Two." During the period of the 1972 Summer offensive, the slogan used was "Let's Make Each Day Count As Twenty Years." Ho Chi Minh himself was fully cognizant of the important role played by popular literature and poetry in the war effort. When North Vietnam was preparing to launch its general offensive against cities in South Vietnam during the Tet holidays of 1968, it gave the order for preparation and attack under the form of a "Happy Tet" poem by Ho Chi Minh. This poem was broadcast by Radio Hanoi, intended for Communist troops in the South:

> This Spring will be much different from previous springs
> Because every household will enjoy news of victory
> North and South will now forever reunite
> Forward! Total victory will be ours.[7]

---

[7]This was Ho's second "Happy Tet" poem ever published. The first one dated back in 1945 when the Viet Minh took over governmental power in Vietnam. The Vietnamese text of the 1968 poem reads:

> Xuan nay khac han may Xuan qua
> Thang loi tin vui khap moi nha
> Nam, Bac tu nay xum hop mai
> Tien len, thang loi se ve ta.

In Vietnamese, Xuan(Spring) also connotes Tet.

Despite its effort to gain independence in culture and language, North Vietnam was heavily influenced by modern Chinese martial music. Most musical songs were composed for choral, not personal presentation. This was perhaps a deliberate Communist effort aimed at stimulating collective activities and work which were deemed more vital to socialism than individual entertainment. As a result, North Vietnamese Communist-style music, although given equal emphasis as other branches of art, did not serve well its propaganda purpose. Many captured NVA soldiers disclosed, however, that they usually furtively tuned in to South Vietnamese radio broadcasts for the simple reason that they wanted to listen to music, the kind of languorous and romanticized music to which human nature feels closer.

Aside from music, North Vietnam also took interest in drama and painting. But as was the case with other arts, drama and painting were also devoted to the objective of promoting Communism and the war of liberation.

In general, over the years of partition, North Vietnam created a culture and a language that specifically befitted its own world and were committed to the service of its own goal. The cultural and linguistic gap between North and South Vietnam gradually widened to the point of transforming them into quasi-foreign countries. The North Vietnamese press once carried a story about a South Vietnamese spy operating in the north being apprehended on a bus. A companion traveller detected oddities in his language which sounded strange to the North Vietnamese and reported the fact to the security police. Without being conscious about it, our operator had given himself away, just by speaking his own language, being himself a native of North Vietnam.

To North Vietnam, the Paris Agreement of 29 January 1973 came into being as an immediate victory in psychological warfare. For one thing, the kind of language written in it was specifically North Vietnamese. This fact could be detected by every Vietnamese. As a matter of fact, North Vietnamese language had become quite an obstacle for the allied effort of intelligence collection. The task of analyzing it was particularly painful for it was not always easy to understand the true semantical meaning of the information collected. To facilitate intelligence analysis, effort was made by South Vietnamese military intelligence to publish a lexicon of North Vietnamese terminology whose third edition in 1973 contained twice as much content as the previous edition of 1968 and five times as much as the first edition in 1961.

The language used by North Vietnam is indeed a language of its own. Its phraseology is also radically different from traditional Vietnamese, influenced as it has been by propaganda technique. The most remarkable feature is repetition. The same idea can be repeated many times in a text; it is presumably intended to be ingrained in the reader's subconsciousness by its repetition. Every year, the leaders of North Vietnam write articles and essays assessing North Vietnamese conduct of the military effort. The same ideas are again and again presented every year in these articles. Only through inquisitive reading and analysis can the reader detect anything novel, but something novel almost invariably is indicative of a significant change. This is because Communists are usually very cautious in expressing themselves and only competent leaders can advance new ideas. In December 1974, for example, North Vietnam's Premier Pham Van Dong declared that during 1975 the South Vietnamese people would witness many events of particular significance. This was immediately interpreted by our intelligence analysts as indicative of a new North Vietnamese military effort during the year.

South Vietnamese Culture and Language

Vietnamese culture and language went through significant transformation in South Vietnam as well as in North Vietnam. As of 1954, the growing American involvement in South Vietnam brought about some cultural influence that outshone and eventually overshadowed the impact of Chinese and French culture. South Vietnamese culture during this period was an amalgamation of traditional and modern tendencies, particularly under the influence of the interplay between modern tendencies and traditional values. Its resulting characteristics were a certain libertarianism verging on permissiveness and a predilection for change.

It was on the cultural front that one could see a real conflict take place, a conflict that diametrically opposed North against South in terms of cultural outlook. Nowhere else did this conflict manifest itself in a more representative way than in music. In South Vietnam, music blossomed in total freedom and diversity, inclined toward romanticism and languorous lyricism. War was also an important subject for musical composition, but more often than not it was represented as a cause for separation and sorrowful laments. Only very rarely was it made the subject of epic music intended to foster heroism and gallantry. There were indeed such works but they were all produced by governmental propaganda and information agencies or the RVNAF psychological warfare department. Thus, in music, all liberties were permitted, even anti-war songs. The line was drawn only at making propaganda for promoting Communism. Strange as it may have seemed, the proliferation of anti-war songs lamenting the sorrows of war occurred at about the same time as the progress of the Communist general offensive campaign in 1968. Simple coincidence or deliberateness, the fashionable anti-war songs were certainly detrimental to the cause of the RVN war effort.

Such permissive libertarianism led to the free introduction of Chinese-style knight-errantry novels from Hong Kong, particularly those written by Kim Dung (Chin Yun). These were serialized in leading newpapers and passionately read by the public. The impact of these outlandish, mythical stories on the lives of the populace and the war in South Vietnam was far-reaching. Several main characters of these stories were so idolized that their thoughts and actions were imitated in daily life. Some people, including a few Vietnamese national leaders, even went as far as calling themselves by nicknames or pseudonyms taken at least in part if not in full from the names of the most famous characters. This fashion for imitating the feats and personalities of knight-errant stories could be found in many instances, for example, in the conference room of the Two-Party Joint Military Commission. A leading character in this series of novels is Lenh Ho Xung. When engaging an adversary in a fight, he uses his own martial style, an unorthodox style which cannot be found in any regular martial textbook and consists of quick-changing variations, and always wins. The RVN military delegation at the JMC applied the same self-styled flexible approach in negotiations which was not based on any official directive or procedure. Its members, as a matter of fact, deliberately contradicted each other when addressing the conference and sometimes talked pure nonsense, just for the fun of confusing their monolithic adversaries. The Communists were greatly surprised and became confused, not knowing exactly what points the other side wanted to make, where the other side's major interest lay, or how the other side proposed to solve a certain problem. But the Communists, too, took advantage of this popular passion for knight-errant novels which were on display and sale almost everywhere. They found the proliferation of these novels an excellent modality to quietly push their propaganda materials by substituting them for the contents, leaving the covers and the first few pages as intact and as appealing as they were.

This widely popular attraction resulted in a competition between newspapers to carry more and more of those stories in serialized form. As a matter of fact, the newspaper with the largest circulation during this period was always one that carried the newest and longest installment of the most appealing knight-errantry story to-date. Another device used by newspapers to achieve wide circulation was a special column devoted to rumors. The stories or anecdotes contained in this column were mostly about current news which might be true or fabricated or a mixture of both, but they were always sensational and mystifying and invariably became subjects of speculation and conjecture.[8] Unknowingly, however, it was those stories that created suspicions and gave rise to rumors to which the South Vietnamese populace were particularly sensitive.

In general, there was an effort to return to the traditional Vietnamese culture in South Vietnam as well as in North Vietnam. It was correctly

---

[8]This refers to the column "Ao Tha Vit" (The Duck-Pond) carried by the "Song" (Live) daily newspaper whose publisher and editor was Chu Tu, a satirist, now deceased. The Vietnamese word "vit" (duck) derives its figurative meaning of "false report" from the French word "canard" from which it is directly translated. Many newspapers later carried a similar column.

surmised by most South Vietnamese intellectuals that the only way to achieve national independence and true identity was through the reinstatement of time-honored traditions and values which had been eroded or debased by war and disorder. Several cultural conventions were held during which it was agreed that contemporary Vietnamese culture should be oriented toward "science, people, and mass." By and large, this effort existed only in form and nothing substantial was achieved over the years. As a result, South Vietnamese culture continued to flourish in libertarianism and even in absurdity.

In contrast to North Vietnam which generally forbids every form of superstition, South Vietnam condoned it. Fortune tellers, astrologers, and mediums conducted a thriving business and their numerous clients included more than a few high-ranking officials. This belief in the supernatural seemed to indicate a certain feeling of insecurity among the populace. There were stories that some field commanders even consulted astrologers for the most appropriate date and time to launch an operation or to go on a combat inspection tour. While North Vietnamese society quietly subsisted along the lines prescribed by the Communist Party, South Vietnamese society was frequently turned upside down by political upheavals and economic misfortunes. This was perhaps the reason why people in South Vietnam were more inclined to search into the supernatural for their own destiny.

Religions in South Vietnam exerted a particularly important influence on politics. Apart from Buddhism and Roman Catholicism which have been established throughout Vietnam, Caodaism and Hoa Hao Buddhism are the two sects that came into being only at the turn of the century, and their influence is limited to the Mekong Delta. Cao Dai and Hoa Hao followers were persistently anti-Communist throughout the war. Their holy lands, located in Tay Ninh and An Giang provinces were bulwarks of resistance against Communist infiltration and attacks. In general, Roman Catholicism always exerted some influence on leading personalities and the elite while Buddhism was the religion of the popular majority. It was the Buddhist struggle movement in 1963 that led up to the overthrow of the First Republic government. Because of the popularity of religion, the Communists always sought to exploit it by using a religious screen for their underground activities or by utilizing the spiritual power of religious leaders as a means to penetrate governmental ranks. Communist agents usually enjoyed relative immunity under the cover of religion. In the aftermath of the Buddhist uprising in 1963, security forces and the national police in particular were especially chary about meddling into religious affairs, and generally chose to stay away from anything related to religion.

Linguistically, the Vietnamese language as it was spoken and written in South Vietnam became more and more enriched and innovative as a result of contributions made by Western culture. The introduction of American subcultural expressions and beliefs, displayed by the "flower children" generation, came to affect Vietnamese young people in particular and gave rise to much sophisticated slang which were subsequently accepted as common usage. In mid-1967, for example, "suc may", meaning "no way", became very popular slang. This apparently harmless expression enjoyed widest acceptance among carefree youths because it connoted playfulness, indolence, and a certain defiance. It was the period of improved security, stabilized politics, and economic prosperity made possible by the presence of US combat troops. Everybody seemed to enjoy the new situation and it was as if the prospect of a bright future was just around the corner. People were carefree and became incredulous of anything that sounded like danger or misfortune, hence the increased popularity of the slang "no way" which was meant to express disagreement or disbelief. In time, the slang became so ingrained into subconsciousness that people were seldom aware of its intended meaning because it was used indiscriminately for almost everything. Unfortunately, the same expression was also used indifferently by intelligence officers when they discussed the validity of certain indicators pointing toward an enemy general offensive in early 1968. Of course, they all thought there was "no way" the enemy would be able to launch such an offensive. That was their first reaction when confronted by hard intelligence, and the slang expression did its job splendidly.

Language, Translation and Cultural Interpretation

Over the years, the culture and language of North and South Vietnamese became separate entities and the gap kept widening. Knowledge about South Vietnam does not necessarily imply the same kind of knowledge about North Vietnam. This is important because people tend to see things through their own perspective and interpret facts according to their own experience. This is a pitfall that was common among the majority of Americans in South Vietnam. Most of them were not aware of the cultural and linguistic difference, and kept inferring their knowledge about North Vietnam from what they knew about the South. Another major obstacle that seriously hampered the American effort to collect data on the enemy was the fact that these data had to go through the distorting lens of translation. If one is to believe the wisdom of the axiom "translating is betraying," then one can always expect a certain amount of distortion at best. There were of course some Americans who had a complete command of the Vietnamese language and in fact spoke it as well as a native, or even better in terms of metaphors and proverbs, but they were a tiny minority. In addition, intelligence as it was practiced in South Vietnam had a special jargon and a methodology of its own that outsiders could hardly understand. The widely admitted reasoning was that not all Vietnamese who were proficient in general English could become good interpreters or translators in intelligence, for aside from a good command of intelligence terminology in both languages, they were also required to have a thorough familiarity with the kind of language used by the Communists. Not very many had this double knowledge. The English language, for example, includes the term "general uprising" which is used to translate the Communist term "Tong Noi Day" (general uprising, literally), But it was found that the same English term was used, indiscriminately, for two other Communist forms of general uprising, "dong khoi" (uprising in unison, literally), and "Tong Khoi Nghia" (general uprising for a cause, literally). As a matter of fact, each of these terms has special connotations that are difficult to include into a ready-made, concise English term. Each of them was also used by the Communists in a discriminating manner for each connoted a certain historical time frame. "Tong Khoi Nghia", for example, referred to the revolution of August 1945, in which the people, at the instigation of the Viet Minh, participated in the seizure of governmental power. In 1968, the Communists called their offensive campaign "Tong Tan Cong, Tong Khoi Nghia" (general offensive, general uprising — for a cause), because they conceived it as a repeat of the August Revolution of 1945, and expected the same kind of popular participation throughout the country. An "Dong Khoi" (uprising in unison) was a term intended only for natives of South Vietnam to incite them to rise up against local governments, an allegorical reminiscence of the first Communist revolt in Kien Hoa province in 1960. Both of these terms referred to specific historical events and if they had been used repetitively, their meanings and psychological impact would have certainly become lost. As a result, in 1972 and again in 1975, the Communists chose a different term, "Tong Noi Day" (general uprising) to replace the previous ones which had apparently become anachronistic. General uprising, as an English term, renders quite adequately the literal meaning of each of these events but for a deeper and more accurate assessment of the event itself, it was not enough for the inquisitive intelligence analyst.

Much has been said about another critical pitfall that occurred during the translation of the Paris Agreement text. The Agreement, which was drafted some time in October 1973, originally intended the National Council of Reconciliation and Concord to be just an administrative body. That was what had been agreed upon by the negotiators. But "administration" when rendered in Vietnamese, can have two meanings and equivalents; one is "chinh quyen" (government) and the other is "hanh chanh" (administration body). The North Vietnamese, by their deliberate choice, opted for the Vietnamese term which means government, and by doing this in all apparent innocence transformed the Council into a form of coalition government. This wickedness was finally detected by a comparison of both English and Vietnamese texts.

In intelligence as well as in certain other fields, the text of a document does not always reflect the true intent of the writer. Sometimes it is necessary also to read between the lines. This is particularly important in intelligence analysis. As far as Communist documents are concerned, the inveterate analyst can always detect something hidden behind the literal meaning of the text. Some call this special ability the sixth sense, or intuition, which is an invaluable asset of the talented analyst. But if the text is translated into another language, this hidden or implied meaning will be difficult to detect, if not entirely lost. Apart from translation, which can be acceptable for intelligence purposes if professionally done, special attention must be given to instantaneous interpreting of speech. In general, our disposition toward interpreting tends to be more tolerant, and bilingual interpreters are not required to meet exacting qualifications. The need for interpreters in South Vietnam became vital when US combat troops were introduced, and it kept growing. Attempts were made to meet this urgent requirement by recruiting civilians with some English knowledge into military service. These interpreters proved to be useful for general work, but their proficiency in English was rather poor and unsuited for specialized work. Humans, being human, never want to expose their weaknesses and deficiencies. The same is true with interpreters who, even though they sometimes don't quite understand what is being said, always try to render it by ad-libbing or inventing things which may be far from the truth. This is one of the pitfalls that plagued the combined intelligence effort in South Vietnam at first. Later, reliance on interpreters was greatly reduced as direct communication between American and Vietnamese counterparts increased and as combined working became an established procedure. The possibility of misunderstanding still remained, but it was more a matter of degree.

Apart from difficulties created by the language barrier, the American intelligence collection effort was also apt to run into some obstacles due to inadequate understanding of Vietnamese psychological customs and manners, expecially those found in local communities. In the Central Highlands of MR-2 for example, there exist many ethnic Montagnard tribes

whose matriarchal social organization gives ruling power to the women.[9]
Any contact made with male members of the tribe inevitably brings about
little result. In the Mekong Delta, particularly in the Ca Mau area
many people made a living by producing charcoal. They built earthen
furnaces in open fields to burn trees and these were registered on
infra-red tapes as thermal spots that initially American specialists
were unable to interpret correctly. This was of course an instance of unfamiliarity with local customs. In imagery interpretation also, several
American specialists at first mistook certain isolated tombs scattered
among rice fields as crew-served weapon positions because on aerial
photos, the configuration of their structures looked almost the same.

Knowledge about traditional Vietnamese architecture can be helpful
in intelligence work in case orientation must be ascertained. As a rule,
most pagodas face the southwest, a market place front always faces north
and a tomb generally lies with its head toward the west. National character
also varies by region or by ethnic group. Vietnamese living in the delta,
for example, are generally shrewd and cunning while Montagnards are ingenuous; southerners are sincere but short-tempered; northerners are
usually tactful and subtle, and most people living in central Vietnam are
incisive and ceremonious. Thorough knowledge about a nation is not always
easy to learn since there are many regional peculiarities that confuse even
local people. The most important feature of the Vietnam war is that it was
a conflict between North Vietnam and South Vietnam, hence a civil war in
some of its aspects. What people usually failed to recognize or took rather
lightly was the deep-seated cultural and linguistic difference between
the warring adversaries, and this was precisely what caused so many failures
and setbacks. A Communist plan of attack which was coordinated with actions
by traitors within our ranks was defeated simply because of the difference
in launching time. The Communist planners apparently failed to realize
that their own official time, aligned on Hanoi time, was one hour later than
Saigon time. When the traitors started firing one hour too soon, they

---

[9] In some tribes, such as the Bahnar and the Jarai, although a woman is usually the "decision-maker" in the family, she has to seek advice from her older brother for important decisions.

exposed themselves and were all arrested. The attack from the outside never materialized because of this initial setback. Another case of failure occurred when a Communist cadre was arrested while visiting his family who lived in a government-controlled rural area. To neighbors who dropped in to see him, he was introduced by his parents as a city-dwelling visitor. While they were chatting a jet fighter happened to fly by at low altitude and creating supersonic booms. Through conditioned reflex the Communist cadre sought cover by crawling under the bed. This took everybody present aback. He had unknowningly given himself away simply by failing to adapt to a new cultural environment.

When they chose the Tet holidays to launch their 1968 general offensive campaign, the Communists were primarily interested in its surprise and totally disregarded its adverse psychological effect. This was understandable because to North Vietnam Tet was merely a custom that needed to be changed because it was both the manifestation of a feudalistic heritage and an occasion for wasteful, luxurious spending. Accordingly, the traditional importance of Tet in North Vietnam was downplayed by Communist authorities. But to South Vietnam, which revered traditions, Tet was as sacred as always because people regarded Tet less as a celebration than a spiritual tie between man and the universe, between the living and the dead, and also between the living people themselves. As a result, the South Vietnamese troops were angrily determined to eliminate the violators of sacred Tet and in the aftermath of the offensive, recruiting was never so successful.

South Vietnam's basic weakness in the war was taking too lightly the enemy's will to carry out his plans. We tended to liken our adversaries to ourselves and assess them according to our subjective thinking. For example, if a Communist plan was disclosed, we usually believed that our enemy would discard it since we always considered everything that had been leaked as too risky. But to the Communists, it was not always so because their goal always outweighed the risks to be incurred, and if the political requirement so dictated, a plan once worked out was usually implemented regardless of the risks caused by disclosure.

In the history of intelligence, there is an abundance of examples of successes in very difficult intelligence and counterintelligence operations. The key to these successes almost always is special attention to minute details. Besides, planners usually consider that any operational scheme is prone to omissions and leaks and accordingly they take extra precautions through contingency planning. In the Vietnam War, such fundamentals were observed in principle but detail was something that usually escaped the planner's mind. The usual contention was that culture, language, customs, manners, and traditions never really constituted true obstacles because both sides were Vietnamese. To intelligence personnel, however, these are precisely the factors of considerable importance that could spell the difference between success and failure.

CHAPTER III

Republic of Vietnam and United States Intelligence
Organizations in South Vietnam

The RVN National and Local Intelligence Coordination Committees

Robert Thompson, a Vietnam specialist, wrote that in 1966, in Saigon, he had been able to identify seventeen different United States and Republic of Vietnam intelligence agencies.[1] He did not name them. However, if we were to take into account all intelligence agencies in the entire Republic, Vietnamese agencies alone actually exceeded this number but fluctuated with time. As of 1965, on the civilian side, there were at one time or another:

1. The Central Intelligence Office (CIO);
2. The National Police (NP);
3. The Directorate of North Vietnamese Affairs of the Office of the Chairman, Central Executive Committee;
4. The Intelligence Directorate of the Ministry of Foreign Affairs;[2]
5. The Directorate General of Administrative Security;
6. The Rural Development (RD) cadre group;
7. The Civil Affairs cadre group;
8. Armed propaganda teams of the "Chieu Hoi" (Open Arms) Ministry;

---

[1] Sir Robert Thompson, Phoenix, Myths and Relevances of the Viet Nam War, (Lugano Review LR 4) James (Paddy) Fitzsimmons, April 1975, p.61.

[2] This organization existed only in name, not in substance.

9. Census and grievance teams.

Military intelligence agencies included the following:

1. The Military Security Directorate (better known as MSS);
2. J-7 of the Joint General Staff (J-7, JGS);
3. The Strategic Technical Directorate (STRATDAT);
4. The Liaison Service;
5. The Research and Documentation Office of the National Defense Ministry;
6. G-2, Special Forces;
7. The Intelligence Directorate of the General Political Warfare Department;
8. J-2, JGS, and subordinate service intelligence staff and units such as A-2 of the Vietnam Air Force (A2/VNAF); N-2 of the Vietnam Navy (VNN); Special Collection Detachment/VNAF; Special Collection Detachment/VNN (Unit 701); G-2's of Army corps, infantry divisions and general reserve divisions; corps and division military intelligence detachments; division long-range reconnaissance companies; S2's of sectors and subsectors with their respective intelligence/security platoons and squads; and the 924th Support Group, J-2, JGS (later renamed Unit 101).

There were also two kinds of Vietnamese intelligence units which came under direct US operational control: the Provincial Reconnaissance Units (PRU) and the Kit Carson Scouts (units made up of Communist defectors).[3]

Though some of the intelligence organizations were later disbanded (North Vietnamese Affairs Directorate, civil affairs cadre, G-2/Special Forces), or merged (the Liaison Service became subordinated to STRATDAT) or disappeared with the withdrawal of US forces (Kit Carson Scouts), there remained a significant number of them.

As an effort to give intelligence a more unified structure, the Social and Political Research Department was established during the First

---

[3]The PRU's were initially created and controlled by CORDS, US Embassy. As of 31 March 1969, they were transferred to the National Police. Each PRU operated under the control of the province chief.

Republic as an agency of the President's Office. It was chartered to control both civilian and military intelligence activities, but its authority was limited to the CIO, NP, MSS and J-2, JGS.

The Social and Political Research Department was disbanded after the 1 November 1963 revolution and the CIO took over control of intelligence organizations in the country. To ensure smooth coordination of operations, a standing committee was established which included representatives of all the agencies involved.

In 1966 the cabinet was augmented with a new department known as the Security Ministry and the Security Minister subsequently took on the additional position of Director, CIO, to control intelligence operations in the country.

Later, the Security Ministry was disbanded, but the CIO remained the highest intelligence agency in the country. Considerations were given to making the Defense Minister or the Interior Minister concurrently Director, CIO, which would shift authority from the President's Office to the cabinet. However, in the end a National Intelligence Coordination Committee (NICC) was established and chaired by the Presidential Assistant for Military and Intelligence Affairs. *(Chart 1)* The office of the chairman of the National Intelligence Coordination Committee was not staffed by representatives of member agencies. Its personnel came from the CIO whose director became secretary general of the NICC. Members of the NICC included the NP, MSS, J-7, JGS, J-2, JGS, and STRATDAT, but the latter was not considered to be a permanent member.

Chart 1 — Organization, National Intelligence Coordination Committee

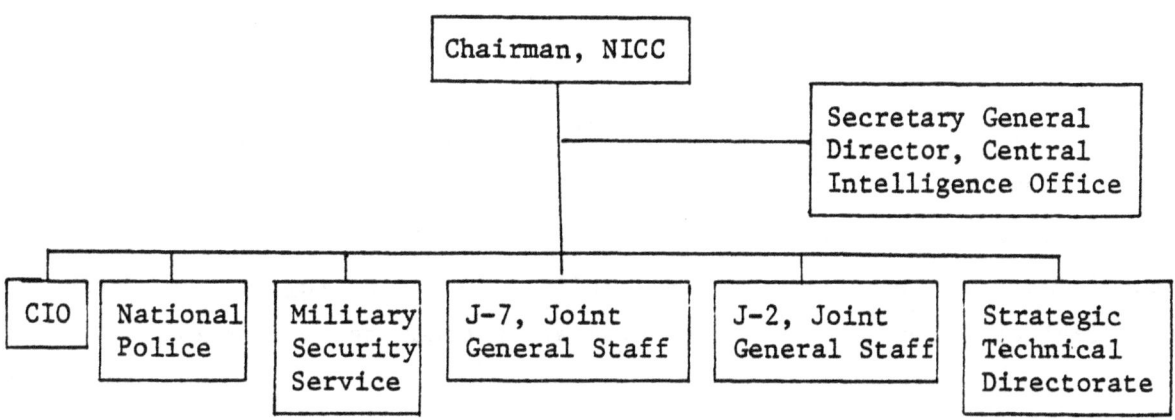

The NICC was supposed to meet once a month. In reality, it met only when needed, once every three to six months, with all member agencies represented. In addition to these meetings, the Chairman's Office worked directly with the CIO, NP, or MSS. Member agencies had to provide the Chairman's Office with copies of all intelligence reports or summaries distributed. Information was extracted from these materials and presented as NICC reports to the President's Office and occasionally to the Premier's Office.

This procedure shows that the NICC Chairman's Office wanted to keep up with intelligence information, both civilian and military, down to the tactical level, when it should have concentrated solely on matters of national concern. This excess led to its being swamped with reports from the member agencies, making evaluation impossible and negating timeliness.

Throughout the years of its existence, the NICC failed to perform its role properly as required. It was unable to establish national intelligence plans and requirements; nor was it capable of arriving at a strategically comprehensive assessment of the military and political situation that the GVN required to face eventualities with confidence.

In addition to the NICC, there were intelligence coordination committees at military region level, but those were established according to the region commanders' individual concepts. They usually included a representative of the region commander (deputy commander or chief of staff) as chairman; the G-2 of the Military Region (G-2, MR) as secretary general; and the chief of the regional MSS and his counterpart at the NP, both serving as members of the committee.

There are no representatives of the CIO, J-7, or STRATDAT on the regional committees. These regional committees did not meet periodically. Their primary purpose was to ensure effective and timely exchange of information which otherwise would have been more difficult, given intelligence agencies' tendency to disregard lateral dissemination for the benefit of their own headquarters. While at military region level, the organization of an intelligence coordination committee was somewhat optional, such organizations at sector and sub-sector levels were mandated by government decrees, beginning in 1964 with a Premier's decree establishing provincial intelligence coordination committees, followed by later directives concerning district intelligence coordination committees. At provincial level, the province chief/sector commander was chairman of the intelligence coordination committee, the sector S-2 was its secretary general; the chief of MSS and his counterpart at the NP were permanent members of the committee. Non-permanent committee members included representatives of the CIO; Unit 101; the Chief, "Chieu Hoi" Service; Chief, Information Service; intelligence officers of US units stationed in the area; US advisors to sector S-2, etc. At district level, the district chief/sub-sector commander was the chairman and the sub-sector S-2 was the secretary general. Committee members included the chiefs of MSS, NP, "Chieu Hoi" and Information sub-services, and representatives of rural development and civil affairs cadre groups.

In addition to providing the mechanics for coordination and exchange of information, the intelligence coordination committee acted as a source control center where agents' reports were screened for validity. At this center, agents' files were maintained in a standardized format that provided for distinctive sections dealing with personal data, collection qualifications, and area of operation, respectively. When there were grounds for suspecting a certain agent, collection agencies compared various parts of the agent's biography and, upon preliminary verification, proceeded toward a complete exchange of biographical information. Upon identifying a fabricator or a contaminated agent, the agency concerned took appropriate action and notified all other collection agencies.

Still another purpose of the coordination committee was to ensure that sources who were available to one member agency, but whose knowledgeability or access was not consistent with the line of priorities handled by that one agency, would be directed to the appropriate agencies or organizations. Members of the Viet Cong Infrastructure (VCI) were the responsibility of the NP, military proselyting cadre were handled by MSS, and military prisoners of war were processed by military intelligence. This operational procedure was designed to provide clear-cut division of responsibilities and delimitation of each organization's collection scope, with no one duplicating the efforts of another, and with each organization having its own distinct targets.

Nevertheless, in 1967 it was realized for the first time that intelligence in Vietnam focused solely on enemy military forces and ignored a no less important force, the Communist political force, also known as Viet Cong Infrastructure (VCI). As a result, a new effort was initiated on a national scale to root out the VCI and the NP was allowed to expand in order to cope with this extensive task.

The need for a concerted intelligence effort led to the establishment of the Phoenix Program in 1968 (Decree 280a/TT/SL, 1 July 1968). This program, originally being an American idea endorsed by the GVN, was administered through existing Provincial and District Intelligence and Operations Coordination Committees (PIOCC and DIOCC respectively). The organizational structure of these committees is shown in Charts 2 and 3. The Phoenix Program sought further coordination than was effected at the old intelligence coordination committees. It provided for coordination between intelligence and tactical operations with the aim of permitting immediate tactical response that would lead to destruction of the VCI.

Many government officials felt that this program, though upgraded to a national policy and enjoying total US support from its inception to cease-fire day, did not live up to expectations. In organization the program's shortcoming was that, while theoretically the concept of entrusting eradication of the VCI to police forces was sound, in reality police personnel in charge of the program at provincial and district levels did not have the qualifications, prestige or experience for such an assignment. Chiefs of NP services and sub-services were all fresh out of training. They were second lieutenants at provincial level and noncommissioned officers at district level while their counterparts in military intelligence or military security were captains or first lieutenants at provincial level and warrant officers or second lieutenants at district level. The military officers were also better qualified and more experienced than their police counterparts.

Chart 2 — Organization, Provincial Intelligence and Operations Coordination Committee

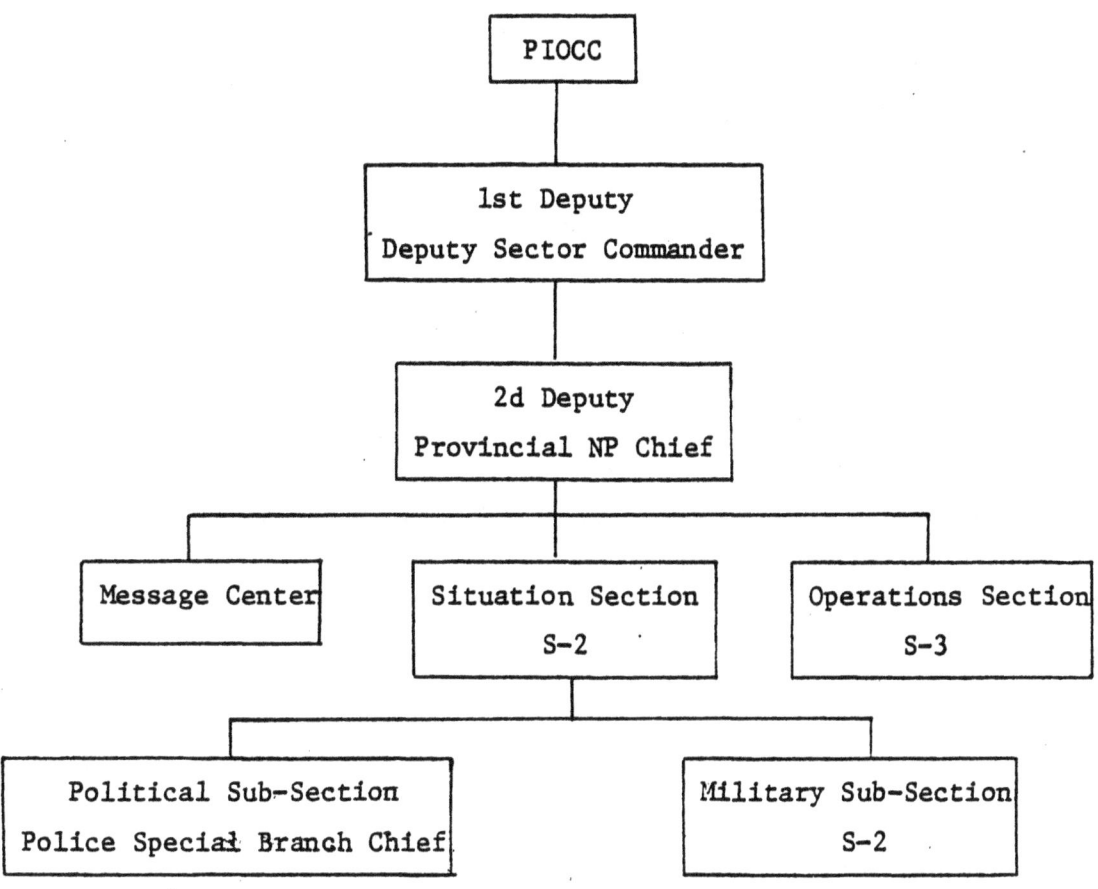

Chart 3 — Organization, District Intelligence and Operations Coordination Committee

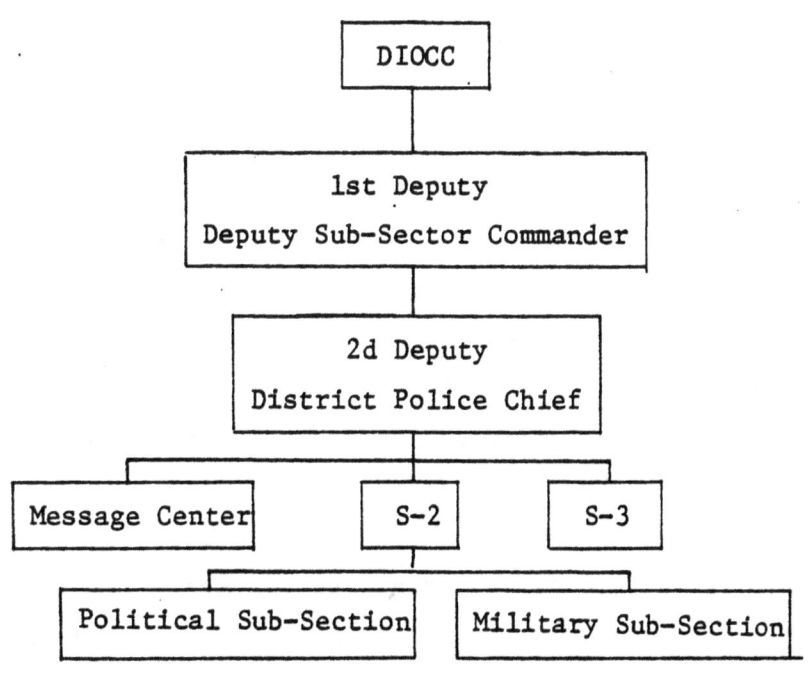

The role of the DIOCC or PIOCC 2d Deputy Chairman called for him to replace the chairman in controlling and guiding intelligence operations in the district or province, coordinating civilian and military intelligence activities, verifying and controlling intelligence sources, maintaining source control files, and advising the sector or sub-sector commander on intelligence operations and the enemy situation. These duties far exceeded what might have been reasonably expected, in qualifications and prestige, of the chief of a police service or sub-service. For this very reason, an inter-ministerial directive was originated which allowed sector and sub-sector commanders to fill the position of 2d deputy chairman of the PIOCC or DIOCC as the local situation warranted, no longer making it a police prerogative. Generally speaking, however, the above situation remained a basic cause of unsuccessful coordination despite the great efforts invested. When the NP became a command in 1971 and its strength was increased to 121,000, it filled 13,000 slots with Republic of Vietnam Armed Forces (RVNAF) personnel who had volunteered to transfer to police status. A number of high-ranking military intelligence and military security officers were also detached to the NP Command to take over key positions and facilitate coordination between this civilian authority and the armed forces. This greatly enhanced the spirit of cooperation between the civilians and the armed forces on the one hand and improved the NP collection capabilities on the other.

In summary, having numerous intelligence agencies does not necessarily guarantee good intelligence. It has been known to produce adverse results. Collection activities may be entrusted to two organizations: a civilian organization specializing in political intelligence and a military organization specializing in military intelligence. These two organizations would support and complement each other. Since each had its own distinct field of activity, there should be no duplication or undue competition. Internally, each organization would be structured with an equally clear-cut division of responsibilities. The relationship between the operational elements and the staff elements would be clearly defined, as would be the interrelation between the various collection areas. Consequently, when weaknesses are identified in a specific field or a specific target area, supplemental plans may be made but no additional agencies would be established. This would help avoid total reliance on higher headquarters and disregard of lateral agencies, or vice-versa. There would be no room for those intelligence agencies which could not collect a single item of interest and spent all their time and efforts doctoring up friendly agencies' reports for dissemination within their own channels.

Vietnamese intelligence agencies which operated jointly with US intelligence organizations were somewhat influenced by the latter. United States military intelligence includes intelligence agencies of the Army, Air Force, Navy and Marine Corps. These agencies are independent from one another. This was not feasible in the RVNAF because VNAF and VNN were but small services. Because they were directly supported by their US counterpart agencies and were able to observe the independence enjoyed by the latter, A-2, VNAF, and N-2, VNN, during 1965-67 wanted to demonstrate their own independence from other Vietnamese services by having their own concepts of organization and operations, their own training programs, their own collection plans and operations, etc.

The organizational concept as applied to Vietnamese intelligence reflected an indiscriminate combination of US, French and Chinese concepts, whereas only the strong points of each system should have been selected and reconciled with the others in keeping with the context of the Vietnam situation. This would have been the best way to arrive at an appropriate organizational concept. Unfortunately, it was not the case with Vietnamese intelligence. Consequently, collection efforts were weakened and resources misused or even squandered. While everyone expected good coordination to provide the solution to all problems, this very same coordination—be it in intelligence or in other fields—remained but a "state of mind."

Vietnamese Civilian Intelligence Agencies

1. <u>The Central Intelligence Office (CIO)</u>

The CIO was established in May 1961. It was given authority to control and coordinate the operation of intelligence organizations in the country to ensure that requirements for intelligence of national scope would be adequately met.[4] This included military and non-military organizations as well as the NP. It had by then become evident that the various intelligence agencies in Vietnam were too self-centered and no agency had access to another's resources. The stated objectives of the CIO were never reached because of the ever-changing internal political situation and the complex nature of the intelligence agencies involved.

The CIO's ultimate missions were: to satisfy requirements for strategic intelligence (primarily political); to conduct counterespionage (security of the regime); and to satisfy special intelligence requirements of the President's Office.

It was last organized as follows *(Chart 4):*

Chart 4 — Organization, Central Intelligence Office

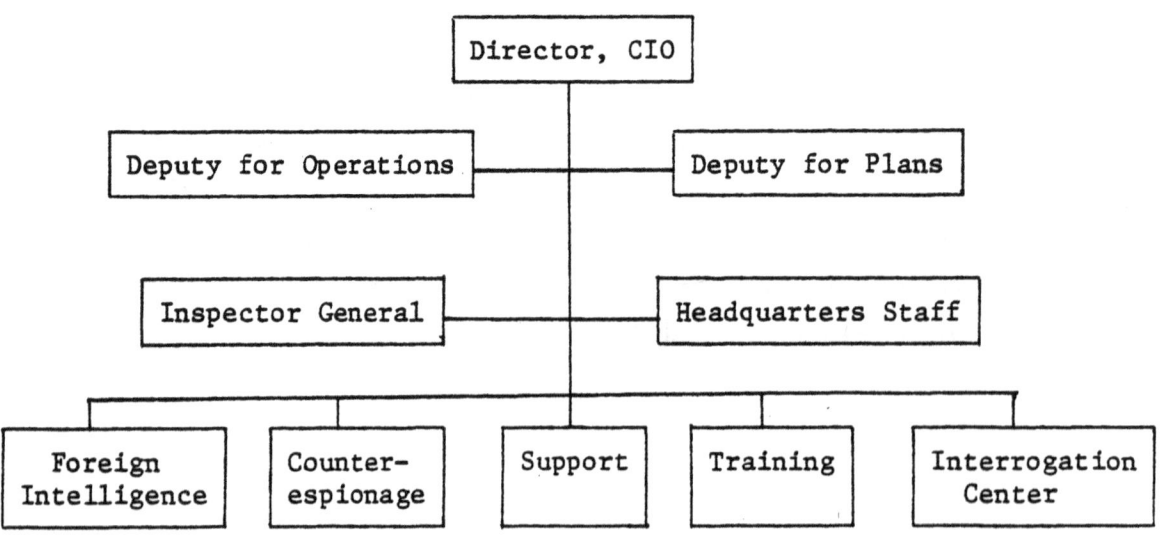

---

[4]First Twelve-Month Report of Chief, MAAG, Vietnam, September 1961, p. 12.

CIO personnel numbered 1,400, 60% of them high-ranking cadre. Intermediate-level cadre made up 20% of the force and the remaining 20% were junior cadre. Personnel of the CIO enjoyed special status and such privileges as draft deferment or military discharge.

The foreign intelligence division operated numerous stations. These stations were the eyes and ears of the CIO in foreign countries. They collected intelligence on both North Vietnam and South Vietnam. They were positioned in friendly countries where there were reasonable prospects for developing collection activities. Among these countries were France, Hong Kong, Thailand, Cambodia and Laos. In Laos alone there were two stations, one in Vientiane and the other in Pakse. Plans had been made to establish stations in the US and Singapore as well, but favorable circumstances did not materialize. Each station had three to five men operating under cover of Republic of Vietnam (RVN) embassy or consular staff. These stations were not successful in their efforts to collect information on North Vietnam because of tight control exercised by its regime over activities of overseas Vietnamese visiting home. Personnel of the embassies of East European countries, some of them indirect CIO sources, were subjected to similar controls in North Vietnam.

At home, the CIO's primary effort was counterespionage. Counter-espionage by the CIO differed from counterespionage by the NP or MSS in scope, nature and sensitivity, and mostly involved cases over which neither of the latter two had jurisdiction. Those were cases involving constitutional institutions like the Upper House and Lower House of the National Assembly, the Inspectorate, and the Supreme Court; executive institutions like the President's Office and the Premier's Office; or influential personalities of domestic political movements and parties.

The support division, in addition to its regular functions, operated radio systems which enabled the CIO to communicate with its elements in the country and those stationed in nearby foreign countries. Its communications branch also handled cryptographic materials for RVN embassies abroad. Communications personnel of these embassies were detached from the CIO. The Foreign Affairs Ministry originally intended for CIO participation in its communications to be limited to specialized training of Foreign Service personnel, but this concept was not accepted. CIO personnel were trained domestically although training materials and instructors were US-supplied.

The interrogation division of the CIO worked with sources of information considered to be of a strategic nature, politically and militarily. In principle, military prisoners of war were first interrogated by military intelligence personnel, then transferred to CIO control upon request by the latter. However, beginning in 1971, the CIO obtained first choice over all sources of strategic intelligence, even if their knowledge was limited to purely military matters. Those selected were evacuated immediately for CIO interrogation and no military agency, even J-2, JGS, was allowed access to these sources.[5] The concept of concentrating all strategic resources into the hands of the CIO was once again evident in 1972 when a presidential directive specified that copies of dispatches sent from Vietnam by foreign correspondents were not to be made available to J-2, JGS, because such distribution was deemed unnecessary.

The CIO's real responsibility remained a political one. In particular, it was responsible for ensuring the security of the regime by watching out for plots against it from within or without. The CIO produced daily information reports and special reports as warranted. Because of its sensitive nature, under certain circumstances it received instructions directly from the President and reported directly to him, bypassing the chairman of the NICC. In these instances, it was not required to inform the Prime Minister.

Consequently, as the CIO effectively turned into the intelligence agency of the President's Office, the NP also became the intelligence agency directly controlled by the Minister of Interior who was also Prime Minister.

---

[5] By order of the Chairman, National Intelligence Coordination Committee.

2. The National Police and Other Civilian Agencies

Police forces experienced several organizational changes between the time they were under control of the Binh Xuyen and 1956; they were subsequently reorganized as a single force in June 1962 and known as the National Police (NP) under the control of a General Directorate which finally became a Command in June 1971. NP personnel strength was increased from 17,000 to 72,000 in 1966 and finally to 121,000 in 1971. The NP force consisted of three major components: (1) Uniformed Police, (2) Police Special Branch (PSB), and (3) Police Field Forces (PFF).

While the uniformed police performed the same duties as uniformed police everywhere in the world, the PSB received special consideration. This special consideration began in 1961 following recommendations from a British advisory group that PSB be effectively organized to cope with the activities of the VCI.

The PSB deployed intelligence nets to collect information on the VCI. The Police Field Forces conducted raids or operations against VCI personnel or targets identified by the PSB. The PFF also served as a reserve for the NP for intervention where needed, such as to quell anti-government demonstrations. The NP Command was organized as follows. *(Chart 5)*.

In the fields of intelligence and security, the NP Command was the principal agency responsible for identifying and detaining VCI personnel. This program was known as "Protection of the People Against Terrorism." Police operations center (POC) patterned after military tactical operations centers (TOC) were established at provincial and district levels. The NP also operated provincial interrogation centers.

In its efforts to identify VCI personnel, the NP relied on police-organized informants' nets, information provided by volunteers, and by such forces or groups as the Popular Self-Defense Forces (PSDF), information disclosed by VCI prisoners, information acquired from human or document sources by uniformed police or the PFF, and on information received from friendly sources such as civilian groups, rural development cadre, or civil affairs cadre.

Chart 5 — Organization, National Police Command

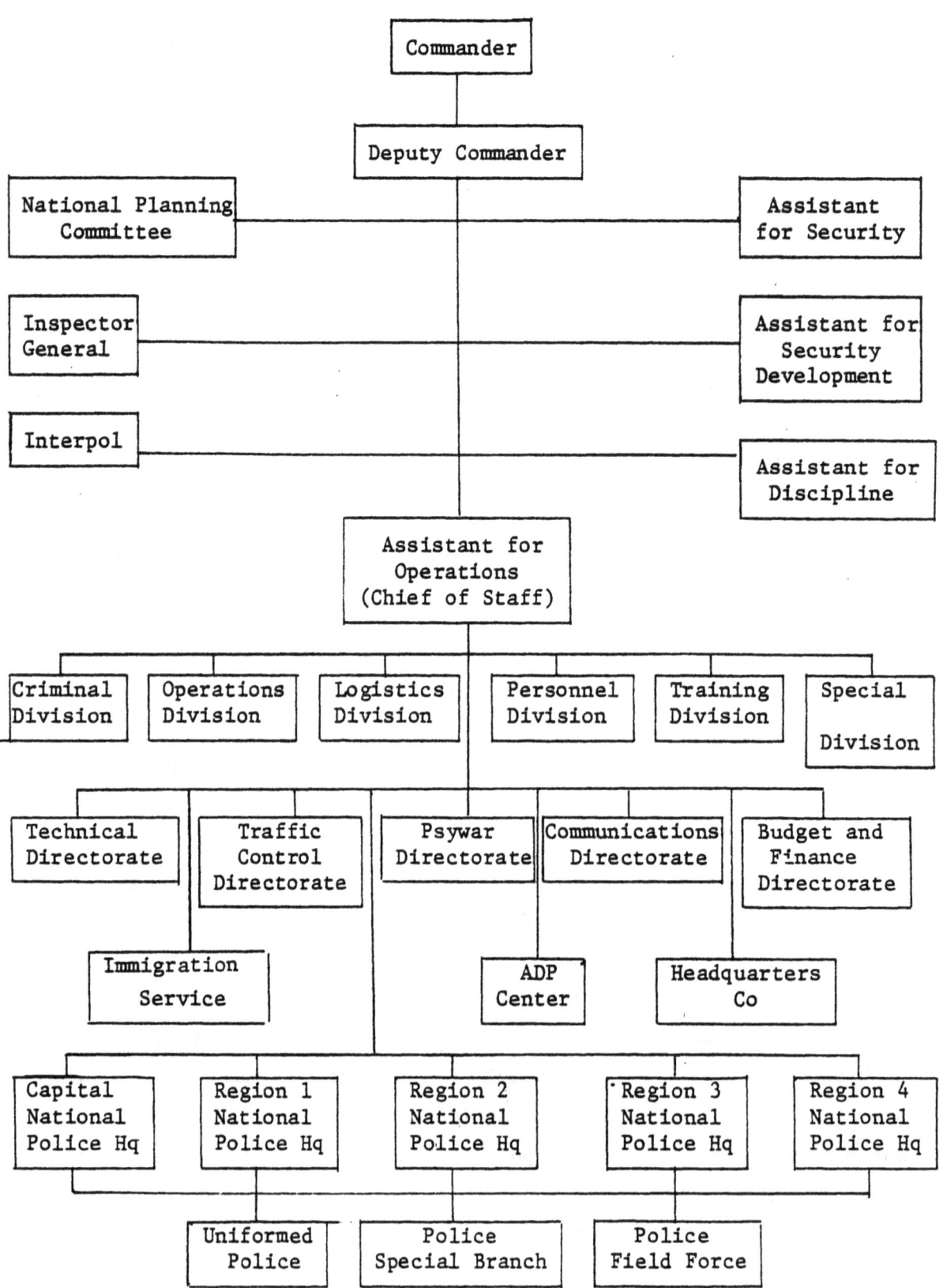

Each rural development cadre team strength varied from 30 to 59 men, depending upon the population of the target hamlet or village. In the initial phase of the pacification effort, these cadre were responsible for population census and classification. The census led to classification of the population into: Communists, Communist sympathizers, Communist defectors, families with relatives in Communist ranks, uncommitted, and nationalists or government sympathizers. Civil affairs cadre were in fact rural development cadre on long-term assignments in specific areas to develop information complementing the above project. Information thus acquired was recorded in charts with appropriate codes and symbols which were in turn forwarded to NP centers.

The next phase of the pacification effort saw the NP proceed to control the population by issuing individual identification cards and establishing family registers which detailed each household's composition by members' names and relationship to one another. In some areas the police went as far as requiring all members of a household to be photographed together for the purpose of identification.

The VCI, already deemed to be a large and effective Communist force which provided supplies, hiding places, guides and propaganda resources, was thought by many to be made up of fanatics with something undefinable in them. In reality, there were two categories: the real VCI personnel imbued with Communist ideology, and those who had been persuaded, bought or coerced into working for the former. The second category consisted of civilians that were like other civilians except that most of them were indigent. Many became part of the VCI out of greed. For example, they purchased drugs and other necessities in government-controlled areas and resold them to the Communists. Some made a living out of this; others did it because of Communist pressure.

People caught in police raids or military tactical operations fell under three categories: the innocent, whom the police commissioner, the district chief, or the province chief were empowered to release; the truly guilty, who were turned over to court-martials; and those who were considered harmful but without enough evidence to warrant legal proceedings. The latter were processed by a provincial security committee which consisted of the province chief, deputy chief for internal security, public prosecutor or presiding judge of the local court, chief of the police service, military security representative, S-2 representative, and a representative of the operational forces or Regional-Popular Forces (RF-PF). This committee was empowered to release, assign residence or detain without due legal proceedings. In the latter case, the terms of detention ranged from a minimum of three months to a maximum of two years. The committee met once a month to review its cases. The police chief presented the charges in each case and, if there were no objections, the committee decided on the spot as to disposition of the case. This trial process was subjected to frequent criticism and opposition as it was an administrative procedure rather than a due process of law, and in most cases the defendant was either not allowed to stand for trial or denied the right to legal counsel.

This method of disposing of the VCI dealt with the branches, not with the roots, of the problem. Sentencing was done mechanically and based solely on effects as recorded in the files; it ignored causes such as weak minds, coercion, or false accusations by people seeking personal revenge, etc. It left indicted people with no way out. In most cases, the suspects were originally not VCI at heart, but in the course of detention they might have been approached and indoctrinated by other detainees who happened to be hard-core Communist cadre; in time they all became real Communist agents. Also the indignation of their relatives at the injustice was readily exploited by the Communists in their recruitment efforts.

The VCI suffered a devastating blow in 1968 when its forces came out in the open during the Tet general offensive. The resulting losses were such that it never again matched the magnitude and performances of the past.

In large cities and suburban areas VCI agents were difficult to identify because they blended with the masses and infiltrated all the heterogeneous elements of society. This prompted the individual policeman to keep away for fear of treading on touchy grounds or touching off a personal vendetta, either because there was no personal gain in sight for him or because he had been bribed to look the other way. In some cases, the police reacted only because they had no choice. The lack of aggressiveness on the part of the police caused people to think it would be foolish to get involved. This was a severe drawback because no one was better informed on what was happening in a city block or ward than the people who lived there. Popular Self-Defense Forces (PSDF) were available everywhere and, though they were not intelligence collection units in the true sense of the term, they were designed in part to serve as a source of information to the NP. In each PSDF combat team, one to three men had received a week of general intelligence training. However, as the designation Popular Self-Defense Forces indicates, these were people's organizations, commanded by city block or ward chiefs, and were loosely structured. The objective in establishing the PSDF was to make it mandatory for those citizens who were not in the service or in the police to participate in security and defense of their own blocks or wards. Because in large cities certain people avoided PSDF guard duty by hiring others to substitute for them, society saw the birth of a new occupation: professional PSDF.

The NP kept tabs on all citizens and reviewed applications for civil service jobs, for which no special security clearance was required. In order to control the ranks of the administration, particularly in the wake of the Huynh Van Trong espionage case in 1971, a new security organization was established which became known as the Directorate General for Administrative Security.[6] Civil servants, too, were cadre of the state and played an equally important role in the conduct of the state. However, their political loyalties had never been questioned and naturally they had never been subjected to security clearances, except when considered for such high positions as cabinet minister or under secretary or directors of important departments. In these cases required clearance by the CIO was based on data furnished by the NP or MSS. In addition to weaknesses in personnel security,

---

[6]See Chapter VII for details on the Huynh Van Trong case.

the civil service suffered from its personnel's ignorance of fundamental security measures required to protect documents and work premises. Classified documents could be lost without being detected, and people who did come upon lost documents usually did not bother to report them. The Directorate General for Administrative Security was designed to fill these gaps but achieved no positive results. Its very first step of establishing personnel files for security purposes met with a negative attitude, if not resistance, from the civil servants who generally objected to preparing detailed personal history statements.

The Directorate General for Administrative Security failed to become an MSS counterpart of the administration although it was patterned after the MSS mission and concept of organization.

Vietnamese Military Intelligence Organizations

When attempting to define responsibility for military intelligence operations in the RVN armed forces, attention is always directed at the role of J-2, JGS, thought by many to be the highest authority in military intelligence and enjoying the sole prerogative for planning, coordinating and controlling all intelligence efforts in the armed forces. Nothing is farther from the truth. This misconception of the role of J-2, JGS, apparently derives from knowledge of the organization and mission of the earlier French "Deuxieme Bureau" and of American military intelligence.

In reality, J-2, JGS, was but a military intelligence agency among others. With regard to authority, it was on a par with MSS; J-7, JGS; and STRATDAT. MSS was responsible for counterintelligence (CI), while J-7, JGS, was responsible for signal intelligence and communications security. STRATDAT, however, was more of an operational unit than an intelligence agency.

The organization of military intelligence in the RVN armed forces lacked a principal agency which would normally prepare a common military intelligence plan, establish common intelligence requirements, and act as the only authority responsible for reporting on the enemy situation.

The intricacies of internal politics had defeated efforts to unify military intelligence organizations. As a result, coordination and cooperation among these agencies were based on personal concepts and convenience of the agency heads involved rather than on established staff policies.

1. The Military Security Department

Contrary to US organizational policies, responsibility for counterintelligence in the Vietnamese armed forces was entrusted to the Military Security Department (better known as Military Security Service or MSS), not to J-2, JGS. The Republic of China's influence was evident in the subordination of MSS to the General Political Warfare Department (GPWD) which came under JGS. However, this subordination was only theoretical because for all practical purposes the MSS usually reported directly to the President or the Premier from whom it received its directives.

While other Vietnamese intelligence agencies were patterned after US intelligence, the organization of the MSS was entirely the product of self-formulated concepts. Though counterintelligence was its avowed mission, one of the MSS unofficial but most critical efforts—which was performed only at headquarters level—was to detect and prevent military coups against the regime. With such a politically-oriented real mission, MSS was organized to become an agency vested with power, authority and influence. It was fully funded by the national budget without need for US assistance. MSS was the only military agency empowered to apprehend, detain, and investigate civilians and military personnel alike without due legal process. MSS commented on appointments within the armed forces, granted security clearances, cleared applications for exit visas or overseas training, and was the key member of annual military promotion boards.

Added to political influence derived from its association with national leaders, this power enabled MSS to organize itself the way it saw fit and to fear no competition or opposition from other agencies.

For instance, MSS was allowed to have its own signal communications system which made intra-agency communications totally free of outside control. The Military Security Department was organized as follows: *(Chart 6)*

Chart 6 — Organization, Military Security Department

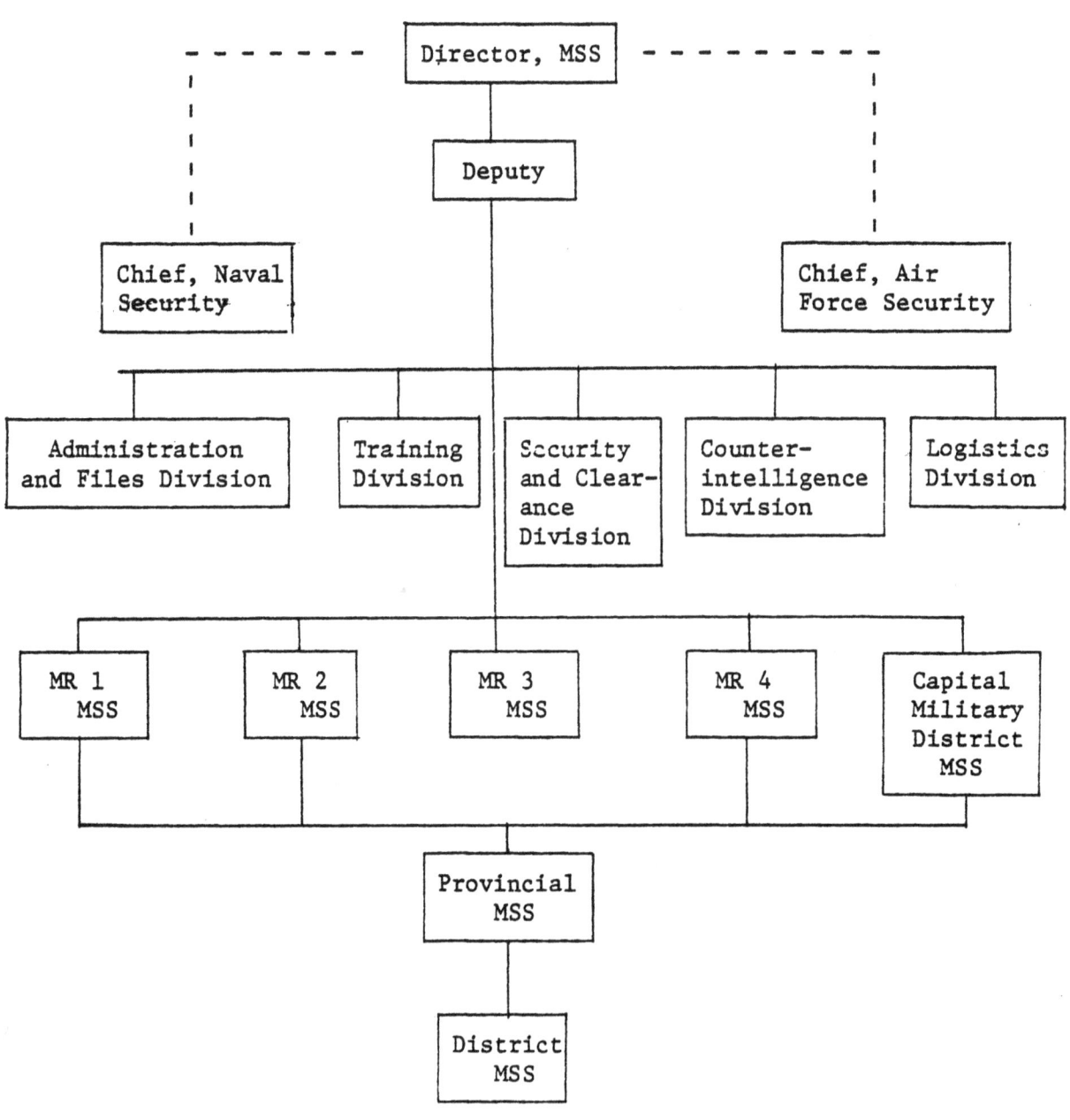

- - - - - operational control

Military Security was 4,328-men strong. MSS headquarters in Saigon had 657 men. The Capital Military District (CMD) MSS had 221 men. Each military region (MR) MSS had 50 men, each province 30, each district 6, each corps 20, and each division 25.

Military Security personnel fell into two categories: the professionals trained and appointed by MSS, and those appointed by the regiments and battalions to serve as security officers or non-commissioned officers.

Military Security's counterintelligence mission called for countering sabotage, subversion, and espionage. Its duties included personnel security, installation security, and document security. Another mission, which was more of a psychological nature, was to safeguard and maintain the morale of troops and prevent desertion.

MSS prepared daily and special reports. Those of a political nature were sent directly to the President's Office and to the Premier's Office. In times of political crises, MSS headquarters staff concentrated maximum efforts on collecting information concerning the opposition. The only bilateral activities involving US elements were those operations which were conducted in coordination with the US 525th Military Intelligence Group against Communist targets in MR 1 and MR 2. MSS supported US forces by conducting security clearances for Vietnamese employees of US agencies, issuing gate passes, etc. Military Security personnel were trained both at home and abroad. Although its organization and mission were different in nature, Vietnamese military security generally operated on the basis of US principles.

MSS did not confine itself to counterintelligence activities. Whenever the occasion presented itself, it also sought intelligence information from counterintelligence nets or through interrogation of prisoners of war.

In summary, MSS was well and strongly organized and was able to retain its independence. It was credited with many successful counterintelligence feats. Had all Vietnamese military intelligence agencies been organized like the MSS, military intelligence as a whole would have earned more respect and consideration.

2. J-7, JGS and the Special Technical and Security Branch

J-7 was a general staff division of the JGS responsible for planning, supervising and controlling signal intelligence and communications security activities performed by units and organizations making up the "Special Technical and Security Branch." In addition to J-7, JGS, the "Special Technical and Security Branch" consisted of Unit 15, Unit 16, Unit 17, and field organizations and units such as signal intelligence centers assigned to corps and divisional technical detachments.

The mission of the Special Technical and Security Branch was to collect and produce signal intelligence and communications-electronics intelligence and ensure communications security for the entire RVNAF and certain key governmental agencies.

The Assistant Chief of Staff, J-7, JGS, was chief of the Special Technical and Security Branch (STS) whose total strength was 3,500 men. The STS Branch was organized as follows: (Chart 7)

Chart 7 — Organization, Special Technical and Security Branch

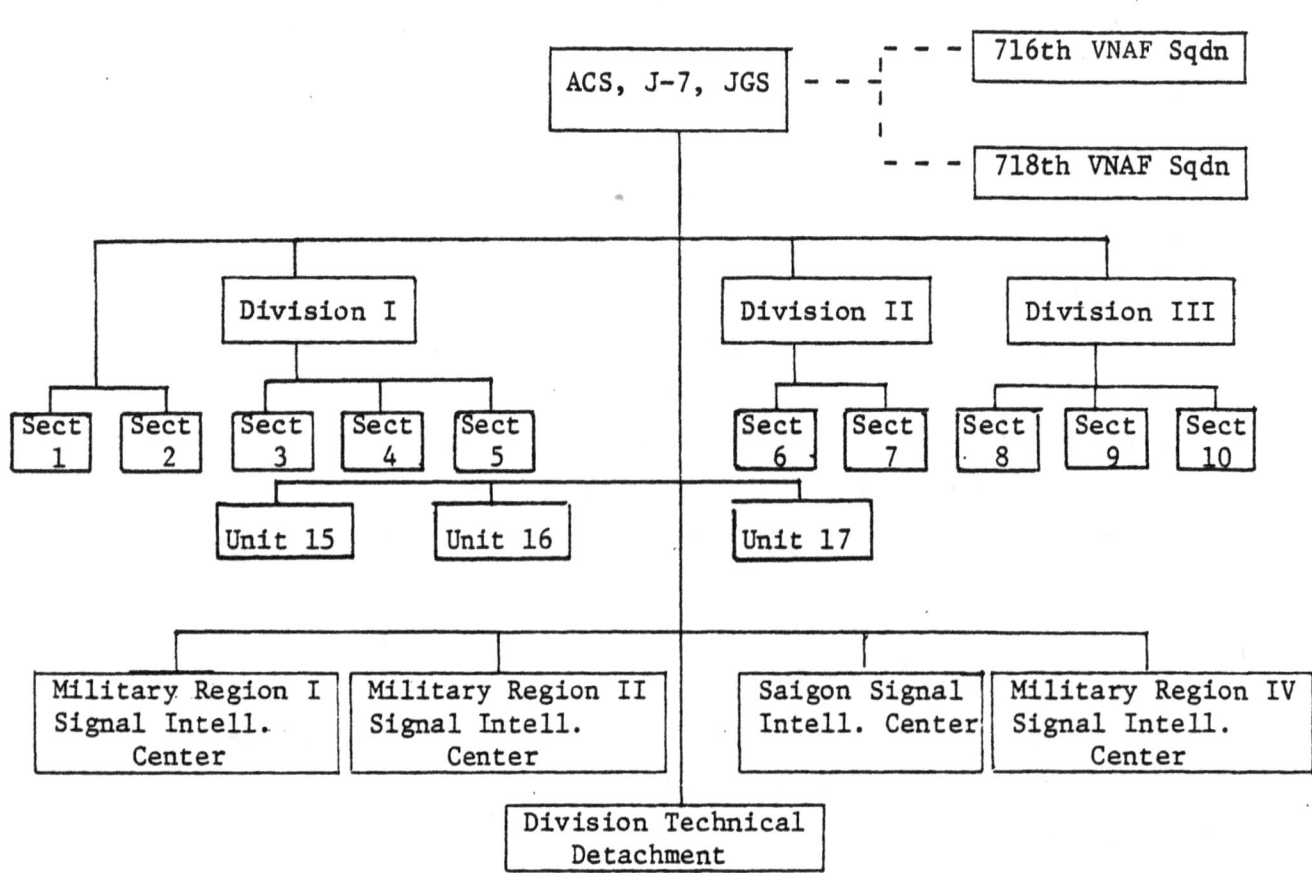

J-7, JGS, was organized into three principal staff divisions, in addition to Sections 1 and 2 which were responsible for administration and personnel. Division I had three sections: 3, 4 and 5. Section 3 maintained liaison with J-2 and J-3, JGS, to obtain updated information on the enemy situation and prepared and distributed technical intelligence reports. Section 4 prepared ARDF (Airborne Radio Direction Finding) information reports, monitored flights, and reported technical changes in enemy radio stations. Section 5 processed enemy defectors' and prisoners of war interrogation reports related to signal intelligence, interrogated these sources when necessary, processed news bulletins from enemy and friendly (BBC, VOA) radio broadcasts to prepare daily information reports, and maintained liaison with civilian and military security agencies in matters related to counterintelligence planning.

Division II was responsible for communications security. It consisted of two sections: 6 and 7. Section 6 processed technical data and prepared communications security reports recommending corrective action. Section 7 studied friendly cryptographic security methods, maintained liaison and coordinated with J-6, JGS, for cryptographic inspections within the armed forces.

Division III was responsible for research, improvement, and coordination of support and training. It was made up of three sections: 8, 9 and 10. Section 8 handled organization, recruitment, operations, support, maintenance and transportation. Section 9 conducted inspections of short-range operational plans. Section 10 trained specialists, monitored training, and prepared training materials.

During the period from 1961 to 1970, Unit 15 was the basic unit responsible for radio intercept. Later this mission was turned over to the four regional/corps signal intelligence centers and the unit became a special unit in charge of code-breaking or decrypting enemy messages.

Unit 16 provided communications security to the RVNAF and a number of key governmental agencies, established reports of communications security violations, inspected cryptographic facilities and classified technical documents, and coordinated with J-6, JGS, to review cryptographic procedures applied in the RVNAF.

Unit 17 was established in 1970 to coordinate with the VNAF 716th and 718th Squadrons in preparing flight plans for signal intelligence missions. Four phases were involved in this preparation: mission analysis, briefing, debriefing, and reporting.

The 716th and 718th Squadrons were subordinate to the 33d Wing of VNAF 5th Air Division. The 716th Squadron had five U-6A aircraft and the 718th had thirty-three EC-47 aircraft.

Of the four signal intelligence centers, three were established at I, II and IV Corps Headquarters in Da Nang, Pleiku and Can Tho respectively, and the fourth was established in Saigon to support III Corps. *(Map 1)* Each center collected information through radio intercept, radio direction finding and transcribing. To provide support for these centers, there were, in addition, four fixed radio intercept stations located at Phu Bai (MR-1), Song Mao (MR-2), Vung Tau (MR-3) and Con Son island.

Infantry divisions, to include general reserve divisions, were each assigned a Technical Detachment to provide direct support in communications intelligence.*(Map 2)* Each Division Technical Detachment was capable of collecting information through radio intercept and radio direction finding, to include CW,Voice(AM) and low-power Voice (FM). Each Divisional Technical Detachment was organized as follows *(Chart 8)*:

Chart 8— Organization, Divisional Technical Detachment

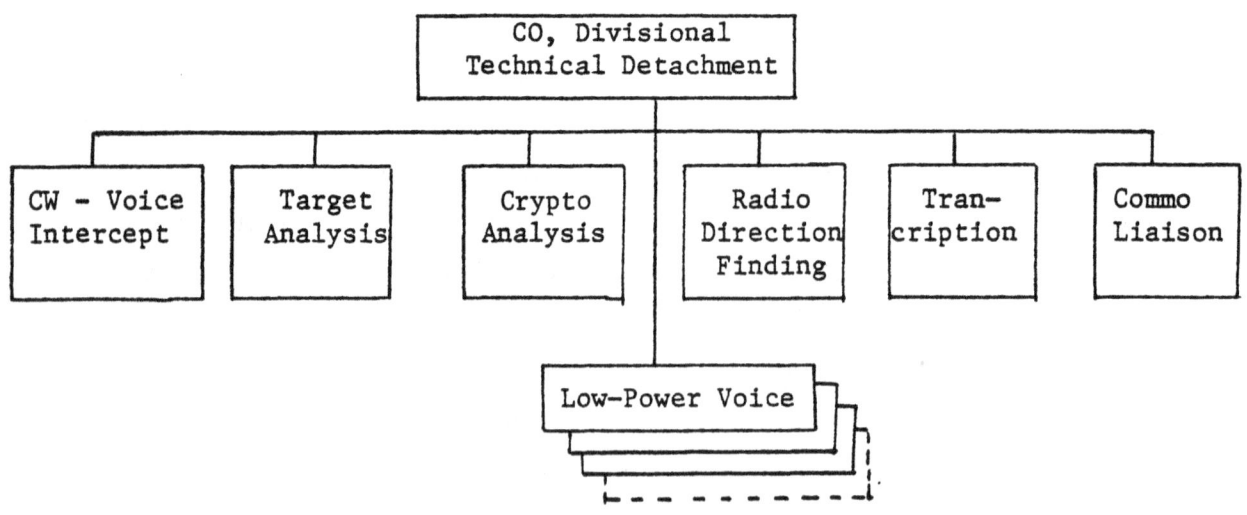

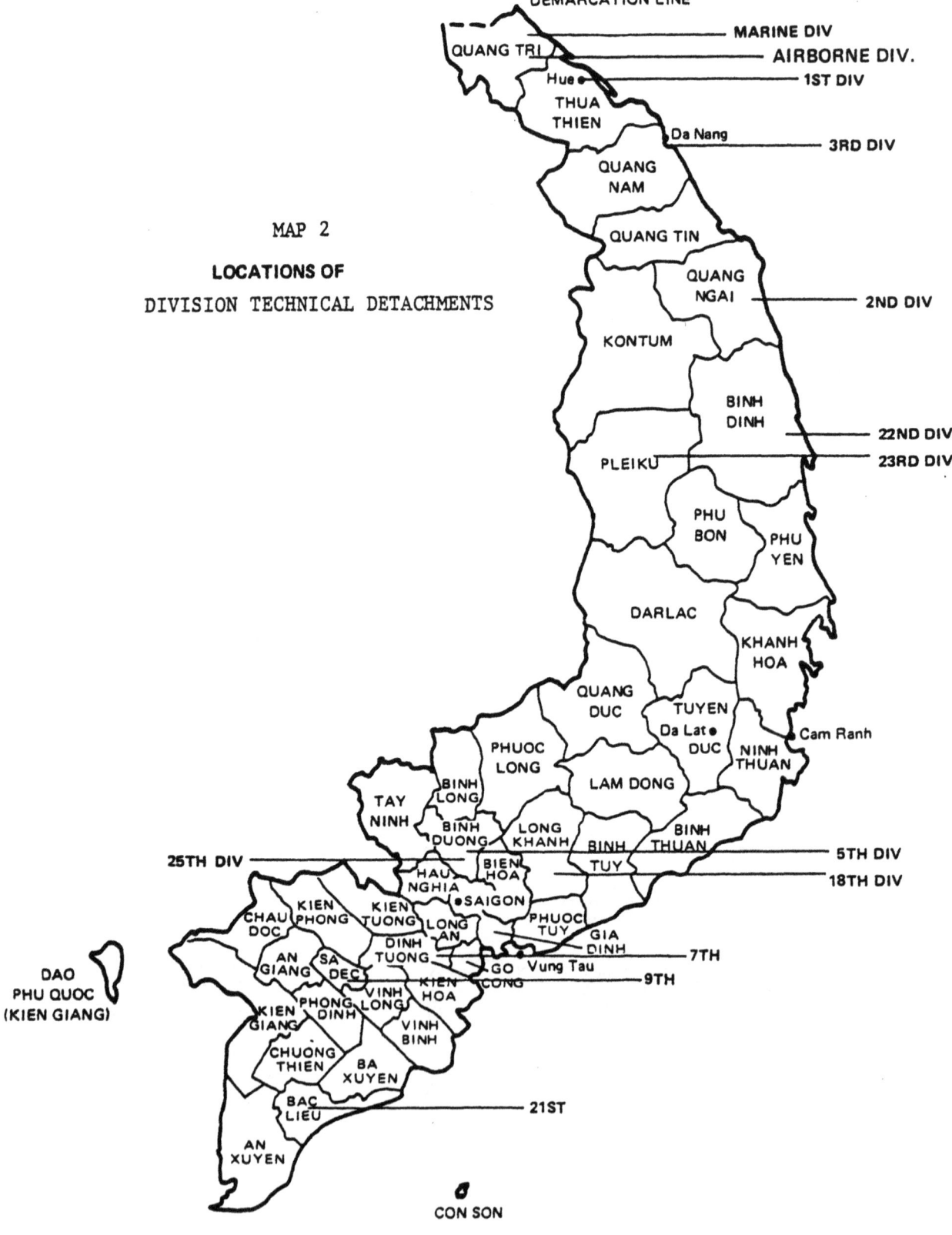

Signal Intelligence Centers and Divisional Technical Detachments reported directly to Corps and Division commanders (or their Chiefs of Staff) respectively. Their reporting channel did not go through Corps or Division G-2's. However, copies of their special reports were always made available to G-2. The major shortcoming of this direct reporting system lies in the fact that intelligence data submitted to field commanders were usually raw and not interpreted. This shortcoming became a real danger when communications specialists tried to analyze and interpret data by themselves as they sometimes did. The Signal Intelligence Center at Da Nang, for example, once submitted a report predicting that an enemy military "high point" was going to occur at a certain precise date. But the expected event never materialized. An investigation later revealed that a communications specialist had taken the liberty to analyze and interpret the raw data collected all by himself.

Techniques employed and controlled by J-7, JGS can be summarized as to include: 1) high-frequency radio direction finding (CW and AM); 2) airborne radio direction finding; 3) ground-based radio direction finding; 4) medium-range radio direction finding; 5) short range radio direction finding; and radio intercept (CW, AM and FM).

High-frequency radio direction finding was not very effective in Vietnam because the length and narrowness of the country did not lend themselves to accurate cross-bearings. This technique only helped determine target areas for ARDF. Airborne communications intercept was performed in conjunction with ground intercept to produce communications intelligence (COMINT) and electronic intelligence (ELINT) data. This technique was very effective in providing accurate and timely information. However, J-7, JGS only had EC-47 aircraft at its service while US forces used sophisticated aircraft such as C-130F, RC-135, RU-21D, JU-21A, etc. Information provided by communications intelligence at the beginning of the US direct participation in the Vietnam war enraptured ARVN unit commanders with its accuracy and timeliness. Beginning in 1970, as US forces phased out, the STS Branch expanded in an attempt to replace them in this field but the gap was not too obvious because US resources and capabilities, though reduced, were still adequate in relation to the needs. Following the 28 January 1973 Paris Agreement, the most significant loss was in ARDF resources as EC-47 aircraft were unable to operate over areas heavily defended by enemy anti-aircraft artillery; they were confined, therefore, to operating over the lowlands and coastal areas. Still, with the expansion of SIGINT and COMINT efforts, signal and communications intelligence contributed substantially to supplementing combat intelligence collected from other sources.

3. J-2, JGS and the RVNAF Military Intelligence Branch

J-2, JGS, as a general staff division of the JGS and command body of the Military Intelligence Branch, was primarily responsible for military intelligence activities in the RVNAF. Its duties were generally limited to combat intelligence, and its span of control, confined to South Vietnam. J-2, JGS exercised no control over foreign intelligence activities which were performed by Vietnamese military attaches under the direct control of the Minister of Defense; nor had J-2, JGS any connection with political warfare intelligence activities which were under direct control of the General Political Warfare Department (GPWD). Since war was the primary national effort, the role of J-2, JGS and the military intelligence branch by extension became more and more pre-eminent over the years. Its position and authority with regard to other intelligence agencies, however, remained unchanged. The chain of command of the Military Intelligence Branch ran from J-2, JGS down to corps and divisions, G-2's and regiments and battalions S-2's, in the tactical structure and down to sectors and sub-sectors S-2's in the territorial structure. (Chart 9) The principal human intelligence (HUMINT) collection agency of J-2, JGS was Unit 101. In addition, the Military Intelligence Center under J-2, JGS control provided technical support in the areas of imagery interpretation, order of battle, targeting, documents, interrogation of prisoners of war and defectors, and exploitation of enemy weapons and equipment. Corps and division G-2's were supported by their respective military intelligence detachments. J-2, JGS also exercised operational control over the operation of A-2, VNAF, N-2, VNN and the RVNAF Military Intelligence School.

Chart 9 —Organization, RVNAF Military Intelligence

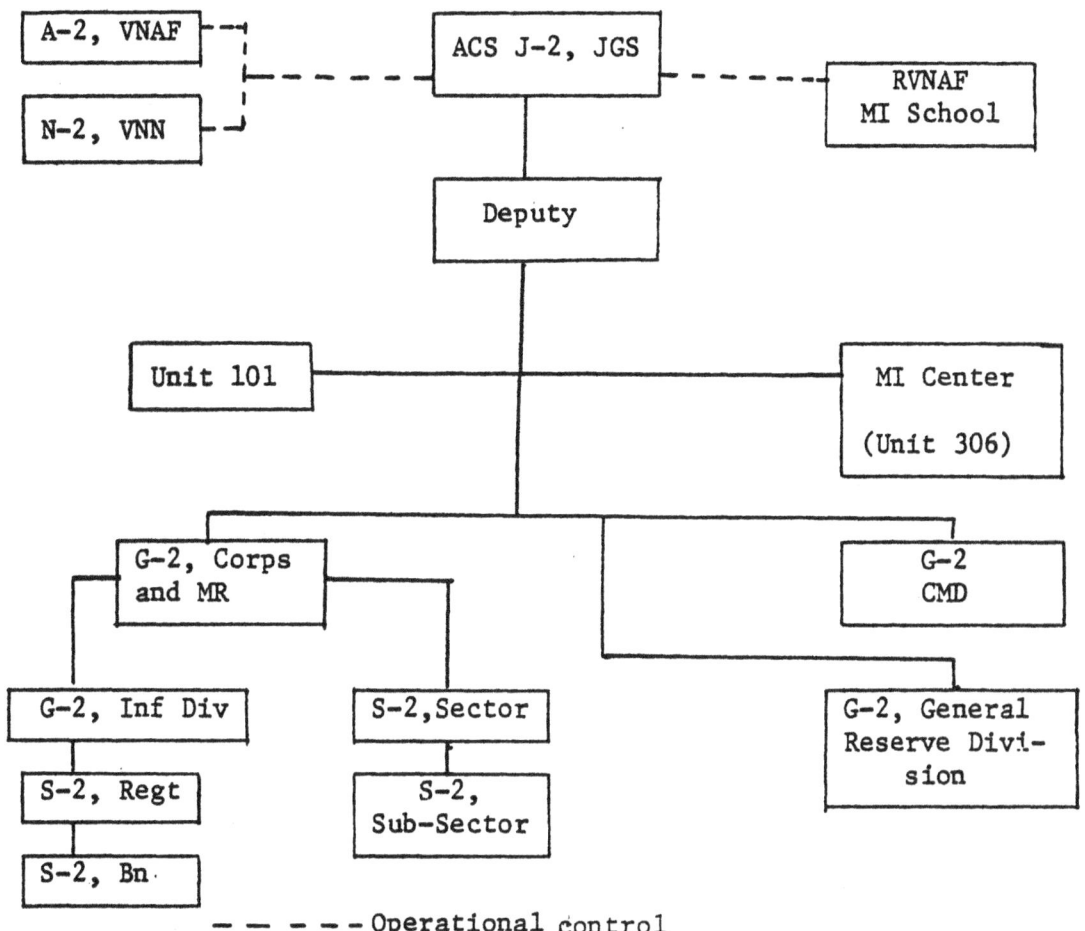

— — — — Operational control

The Military Intelligence Branch had 4,328 men. This did not include divisional and regimental reconnaissance companies or the Sector security/intelligence platoons and sub-sectors security/intelligence squads. The Military Intelligence Branch received its charter in 1971. Those who held positions in military intelligence organizations and had received military intelligence training or had operated in this field for at least a year were considered members of the Military Intelligence Branch. Military intelligence personnel at all levels were appointed by authority of the Assistant Chief of Staff J-2, JGS, who was also commander of the Military Intelligence Branch, or upon recommendation by tactical commanders subject to ratification by the ACS J-2, JGS. Most appointments fell in the second case. Until the charter of the Military

Intelligence Branch was promulgated, MI staff at all levels were usually subject to full control by tactical commanders and were required to comply with the latter's directives no matter how they conflicted with intelligence standing operating procedures in the armed forces. Some commanders of large units went so far as directing their G-2's not to report significant information on the enemy or tactical situation to J-2, JGS. In some cases liaison officers detached to Corps from J-2, JGS were even denied access to daily briefings or the use of local communications facilities to transmit information to their central headquarters. This snubbing occurred at a time when excessive military and civilian powers were given to field commanders, who usually reported directly to the President's office. Because of the lack of real powers over subordinate levels and the lack of a sole-user communications system, intelligence information collected by Vietnamese agencies and units during this period were routed to J-2, JGS through MACV (Military Assistance Command, Vietnam) channels rather than through local communication facilities. Information sent through RVNAF channels came in very late. This situation was gradually improved as more operational responsibilities were shifted to the RVNAF and JGS intelligence support to the local levels became more effective. From the time of the 1972 Summer General Offensive onward, military intelligence operational activities proved to be very effective and the only obstacles encountered were caused by insufficient resources. J-2, JGS was organized as shown in Chart 10.

During the period from 1967 to the cease-fire, J-2, JGS exercised operational control over four combined US-Vietnamese intelligence centers in addition to Unit 101 and the MI Center. Depending on its functions, each staff division of J-2, JGS was responsible for coordinating and supervising the activities of one or many centers and/or agencies as shown in Chart 11.

In its responsibility for preparing military maps, J-2, JGS received technical support from the National Geographic Directorate in Dalat and the Military Topography Company in Saigon. The situation room was not

Chart 10—Organization, J-2, JGS

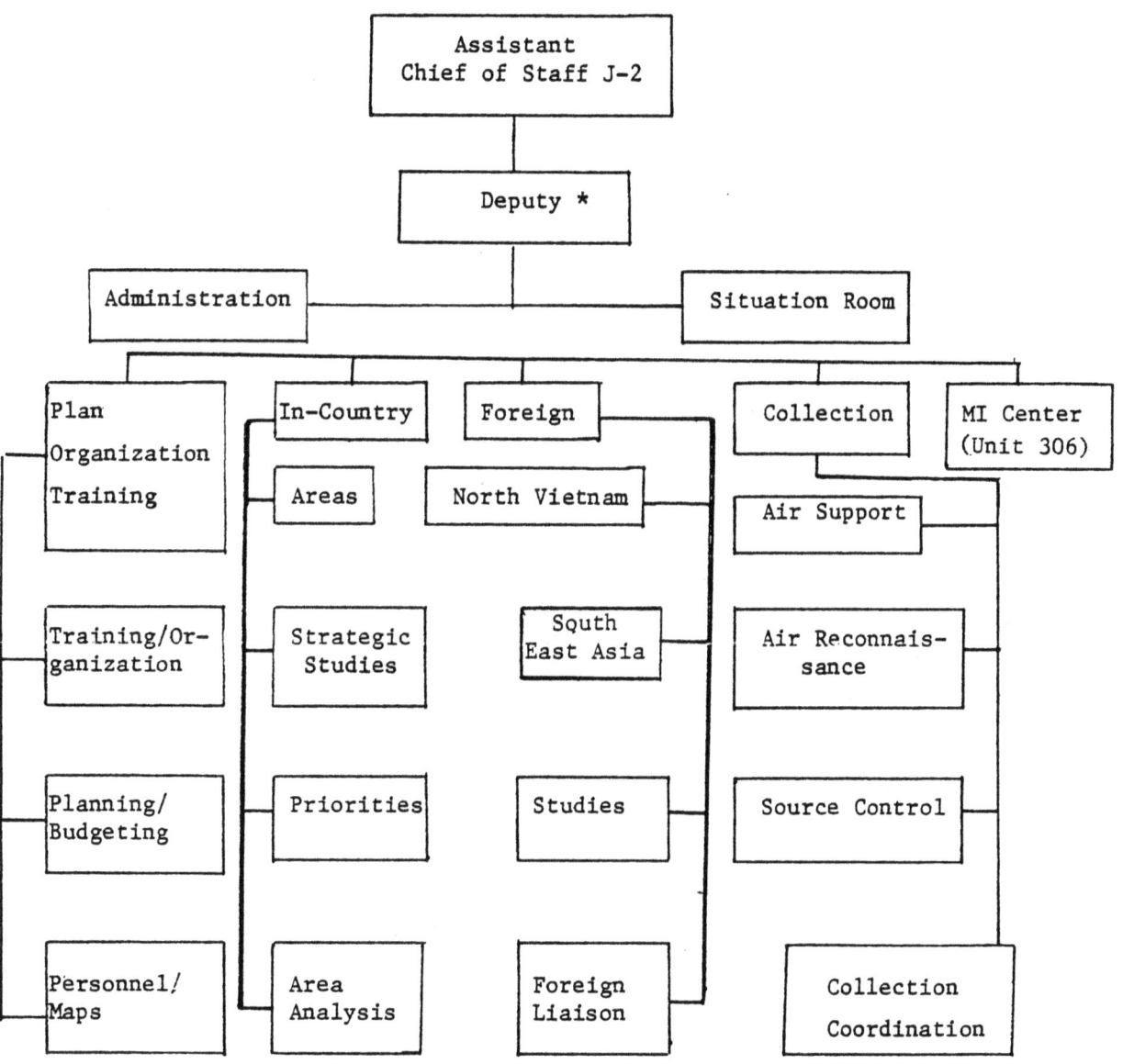

*Also commander of Unit 306 (MI Center).

Chart 11—Coordination and Supervision of Combined Intelligence Centers

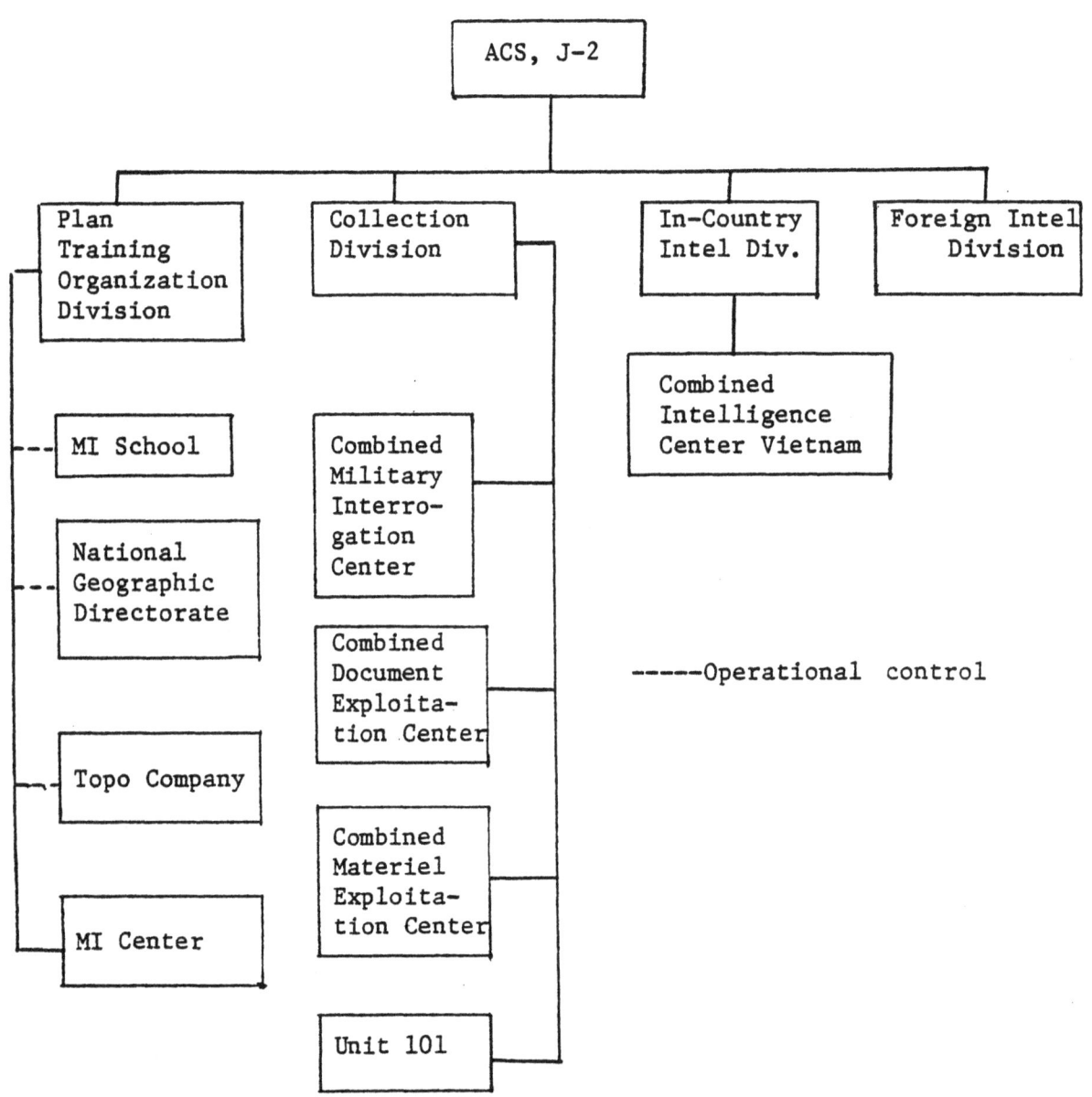

authorized in the Table of Organization and Equipment (TO&E) but was created out of necessity. This room was equipped with hot lines for direct communications with corps and division G-2's when the situation was serious. It operated around the clock and was staffed with field-grade officers who performed liaison duties for the purpose of exchanging intelligence information and tactical information, recording information requirements and support requirements of each MR; processing requests for aerial photographic reconnaissance, answering questions related to the identification of enemy units and infiltration groups. The situation room served as an operations center for J-2, JGS. Important tactical information was always reported immediately by subordinate G-2s. Situation developments were thus reported as they happened. For instance, information on enemy tanks moving into Ban Me Thuot city at 0330 hours on 10 March 1973 was reported and received as the action was in progress. Everyday, whenever the enemy attacked or clashes occurred, enemy unit identification was provided within the day upon processing of captured enemy documents or prisoners of war. These data enabled J-2, JGS daily situational reports to be accurate and timely. In addition to daily reports, J-2, JGS compiled weekly and monthly reports, semiannual reports, and annual recapitulative reports. Occasionally, J-2, JGS was also required to produce intelligence estimates, situational assessments, and special studies. Though entrusted with such an encompassing responsibility as monitoring the enemy situation, J-2 was only vested with the authority of a staff agency, and most people were unaware of its material limitations.

4. ARVN Combat and Territorial Intelligence Organization

G-2's of corps and military regions operated the combat and territorial intelligence systems. At this level, each G-2 was directly supported by a military intelligence detachment and a prisoner interrogation center, whose strength was authorized by separate TO&Es. Their aggregated strength was 164 men of whom 27 were assigned to corps G-2. G-2, Corps was organized as follows (*Chart 12*):

Chart 12—Organization, G-2/Corps

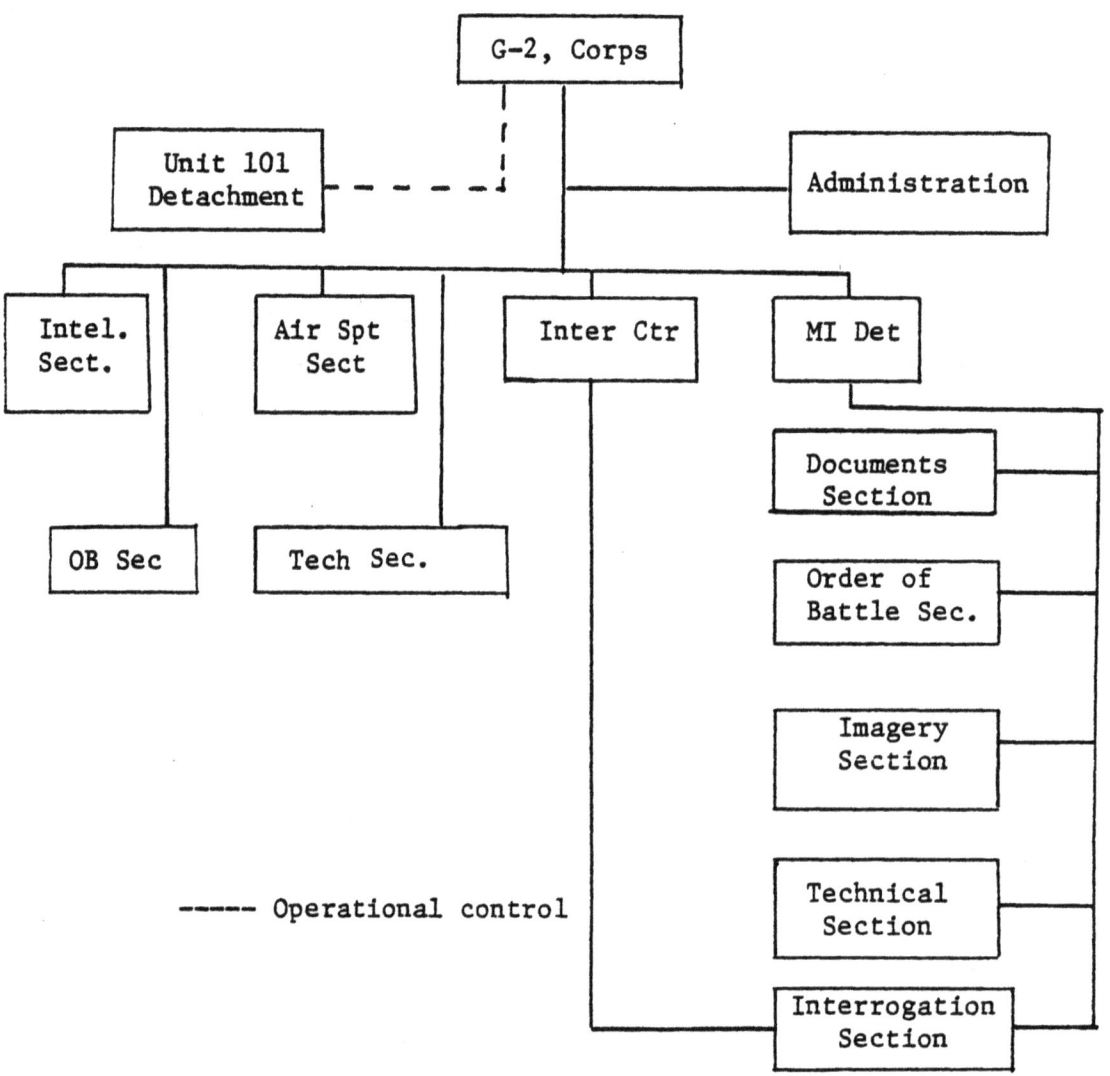

A corps military intelligence detachment had an authorized strength of 62 men and was usually commanded by the deputy corps G-2. Its interrogation section became part of the corps interrogation center when the latter was established. The Intelligence Section's mission was two-fold: collection and production. To carry out its collection mission, G-2, Corps organized agent nets and penetration/reconnaissance teams. Penetration/reconnaissance teams were made up of former Communist defectors or prisoners of war. In the highlands, penetration/reconnaissance teams consisted of Montagnard personnel trained and dispatched according to

specific operations plan. Agents operating for corps G-2 were very
limited in numbers. Being carefully screened and trained, they proved
reliable. Corps did not have long-range reconnaissance or special reconnaissance companies like divisions and regiments. Its penetration/reconnaissance teams consisted entirely of volunteers from subordinate combat
units. G-2, Corps was responsible for monitoring the enemy situation in
its related military region and providing guidance and control over all
combat and territorial intelligence collection activities. Thus it
played a very important role, particularly after the deactivation of
division tactical areas (DTA) in 1970.

A Division G-2 had an intelligence section, an air support section
and an order-of-battle section; it was directly supported by a division
military intelligence detachment. Each Division G-2 had 19 men whereas
the military intelligence detachment had 46. Until 1970, G-2, Division
was also G-2, Division Tactical Area. After being released from territorial responsibility, it was able to concentrate exclusively on combat
intelligence. As an additional tool for intelligence collection, G-2
Division was attached a long-range reconnaissance or special reconnaissance
company whose main mission was to carry out intelligence plans prepared
by G-2. The tactical conduct of these intelligence operations was planned
by G-3. Reconnaissance companies received special training at the Ranger
Training Center in Duc My and proved to be daring, combat-experienced
units. Because of their combat audacity they were gradually used more
as a reserve or reaction unit for special combat situations rather than
for intelligence gathering purposes. Division G-2 was the key level in
combat intelligence, constantly monitoring the situation, pressing the
units to report and turn in captured documents, new weapons, and preliminary information from interrogation of prisoners of war and defectors.
The main obstacle that hampered its effectiveness remained the lack of
facilities to ensure expeditious movement of materials from the field
to base camp and from there on to corps and above. At the regiment level,
the S-2 staff was composed of two officers and two NCOs. They operated
an OB section, an IPW/DOC section, and Agent Nets Section and a long-
range reconnaissance section. At battalion level, there was only one

officer, the S-2, and one NCO, his assistant. The primary mission of the S-2 at battalion level was the interrogation of POW's and the exploitation of captured documents. Sector and sub-sector S-2s were responsible for territorial intelligence. Their collection targets were enemy provincial and district units, guerrillas and infrastructure. S-2 personnel were limited to Regional Force (RF) status. A sector S-2 had ten men and a sub-sector S-2 had only four (one officer, two noncommissioned officers and one enlisted man). Because territorial intelligence personnel were selected from RF ranks, there was no way of reinforcing S-2 staffs as desired nor was it possible for the territorial S-2's to share some of the Regular Army's intelligence personnel. Meanwhile, the S-2 responsibility was a very heavy one, with a vast territory to cover yet without adequate collection means to provide the coverage except for a security/intelligence (SI) platoon for sector level and a SI squad for sub-sector level. These units had the mission of collecting and verifying intelligence information. Each platoon had 28 men organized as follows (*Chart 13*):

Chart 13—Organization, Sector Security/Intelligence Platoon

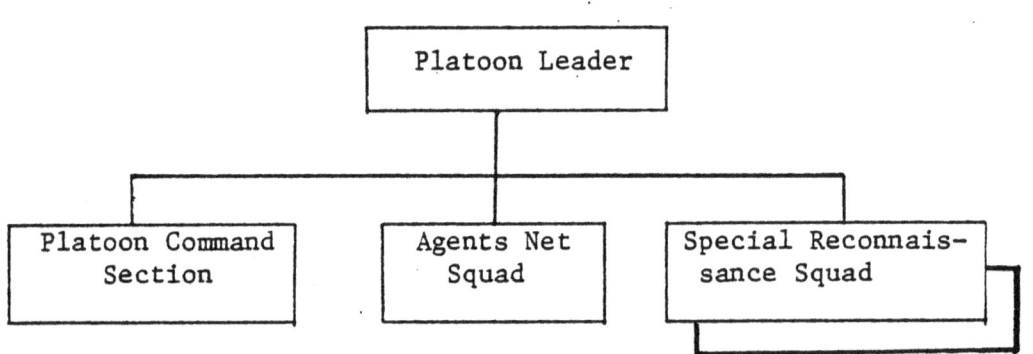

A sub-sector security/intelligence squad had 12 men divided into three teams: one agent team of two men and two special reconnaissance teams totalling seven men. Despite their organizational purpose, SI platoons and squads were usually assigned escort and guard duties instead of intelligence collection.

The sector and sub-sector S-2's lacked everything for their operation, even office supplies. There was a time when each S-2 was given a duplicating machine but those were not used for long because they usually ran out of printing ink and paper. Sources in a province who were in a position to provide information on the VCI came under NP jurisdiction and agents nets were not effective because they were short of means. As a result, only information derived from the processing of defectors, documents, and prisoners of war captured by the RF/PF was available, and that also was scarce. The S-2's were also employed by the province and district chiefs in miscellaneous duties unrelated to their intelligence mission.

It may be said that tactical intelligence at sector and sub-sector levels was very inadequate but corrective action or improvement could hardly be expected when basic equipment needs could not be met. In Vietnam, priority for improving intelligence capabilities at the lower levels was given to the NP rather than to the RF. This practice proved effective at an earlier stage but gradually deteriorated as supporting means were reduced and eventually terminated with the advent of the cease-fire agreement on 28 January 1973.

5. Vietnamese Air Force Intelligence Organization

A-2's mission was to collect information on the organization, equipment and capabilities of the North Vietnamese Air Force, the conditions of airfields in North Vietnam and of those in South Vietnam susceptible to use by the Communists, and North Vietnam's air defense and radar systems. A-2 was also responsible for providing bomb damage assessments (BDA).

A-2 had a collection section, a targeting section, an imagery interpretation center and a special collection detachment. *(Chart 14)* Its authorized strength was 638 men.

Chart 14 —Organization, Air Intelligence

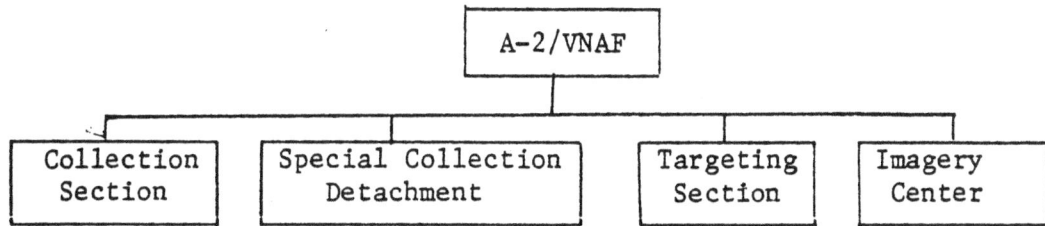

The collection section assigned collection missions and monitored the enemy situation nationwide, with special emphasis on locations of friendly airbases and areas of intense enemy air defense activities. The collection section also kept track of the various types of air defense armament used by the enemy, with special priority being given to such weapons as the heat-seeking SA-7 missile. The special collection detachment had 168 men assigned to a headquarters in Saigon and six collection teams, 17 men to a team.

The targeting section conducted briefings and debriefings for bombing missions whose targets were designated at the national level, and coordinated with air support squadrons in the conduct of photographic or observation flights. Once a photo mission was completed, films were delivered to the Imagery Center for processing and interpretation. Results were then forwarded to the users, J-2, JGS, and the air division concerned. This process took three days and therefore on many occasions results were no longer consistent with tactical developments. Air reconnaissance support was limited to military regions 2, 3 and 4. In MR-1, the highlands of MR-2 and the joint boundary area of MR-2 and MR-3, air reconnaissance support could not be provided due to the intensity of enemy air defenses. As a result, VNAF had to depend on the US "Buffalo Hunter" program for air reconnaissance over these areas.

The Imagery Center was capable of producing selected prints and duplicating positives of aerial photos provided by the USAF as well as making mosaics of photos obtained by VNAF RC-47's despite the obsolescence of its equipment and the scarcity of print paper. In June 1974, a fire broke out at the center because of deteriorating electrical wiring and its activities were subsequently curtailed. Because of the extremely limited number of photo reconnaissance aircraft at its disposal (four RF-5's and four RC-47's), the inadequacy and obsolescence of camera equipment, the threat of enemy air defenses, the Vietnamese Air Force had to depend on US support for 95% of in-country aerial photographs during the period following the cease-fire.

6. <u>Vietnamese Navy Intelligence Organization</u>

The VNN's primary mission was to detect Communist seaborne infiltration. This infiltration took on more magnitude and significance beginning in March 1970, after Sihanoukville had ceased to be an entry point for logistical supplies shipped from North Vietnam. After the Paris Agreement, the US Navy discontinued its patrolling off Vietnamese territorial waters while VNN was only capable of coastal patrols and interception and riverine missions. N-2 scope of activity was subjected to the same limitations. N-2, VNN was organized as follows (*Chart 15*):

Chart 15—Organization, Naval Intelligence

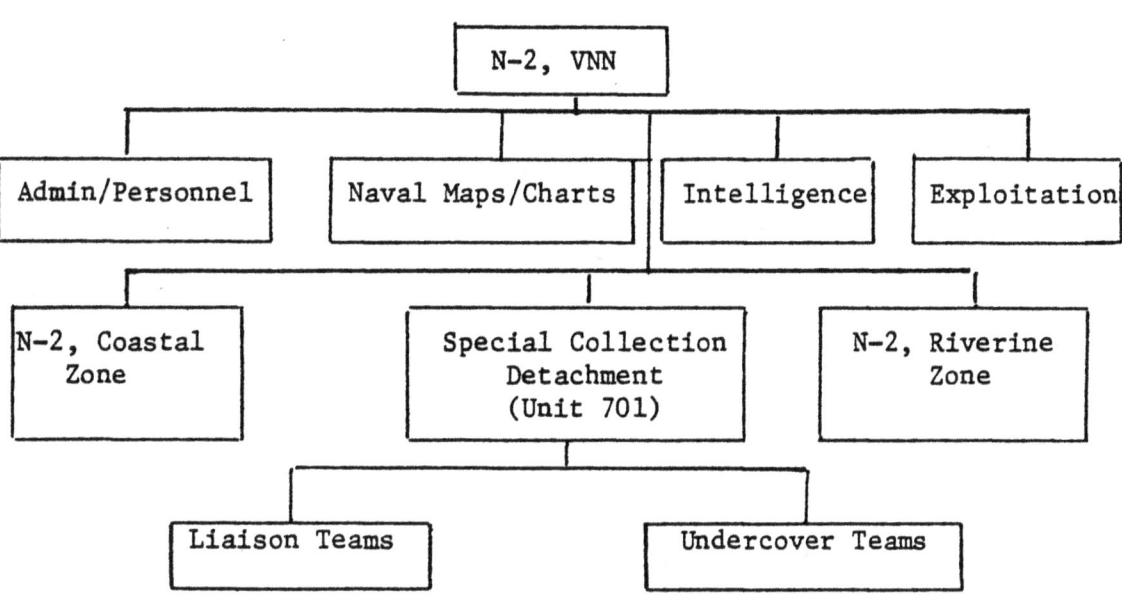

N-2 had a mobile interrrogation team which provided interrogation support to naval intelligence units when needed, as in the case of interception of North Vietnamese fishermen lost in MR-1, or foreign fishing vessels violating Vietnamese territorial waters.

The VNN special collection detachment was strongly developed after the cease-fire. Although its authorized strength was 124 men, the Chief of Naval Operations increased it to 230 to step up naval intelligence activities. The special collection detachment conducted both covert and overt operations. Covert operations were conducted by six teams which organized agents nets to operate in coastal and riverine zones. Overt operations were conducted by the Naval Intelligence Liaison Officers (NILO) who were assigned to 28 stations located throughout the country with the mission to collect and exchange information. These officers also functioned as case officers. The collection teams communicated with the detachment headquarters through single side-band, and FM radios.

In July 1970, the special collection detachment was redesignated Unit 701. Its collection operations were also reorganized to involve personnel of the unit disguised as civilians who operated fishing craft or in fishing villages to monitor Communist seaborne infiltration and smuggling activities.

In general, both VNN and VNAF were not capable of conducting sea reconnaissance either by air or by naval craft; nor were they equipped with telephoto cameras to photograph and identify the various types of vessels. Naval craft at sea provided information on Soviet or Chicom ships loaded with bulky cargoes. VNN repeatedly reported sightings of Soviet ships in territorial waters off MR-1 and MR-2 after the cease-fire but no infiltrations were detected. Apparently, since expanded logistical roadways in-country and in lower Laos more than adequately supported the needs of Communist units, sea infiltration was no longer as much needed as before.

United States Intelligence Organizations in Vietnam Before The Paris Agreement

There were too many Vietnamese intelligence organizations, as was commonly observed. Each of those usually coordinated with a counterpart US intelligence agency, which proves that the latter were just as numerous. These agencies were either under civilian control or military control. The civilian control was exerted by one of two agencies: the Office of the Special Assistant to the Ambassador (OSA), or the Civil Operations and Revolutionary Development Support (CORDS).

OSA collection efforts were directed at internal RVN politics and the Communists and closely coordinated with Vietnamese intelligence agencies such as the CIO, NP and J-7, JGS.

CORDS focused on intelligence coordination for the purpose of rooting out the VCI. This effort was also known as the Phoenix Program which was operated from national to district levels. US personnel assigned to CORDS were OSA or military officers. At sector level they were also intelligence advisors to the province chief.

The military control was exercised by MACV, J-2. Under MACV, J-2 there were three service intelligence organizations: G-2, US Army, Vietnam (USARV), the Office of Special Intelligence (OSI), 7th Air Force, and the Office of Naval Intelligence (ONI), US Naval Forces, Vietnam.

US Army Intelligence in South Vietnam consisted of the following organizations: G-2, USARV; G-2, III MAF, I FFV, II FFV; G-2, Divisions; S-2, Brigades and 5th Special Forces Group; and S-2 Battalions.

Also under MACV, J-2 were the 525th Military Intelligence Group, the 509th Radio Research Group; and the 1st Military Intelligence Battalion (Aerial Reconnaissance Support). In the beginning, the 525th Military Intelligence Group consisted of the 519th Military Intelligence Battalion, the 135th Military Intelligence Group, the 149th Military Intelligence Group, and military intelligence advisors. The 519th Military Intelligence Battalion was organized into four companies, each coordinating with a combined US/RVNAF intelligence center. Later, military intelligence advisors were organized into a company under control of the 519th instead of being directly subordinate to the 525th. This team had been established to provide intelligence advisors to four corps, 12 divisions, 43 sectors, totalling 622 men.[7]

The 135th Military Intelligence Group supported MACV J-2 and United States Army, Vietnam, in counterintelligence. This unit also provided advisors to and coordinated activities with the Vietnamese Military Security Department (MSS). The 149th Military Intelligence Group provided advisors to and coordinated bilateral collection operations

---

[7] Major General Joseph A. McChristian, The Role of Military Intelligence, 1965 - 1967, (Vietnam Studies, Department of the Army, Washington, D.C.: 1974).

with the 924th Support Group (Unit 101). The 509th Radio Research Group operated the intelligence communications system between MACV and subordinate units. The 1st Military Intelligence Battalion (Aerial Reconnaissance Support) provided imagery interpretation of aerial photos taken in-country. It was composed of: Detachment A stationed in Bien Hoa, Detachment B in Da Nang, Detachment C in Can Tho, Detachment D in Nha Trang, and the 45th Military Intelligence Detachment in Hue and Phu Bai.

By the time of the cease-fire, the 525th MI Group had been reorganized to include: the 571st Military Intelligence Detachment in MR-1, the 572d Military Intelligence Detachment in MR-2, the 573d Military Intelligence Detachment in MR-3, the 574th Military Intelligence Detachment in MR-4, the 575th Military Intelligence Detachment in charge of counterintelligence, the 358th Aviation Detachment, and the 504th Signal Detachment.[8]

US intelligence organizations in Vietnam played a dual role: advisory and coordinating. With sophisticated equipment, substantial resources, expertise, and modern operating methods, US intelligence helped Vietnamese intelligence improve gradually and move into real professionalism.

---

[8] OPORD 215, After Action Report, COUNTDOWN (DA: 4 June 1973).

CHAPTER IV

Intelligence Cooperation And Coordination

Concepts And Problems

There is general agreement that, in the Vietnam war, though US-Vietnamese cooperation and coordination existed in every field and sector, they were nowhere as concrete and distinctive as in the area of Intelligence. A common mission, common objectives, common efforts, and similarity in organization and operational procedures, all contributed to this cooperation and coordination. United States and Vietnamese intelligence organizations had their own assets and liabilities. The United States had sophisticated equipment, lavish means, effective techniques and management, and large-scale organizations. However, they lacked basic knowledge of the enemy, the language and the culture; furthermore, personnel were often replaced after a year's tour of duty. Vietnam didn't have sophisticated assets but Vietnamese intelligence personnel were more experienced and knowledgeable about the Vietnam war, about the enemy and his psychology and techniques, and especially important, they shared a common language with the enemy.

Bilateral cooperation and coordination increased the effectiveness of intelligence activities and joint operation helped each side to overcome its own limitations. However, the spirit of cooperation was the prime factor in determining success or failure of the intelligence program. This spirit was perceived by a high-ranking US intelligence official to be one of "mutual sincerity, openness, confidence and respect."[1]

---

[1] McChristian, *Military Intelligence*, Department of the Army, Washington, D.C. 1974, p.p. 11 - 142.

Cooperation and coordination must be based on joint agreements. These agreements must lead to clearcut directives for each side to follow, thereby precluding difficulties, misunderstandings, and loss of timeliness. When US forces were committed in Vietnam other problems arose, among them disputes over sovereignty and status of forces. Within the intelligence field, there were difficulties in exchanging information because restrictions imposed by national defense and security laws conflicted with the need to make information available to those concerned. However, all foreseeable difficulties were resolved officially with agreements that were either signed by both parties or were tacit. The foundations for these agreements were laid by the 27 September 1965 agreement between Commander, United States Military Assistance Command, Vietnam, and the Chief, Joint General Staff, Republic of Vietnam Armed Forces.

Weapons and equipment were classified as either common or sophisticated, with sophisticated weapons being those seized for the first time in the Vietnam theater. The common types were resolved according to status-of-force agreements which provided for the capturing forces to keep what they had captured. The sophisticated weapons, that is those captured for the first time in the Vietnam theater, were Vietnamese property. On the second capture, these items might go to the US side. On subsequent captures either side might keep the items. In reality, the Vietnamese side did not have the capability to test really sophisticated pieces of equipment and the US side was allowed to keep them for testing before returning or transferring them to Vietnamese custody. To facilitate the testing process no time limits were set. Test results were to be made available to the Vietnamese side. Actually, the agreement was carried out in a looser manner, as in the case of the SA-7 heat-seeking missile used for the first time in the Vietnam war during the 1972 general attack. Because of testing needs all captured SA-7s were turned over to the US side, and the Vietnamese had only a plastic mock-up of the weapon.

There were no problems in the area of captured documents because they were easily reproduced. All handwritten, printed, typewritten, drawn or engraved materials; tape recordings; photographs; films and seals were considered to be documents.

The US side transferred all prisoners of war and "Hoi Chanh" (defectors) to Vietnamese control. Though the US never officially declared war on the Vietnamese Communists, the 1949 Geneva Convention on Prisoners of War provided for a country to be allowed to entrust custody of its PW to another country as long as both fulfilled their obligations concerning good treatment of these prisoners. Consequently, PW of US or Free World Military Assistance Forces (US/FWMAF) were evacuated through US channels to the central Combined Military Interrogation Center (CMIC) in Saigon or CMICs at corps or division level, or Republic of Vietnam (RVN) operated PW camps.

On the RVN side, the difficulty was not in making Secret or Top Secret documents available to the US. Problems were frequently occasioned by US requests to downgrade materials, mostly Communist documents, for distribution to US information agencies or the US press corps. Vietnamese laws prohibited the distribution of Communist documents. Once downgraded the documents were exploited by the US press and were eventually published by the Vietnamese newspapers as translations, which frequently led to criticism of the Vietnamese press and US journalistic privileges.

Combined Intelligence Activities

In Military Intelligence, cooperation and coordination were conducted in one of two modes. The first mode provided for US personnel to function both as advisers and colleagues. The second mode gave them a strictly advisory capacity. The first type of relationship was established at Joint General Staff (JGS) level, the four combined intelligence centers, Collection Unit 101, J-7, JGS and subordinate elements, and the Military Security Department (better known as MSS). The second type of relationship existed at corps and division G-2s, sector and sub-sector S-2s and local MSS services.

Among combat units, intelligence cooperation and coordination were effected by detaching Vietnamese Military Intelligence Detachments (MIDs) to US/FWMAF corps, divisions and separate brigades. Sector S-2s assigned intelligence personnel to cooperate with US units conducting mobile operations on their respective territories. Division Tactical Area (DTA) G-2s assigned personnel to US units involved in interprovincial operations to assist in exploiting human sources and documents. Operational units also enjoyed support from "go-teams"[2] of the combined US/Vietnamese intelligence centers which were dispatched upon clearance by J-2/USMACV and J-2, JGS.

J-2, JGS And J-2, USMACV

During the initial period of US participation in the Vietnam war, cooperation and coordination between J-2, MACV and J-2, JGS were performed through a US liaison team permanently installed at J-2, JGS and consisting of four officers (two Army and one each from the Navy and Air Force) and a noncommissioned officer. The task of this liaison team was more administrative than professional, and little was accomplished in terms of information exchange or situation estimates. This situation improved during the next period when Major General Joseph A. McChristian was assigned as Chief J-2, MACV. For the first time, there were initiated weekly intelligence briefings conducted by US and ARVN staff officers. During these briefings, both parties compared and exchanged information received during the week and presented their respective assessments and estimates concerning enemy capabilities for the following week. Still, coordination was generally limited to staff officers. There were occasional consultations between the two J-2 chiefs but these meetings were not part of any established procedure nor did they relate to anything

---

[2] Team of US and Vietnamese specialists dispatched from Saigon to support combat units when required.

other than work policies and administration. As a matter of fact, the
Chief J-2, JGS and his US counterpart met only when needed and generally
with the purpose of acquainting themselves with organization, operation
and training of each side. The exchange of information, as a result,
lacked spontaneity and timeliness. But it was also during this period
that the idea of combined activities took shape and was implemented with
the activation of combined intelligence centers whose operations were
intended to benefit both MACV and the JGS.

Not until 1969, however, did intelligence cooperation and coordination between MACV and the JGS become really close and effective. This
was due to the professional interest given to the combined intelligence
effort by the Chief J-2, MACV, Major General William E. Potts. In addition to weekly combined staff meetings, the Chief J-2, MACV also took
the unprecedented step of discussing the situation and exchanging professional viewpoints with his counterpart and generally made himself
available for every worthy discussion. It was also due to his dedicated
and untiring effort that combined intelligence activities were greatly
enhanced and became instrumental in improving the effectiveness of
Vietnamese military intelligence.

At the combined intelligence centers and Collection Unit 101, coordination and collaboration materialized in the form of bilateral US/
Vietnamese activities. There were four combined intelligence centers:
Combined Intelligence Center, Vietnam (CICV); Combined Document Exploitation Center (CDEC); Combined Military Interrogation Center (CMIC);
and Combined Materiel Exploitation Center (CMEC).

Each center had two elements, one Vietnamese, the other US, each
with its own director. These two elements shared the same installations
and facilities. Personnel were integrated in individual sections.
Documents were compiled bilingually. There were a few differences such
as in organization and strength.[3]

---

[3] The organization of the four Combined Intelligence Centers is described here at the initial stage of operation in 1967.

Combined Intelligence Center, Vietnam (CICV)

This center was conceived in 1965 and its building inaugurated on 17 January 1967 although the various US/Vietnamese sections of the center had previously and individually initiated coordination of activities. The center operated around the clock with permanent and rotating teams.

The mission of CICV was to compile and provide intelligence data to the J-2s. These data were related to: terrain, weather, lines of communication (LOCs), bridges and culverts, and local area features; Vietnamese Communist order of battle (OB), Communist base areas, infiltration corridors, bombing targets, bomb damage assessment (BDA); imagery interpretation (II). CICV was organized as shown in Chart 16.

The center had six major operating sections. However, the RVNAF element did not staff the Technical Intelligence and Research Analysis sections because RVNAF had a separate center for technical intelligence and its research analysis function was carried out by the Studies Section of J-2, JGS. The Area Analysis Section, though an organic element of J-2, JGS, was integrated into CICV's organization in order to match the US structure. The US Operations Section functioned in a production capacity which involved assigning priorities, editing, and distributing documents and messages. It also had a communications center which enabled it to communicate by teletype with major US units and senior US advisers for the purpose of timely dissemination of intelligence information needed for tactical operations. The RVNAF Operations Section's only duties were to receive and/or dispatch correspondence and documents. It was consequently given the additional assignment of handling supplies. The Vietnamese element did not establish a Liaison Section because there already was one at J-2, JGS. Nor was there a Collection Requirements Section on the Vietnamese side because each specialized section handled its own requirements. The Automated Data Processing (ADP) Section provided intelligence data from Intelligence Data Handling Systems (IDHS), using IBM 360-30 computers. Because this was a very new technique, the Vietnamese side did not have specialists to staff the section among its two officers, six noncommissioned officers and enlisted man. Later, the two officers were sent to the US for training in the operation of the 360-30 computer while the noncommissioned officers received on-the-job

Chart 16— Organization, Combined Intelligence Center, Vietnam

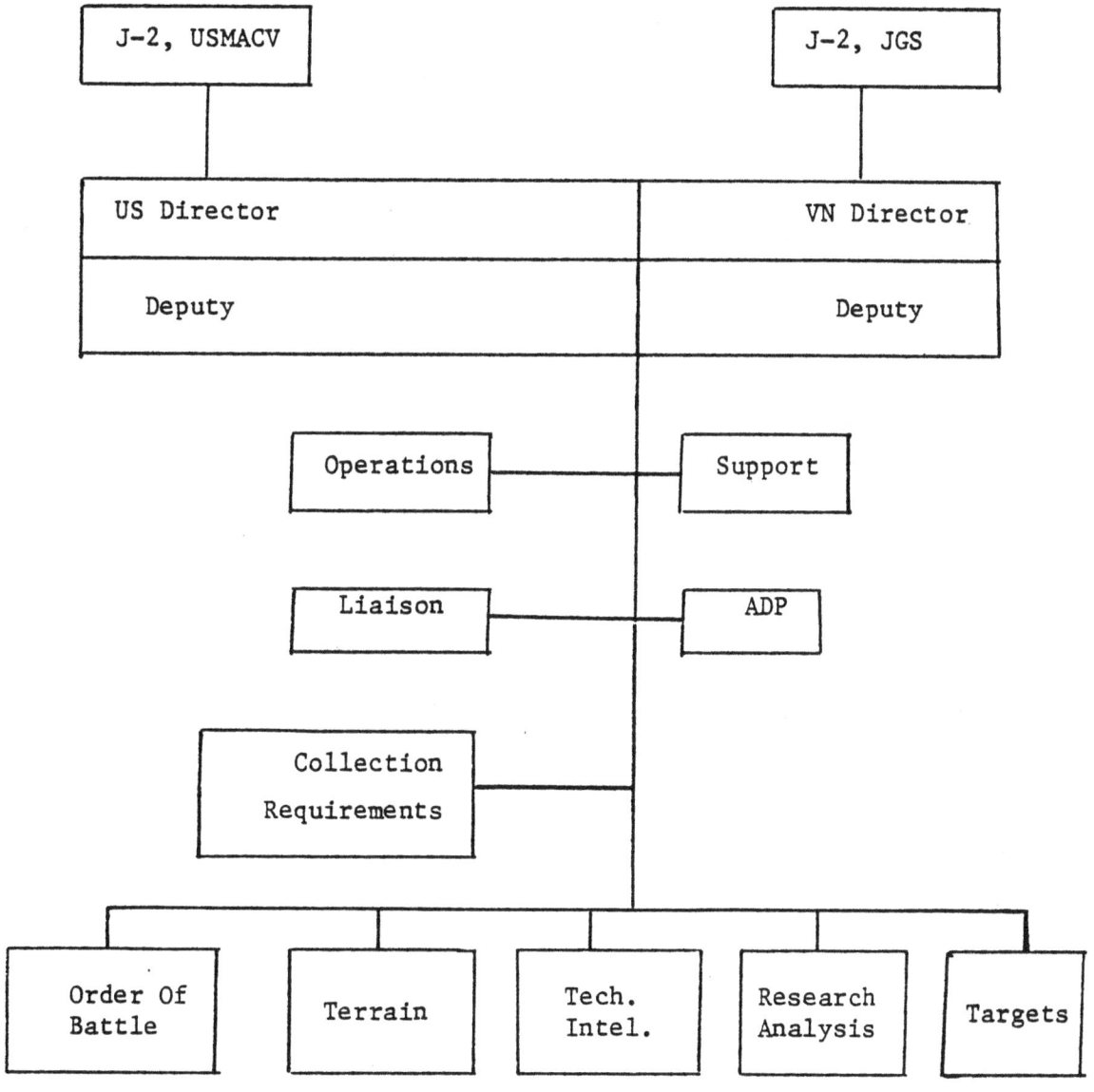

The US element had 651 men and the RVNAF 164.

training. Intelligence Data Handling Systems thus proved to be more useful to the US side than to the Vietnamese.

The Order of Battle (OB) Section of each side had three elements. The first element handled military OB and consisted of five teams: four for the four military regions of the republic and one providing coverage of North Vietnam, Laos and Cambodia. The second element studied and monitored infiltration routes and units. The third element was in charge of political OB and information on the Viet Cong Infrastructure (VCI). In the area of OB, though close bilateral coordination was effected right on the spot, the two sides differed on enemy strength figures, with RVN-computed figures always the higher. The reason for the discrepancy was that authority to accept enemy strength and forces rested on J-2, JGS on the Vietnamese side, while on the US side acceptance had to come from Commander in Chief, Pacific (CINCPAC), the DIA, and the acceptance procedure, on the RVN side almost proved, in a few instances, more flexible. In OB considerations, strength figures on guerrilla and VCI forces were usually not very accurate, especially after the general offensive of Tet 1968, when most of the heavy losses sustained by the enemy were actually borne by the guerrillas and the VCI. Efforts to keep a close count of the VCI ran into difficulties because sectors and sub-sectors did not have accurate figures or did not report them objectively. This reporting depended on each commander's personal appraisal of the local situation. A sector maintained a steady 100 in its count of the local VCI while submitting monthly reports on the number put out of action. In reality, even the Communists did not have these figures. This was precisely why in 1969 they sent inspection groups to each locality to conduct an on-the-spot census. Communist documents admitted that even their own provincial and district officials were unable to keep count of their membership.

As regards enemy units, it was conceived that they must be categorized into Main Force, Local Force, guerrillas or VCI and identified as Viet Cong (VC) or North Vietnam Army (NVA). This second classification was very important because on the one hand North Vietnam always denied it had any forces in the South, and on the other RVN was endeavoring to prove that the war efforts originated in the North. Classification was based upon the following definitions:[4]

North Vietnamese Army (NVA) Units: a unit formed, trained and designated by North Vietnam as an NVA unit and composed completely or primarily of North Vietnamese. Depending upon their subordination, these units may be categorized as Local Force or Main Force.

Viet Cong (VC) Units: a unit formed and trained in South Vietnam (or in some instances Cambodia and Laos) whose original composition consisted primarily of people residing in South Vietnam. Depending upon their subordination, these units may be categorized as guerrilla, Local Force, or Main Force.

Main Force (MF) Units: those VC or NVA military units which are directly subordinate to the Central Office of South Vietnam (COSVN), a Viet Cong military region, military subregion or front.

Local Force (LF) Units: those VC or NVA military units which are directly subordinate to province and district party committees and normally operating within the territorial jurisdiction of their respective control headquarters.

Guerrillas: guerrillas are fighting forces usually organized into platoons and squads, directly subordinate to the party apparatus at village and hamlet level. Although they form a full-time part of the enemy's offensive threat, the amount of time devoted to guerrilla duties by the individual guerrilla varies. At times guerrillas operate outside their home villages and hamlets, often with LF and MF units. Typical missions include limited offensive operations, harassment, sabotage, propaganda, protection of party committees, collection of taxes, and also security and reconnaissance for MF and LF units.

Vietnamese Communist Infrastructure (VCI): the VCI is the political and administrative organization through which the VC seek control of the people of the RVN. It embodies the Communist party control structure and the leadership and administration of front organizations from the national through the hamlet level.

---

[4] MACV Directives No 381-4 issued on Nov. 19, 1968 and July 4, 1972.

The VCI includes individuals who are members or probationary members of the Vietnamese Communist Party, also known as the People's Revolutionary Party, and those non-Communist members who perform an enemy cadre function described in the "Current Breakout of VCI Executive and Significant Cadre" (also known as the "Green Book"), published by the Government of Vietnam (GVN). The VCI does not include members of the enemy military forces who would qualify as PW according to the Geneva Convention rules.

Another aspect of the OB problem was that, when referring to enemy strength and forces, everyone usually implied those physically present on South Vietnam (SVN) territory with no consideration given to those positioned in border areas of Cambodia, Laos or North Vietnam (NVN). Such limited thinking led to misconceptions as to the status of conflicting forces. For instance, it was believed that the Communists had only 300,000 men against the combined 1,500,000 US/RVNAF troops. These 300,000 Communist troops in the South were trained, supplied and replenished by units stationed across the border. In Laos, Rear Service Group 559 alone had 50,000 men to move supplies from NVN to SVN by way of the Ho Chi Minh trail.

In 1970, when the tactical situation compelled major Communist units in Military Regions 3 and 4 (MR-3 and MR-4) of the RVN to seek refuge in Cambodia, the overall Communist strength in SVN dropped, but this very same fact created an illusory situation as Communist divisions could reinfiltrate within a day or two, with their combat capabilities reinforced through rest, training, and replenishment received while on Cambodian territory. Misconceptions could not be dispelled despite the fact that these units were carried in OB holdings as "units in border areas".

Disagreements over enemy strength and forces occurred right within the RVNAF, between J-2, JGS and the corps, divisions and sectors, though authority for acceptance of enemy units had been clearly defined, with the JGS level handling units of battalion-size and higher, and military regions/corps assuming responsibility for companies and smaller units. Quarterly OB discussions with the various units involved accomplished nothing more than reducing the discrepancies.

In late 1972, as the drafting of the Paris Agreement was nearing completion, the RVN side felt the need to demonstrate the presence of the NVA in the South and subsequently insisted that an OB book be compiled that would identify by composition all NVA units in the South. The need was justified but realization was not that easy. Finally, based on all information gathered over a period of three years, from 1970 through 1972, rosters of NVA personnel in each unit were compiled and those thus identified numbered up to 115,000.

The Area Analysis Section on the Vietnamese side was an old organic element of J-2, JGS. Its activities were strictly based on reporting from local agencies as to the status of the population, LOCs, bridges and culverts, etc., and this reporting was generally late. One of the important assignments of the section was to prepare area geographical studies and gazetteers. The area geographical studies described geographical features of the areas studied while the gazetteers listed place-names along with details on each place such as description, grid coordinates, other known names, etc. Another assignment was to update friendly maps and study enemy maps. Following an operation that yielded 127 Communist map sheets related to SVN territory and scaled 1:100,000, the Area Analysis sections of the US and Vietnamese elements coordinated closely to publish a new gazetteer and a study of Communist military symbols. Thanks to lavish equipment and new techniques available to the US element, the VN element learned to establish a data base and conduct area analyses, which were produced at an area scale of 1:250,000 and were referred to as encyclopaedia of intelligence. Thanks to adequate supplies of aerial photographs, map revising and updating of information on the conditions of LOCs took less time than before. In particular, studies on rice-growing areas were undertaken by the Area Analysis Section in coordination with the II Section for the purpose of estimating rice production potentials and monitoring rice-growing in both government and Communist areas. The resulting documents proved essential to the Ministry of Land Reform. In addition to its regular assignments, the Area Analysis section responded to special assignments such as preparing area geographical studies on Cambodia and Laos for cross-border operations. These studies were completed in two weeks.

The Imagery Interpretation (II) Section was the largest Vietnamese section of CICV because it was a division of the Military Intelligence (MI) Center of J-2, JGS prior to becoming an organic element of CICV.

A difference in interpretation scope was that the US side's imagery interpretation extended to infrared photographs and Side Looking Airborne Radar (SLAR) resolution while the VN side's was limited to aerial photographs. The II Section consisted of two elements: interpretation and studies. The Interpretation element had five teams, four in charge of the in-country military regions (MRs) and one in charge of NVN, Laos and Cambodia. It also had a support team with a film library and a photo laboratory. Coordination with its US counterpart gave the VN element the opportunity to use sophisticated equipment such as the 85-view computer, Itek rear projection viewer and the CAF model 910 Ugalid printmaster. Among these the Itek rear projection viewer was the most popular as it was capable of magnifying an aerial photo 30 times.

Aerial photos were one of the favorite sources of intelligence for briefings, debriefings and intelligence studies. Around June 1972, after Quang Tri City had fallen, enemy 130 and 122-mm field guns continually pounded on Hue City. Enemy gun positions had to be located but direction-finding radars could not help determine these positions. Aircraft were finally called in to continually photograph the suspected positions in an attempt to catch the guns as they were being pulled out of their camouflaged positions or when they opened fire. Films taken by aircraft from the 460th Tactical Reconnaissance Wing were processed for immediate photo readouts and Hot and Immediate Photo Interpretation Reports (HOPIRs and IPIRs). Results were immediately relayed to the Tactical Air Command and the artillery for firing on them before the enemy was able to move the guns out of the identified positions. This procedure proved more effective in reducing enemy attacks by fire than B-52 strikes.

In imagery interpretation, the US side usually provided preliminary reports to US units and US advisors to RVNAF units. The VN II element at CICV made prints from negatives with Vietnamese captions and sent them to RVNAF units, verified earlier readouts or conducted interpretation phases 2 and 3, i.e. supplemental photo interpretation reports or SUPIRs. When interpretation differed because of translation or the quality of the prints, other photos were taken for verification. Differences frequently occurred in identification of armored vehicles and tanks which came in increasing numbers and types. The US-compiled interpretation keys proved very useful to the Vietnamese specialists who were not familiar with this type of enemy equipment.

The Targets Section provided targets to both Tactical and Strategic Air Commands (TAC and SAC); this mission was carried out exclusively by the US side. On the VN side targets were the responsibility of corps and division G-2s working in coordination with the combat units. At JGS level the Targets Section was only required to establish target folders for follow-up purposes, particularly on B-52 missions. The VN Targets Section focused mainly on observing the status of enemy base areas and infiltration routes. Each base area (BA) was given a three-digit numeral designation for identification purposes, as opposed to the Communists' own designations. Base areas in MR-1 were given a 100 series, MR-2 a 200 series, MR-3 a 300 series and MR-4 a 400 series. Base areas in Laos received a 600 series and those in Cambodia a 700 series. Factors considered in observing and determining the status of an enemy BA were US-established. The same technique was used in conducting pattern analyses. Vietnamese corps and division commanders appreciated this technique very much because the thorough recapitulation of information on a specific area (with up to 30 different types of information) was in itself a factual assessment and needed no further explanations. This information was categorized and normally presented in eight different overlays placed on a master map and with the following information plotted: enemy units and their movements in the areas as indicated in ARDF reports; information obtained by SLAR or Red Haze; information derived from aerial photos and aerial reconnaissance; information derived from PWs, "Hoi Chanh" and documents; information reported by agents; types of incidents recorded in the area; enemy air defenses, and information resulting from intelligence studies of the area. These overlays were updated every three months. Data for the pattern analyses were provided to the Targets Section on an as-soon-as-possible basis. The Targets Section notified the units or agencies concerned. To the corps and divisions, this notification only served to verify information provided by US intelligence advisers, which in most cases meant 12 or 48 hours before.

Combined Document Exploitation Center (CDEC)

This center was organized on 1 October 1965. Prior to that the US had a liaison element and a team of Vietnamese civilian translators. As a combined MI center, it had both VN and US elements, each with its own director. United States personnel numbered 101. In addition, there were an estimated 100 Vietnamese civilian employees of the US element who performed as translators or typists. On the VN side, the Table of Organization and Equipment (TOE) strength was 69 men. The CDEC was organized as follow: *(Chart 17)*

Chart 17 — Organization, Combined Document Exploitation Center

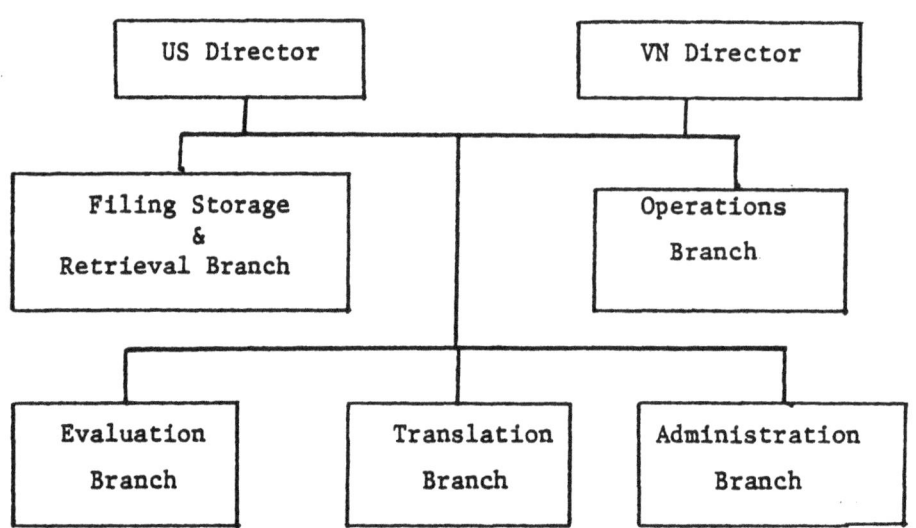

The VN element did not have a translation team but the US element had the capability to translate Vietnamese, English, French, Chinese, Cambodian and Japanese. Documents were always considered to be a very valuable source of information. However, prior to the establishment of CDEC the evacuation of documents from the capturing unit to the Document Exploitation Section sometimes took up to six months. During this time documents were exploited at numerous levels prior to reaching the national level. This caused delays, inability to verify circumstances of acquisition, losses or mix-ups, and inconsistencies. Also analysts along the way tampered with the originals. After exploitation, the results were late in reaching the affected areas or the capturing units because they were forwarded through military postal channels and the recipient units might have been on tactical operations in remote areas. In this case the mail ended up at their rear base camps.

RVNAF document evacuation channel is shown as follows:[5] *(Chart 18)*

---

[5] J-2, JGS Directive No 170-1 issued in 1969.

Chart 18 — RVNAF, Document Evacuation Channel

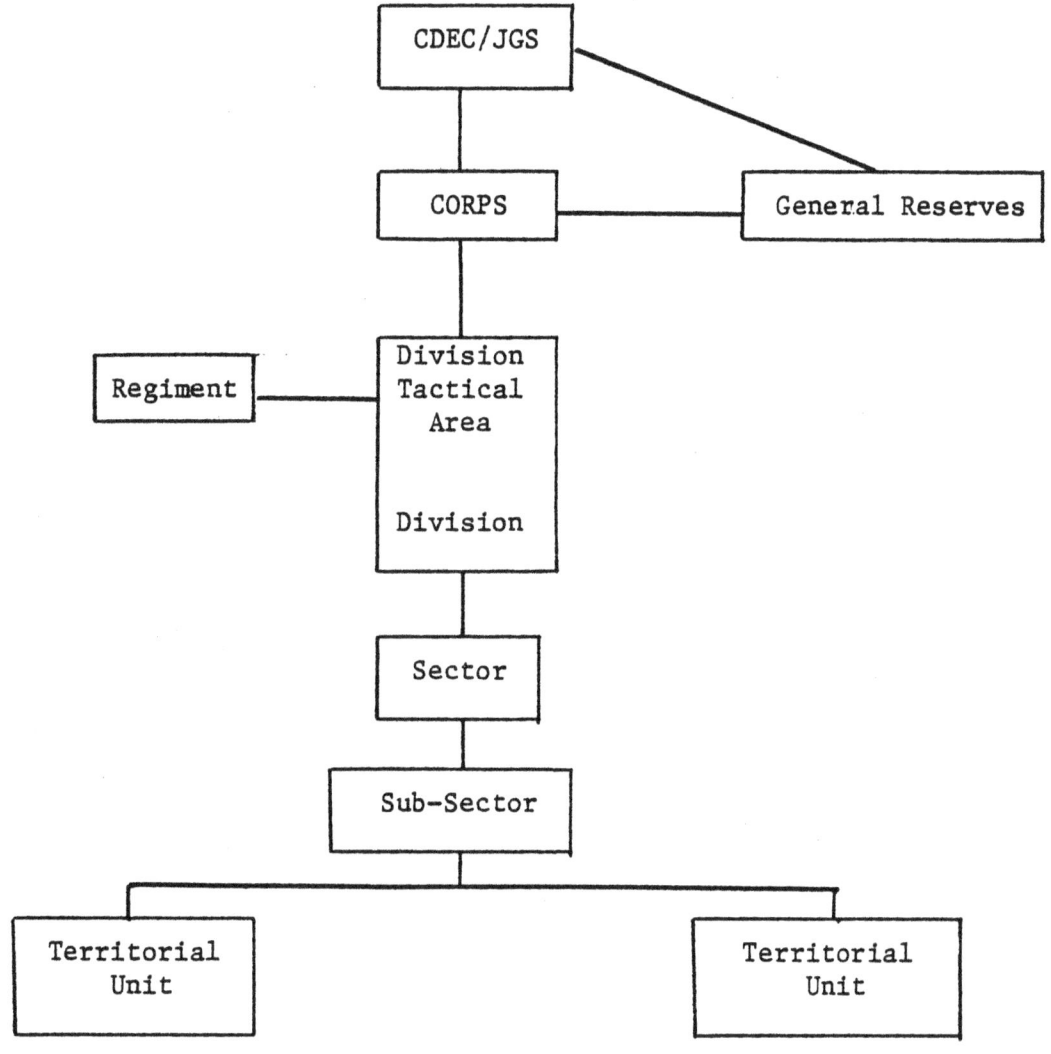

To overcome this problem, intelligence advisers to RVNAF units and J-2, JGS met the TOE needs of corps and divisions by providing each with a document copier, but after a while difficulties occurred because the machines broke down and there were no qualified personnel to repair them, or the units had no funds to purchase the fluid and paper necessary for the copying process. Coordination with US agencies to whom lavish means were available helped solve the problem. When there were important documents to examine, go-teams were dispatched to do the job right on the spot or photograph the documents for the units while the originals would be taken back to CDEC for exploitation. At the center, information was exploited within 12 to 24 hours and the units received feedback within 48 hours thanks to daily or special flights. Routine documents were forwarded to CDEC in the same, timely manner. Expeditious and professional exploitation boosted the unit commanders' confidence and made them more willing to urge their subordinates to send the documents in instead of keeping them for a long time as they had previously done.

Storage of documents became easier through the use of 35mm microfilm and/or the ADP systems of CICV. Research was made easier through retrieval by filing systems which projected the documents on an 8 x 10 in. screen and reproduced them within five seconds per page for hard copies. Copying document exploitation reports was made easy and quick thanks to Xerox machines which reproduced, photographed, and made enlargements or reductions.

In 1968, captured documents numbered 900,000 pages, Exploitation results showed that only an estimated 10% had intelligence value. This center was restricted to exploiting documents captured in the field and thus did not have access to reference or Communist publications commercially available in such countries as France or Hong Kong. This latter type of material was processed by the US Document Exploitation Center in Japan. This arrangement was detrimental in terms of timeliness and essential elements of information (EEI). Also, in exploitation and interpretation of documents the US and VN elements worked independently of each other. However, results were later communicated to the counterpart element.

On many occasions exploitation results differed because most of the documents were handwritten and hard to read, and abbreviations were frequently found. The US side was handicapped in that it was difficult for US specialists to resolve such conflicts when they were totally dependent on their Vietnamese employees to process the materials. On the VN side, however, when there were important documents or documents which generated differing interpretations, they were immediately retyped into many copies for distribution to the most experienced intelligence officers of J-2, JGS who would each prepare his own interpretation and comments. This method proved very effective.

Most available documents had been captured by US Forces, primarily because in the first years of their involvement they were responsible for tactical operations while RVNAF units worked in pacification. Moreover, the US military were trained to focus maximum attention on documents. The documents were all in the Vietnamese language and since US personnel could not tell the value of each, they turned in all captured documents.

The routing of Communist documents captured by US and allied forces is shown as follows: *(Chart 19)*

Chart 19— Routing of Communist Documents
Captured by FWMAF

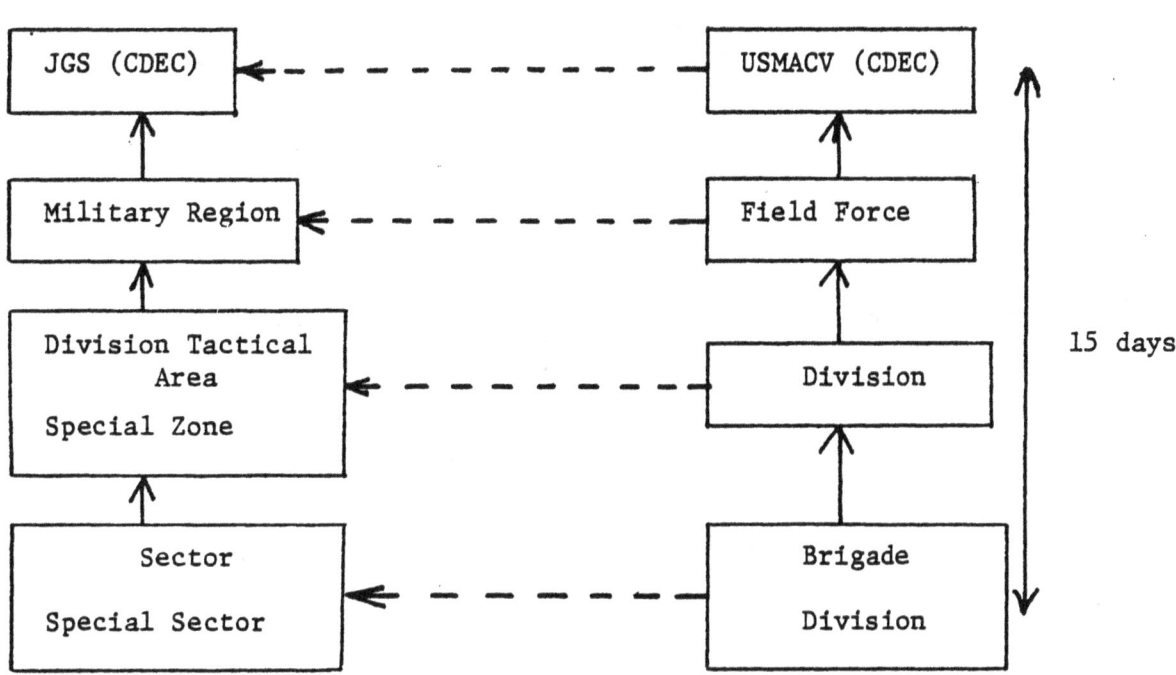

Symbols:

⟵———— Routing of documents through intelligence channels or directly to CDEC

⟵ — — — —Information exchange channels.

RVNAF units paid minimum attention to capturing documents and immediately discarded those they came upon which they considered to be propaganda. In 1971, a unit of the 7th Infantry Division, RVNAF, staged an ambush in My Tho. The reported results were that two enemy junks had been sunk, five enemy troops killed in action (KIA) and seven K54 pistols captured. When the guns arrived at division headquarters, the division G-2 observed they were of the latest model and that the holsters bore a gold star, all indicative of the high ranks of the users. However, no documents were found. Preliminary investigations showed that the ambushing unit did capture a number of documents but did not give them any consideration because they were too busy searching for additional weapons in the river. Finally, the 7th Division's G-2 had the unit return to the site and a few remaining documents were found. These indicated the Communist team ambushed was made up of battalion and provincial unit cadre.

In this particular case the psychology of the troops was such that they believed capturing documents was not as important as other combat achievements and would cause the operation to be prolonged, pending the exploitation of the documents. Therefore they were not too eager to turn in documents. Still, the Vietnam war did demonstrate that knowledge of Communist strategic courses of action was gained through captured documents. Through lavish means of communication, transportation and operation, and through expeditious and professional exploitation, CDEC made documents an abundant and accurate source of information, and the most trusted in the area of combat intelligence.

Combined Military Interrogation Center (CMIC)

From 1959 to 1965 Interrogation was an organic section of the MI Center/ J-2, JGS. In 1961 the US appointed an officer and an NCO to be advisers to this section. By 1964 the number of US advisers had increased to 50 men. On 31 January 1967 CMIC was officially activated to perform the mission of interrrogating important PW and "Hoi Chanh", who were selected for their strategic knowledgeability. These "selected" and "strategic knowledgeability" factors were set forth because, in addition to CMIC in Saigon, there were CMIC of the corps, interrogation sections of the corps and division Military Intelligence Detachements, and interrogators of the sectors. The central CMIC was designed to accommodate up to 63 sources and had 28 interrogation rooms. The Interrogation Center compound was divided into three areas: VN area, US area and joint areas (organizational outlays shown in *Chart 20*).

The US element had two divisions: support and operations, while the VN element had three: operations, exploitation and editing. The VN exploitation division had two sections: requirements and interrogation. Requirements levied EEI on each PW or "hoi chanh". These EEI were based on general requirements of G-2, JGS or friendly units. The Interrogation Section had several teams, some in charge of geographical areas such as MRs 1, 2, 3 and 4; others specializing in political, military or economic affairs, or infiltration, etc. Reports prepared by the interrrogation teams were forwarded to the Editing Division which synthesized them for clarity, prepared sketch maps of bases from the information obtained, etc. Technical information was submitted to specialists from the engineer, signal, artillery, ordnance, etc. corps for review. This activity on the US side was the responsibility of its Reporting Section. This section also translated Vietnamese interrogation reports into English.

The US element of CMIC had a TOE strength of 98 men plus 40 Vietnamese civilian employees and 12 Vietnamese Military translators (two men and ten women). It was organized as follows: *(Chart 21)*

Chart 21 — US Element, Combined Interrogation Center

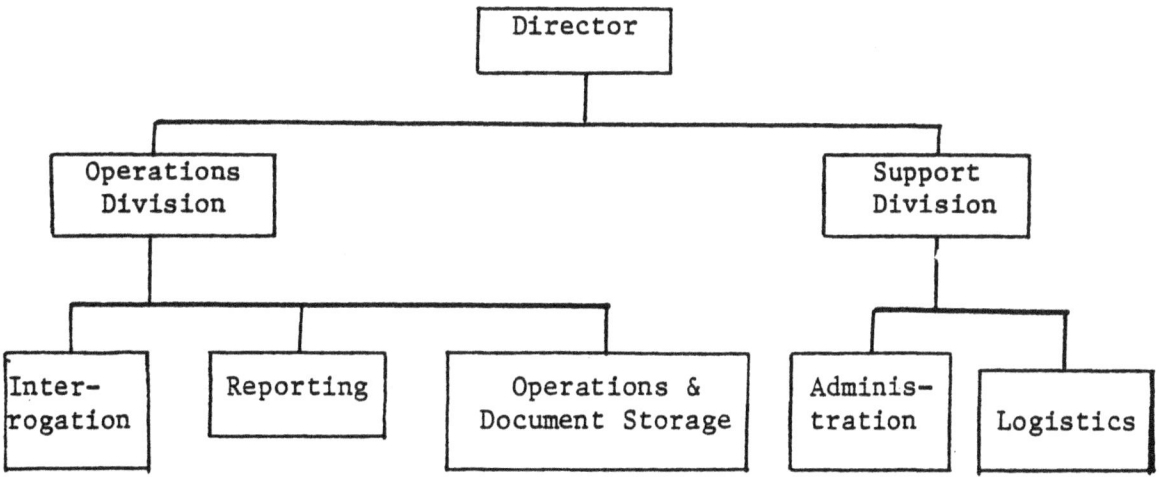

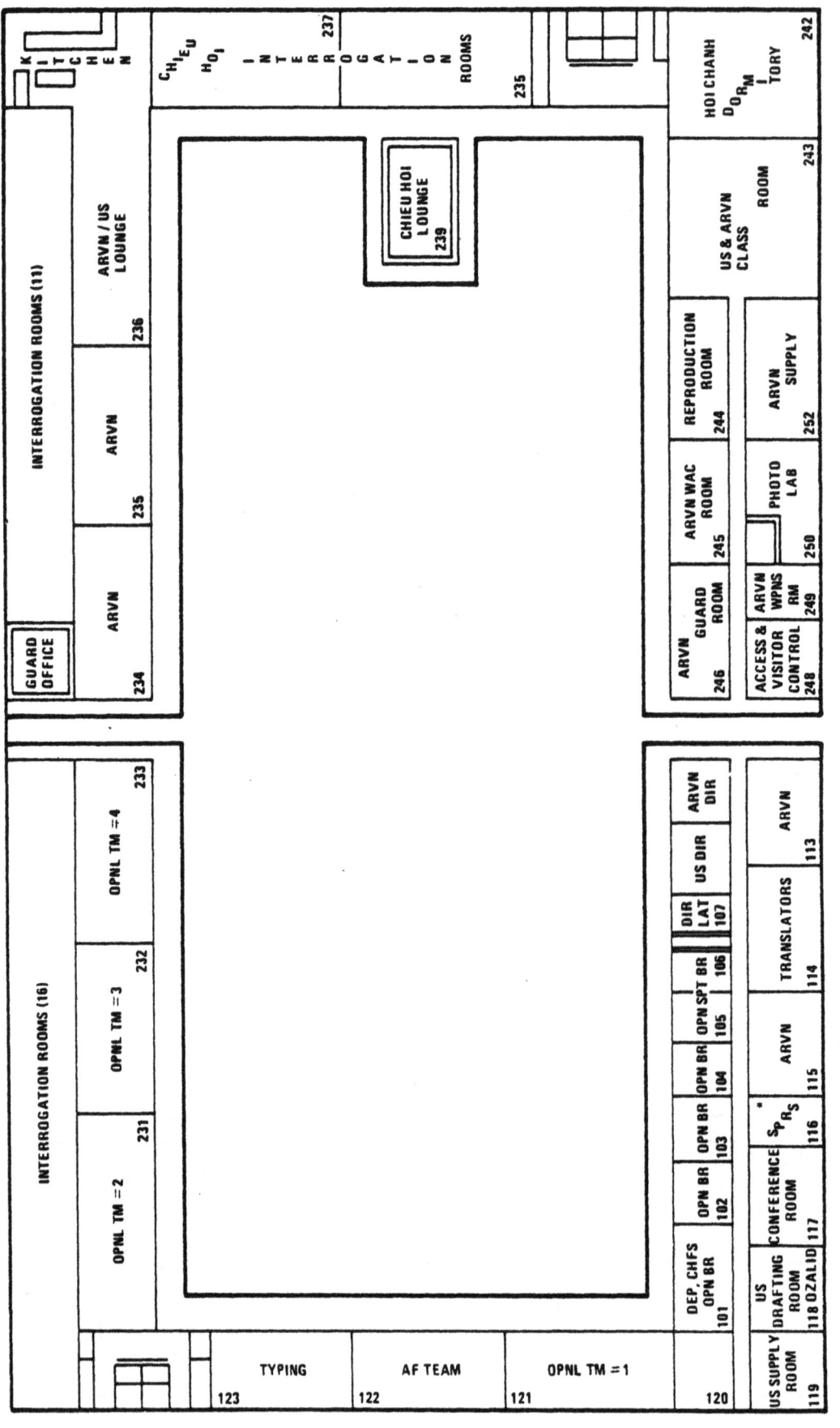

Chart 20 — COMBINED INTERROGATION COMPOUND LAYOUT

The VN element had 97 men excluding a Regional Force (RF) company detached from Gia Dinh Sector to assume guard and defense duties at the compound. The VN element of CMIC was organized as follows: *(Chart 22)*

Chart 22 —ARVN Element Combined Interrogation Center

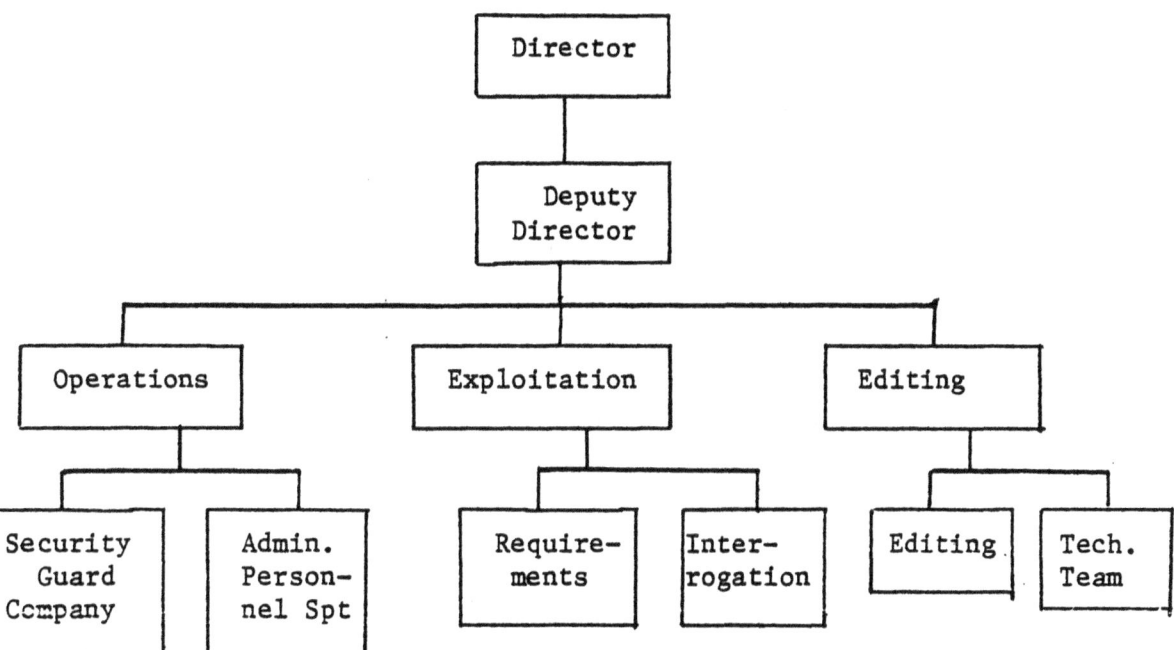

The interrogation process normally proceeded as indicated in Table 1. When sources arrived at CMIC they were divided into two groups. One group was interrogated by the VN element, the other by the US element. If there were only one source, the VN element usually interrogated him on the first day, and the US element had access to him on the second day This procedure was changed in April 1971 after it had been determined that a day was not sufficient for any one side to complete its assignment. Subsequently, the Vietnamese were given three days and the Americans two. If the source was deemed to have information which responded to the special needs of the VN or the US element, that element was given priority for interrogation. Interrogation results were exchanged for corroboration and complementing.

Originally, US personnel selected for interrogation assignments were those who could speak Vietnamese, of whom there were very few. Those

Table 1 — Interrogation Process

Interrogation Section	Requirements Section	Editing/Operations Sections
Source arrives CMIC		
Preliminary contact ⟶	Preliminary report prepared	
	EEI prepared	
	Interrogation requested ⟶	Contact coordinated
⟵	Interrogator notified ⟵	Source received
Actual interrogation ⟷	Additional contact made with interrogator	
	Results reported	
	Additional questions, guidance	
Interrogation report prepared ⟵		
⟶	Interrogation report reviewed ⟶	Reports reviewed & corrected
		Reports printed & published

who spoke fluently enough to debate with the sources were even fewer. Gradually, US element interrogation had to be conducted through Vietnamese male or female interpreters, all noncommissioned officers, and could not be as effective as the VN element interrogation. The VN element had interrogation specialists who were all officers with long-experience in interrogation, with facility in the Communists language, and with knowledge of Communist organization and OB. Thus these VN interrogators were able to immediately detect any attempts to make false statements. Many of the sources did lie because the common psychology of PW and "hoi chanh" was a mixture of suspicion, fear, and a desire to receive better treatment. It prompted some to lie about their positions or ranks or to exaggerate in their reporting. All sources who came to CMIC were subjected to fingerprinting, photographing and haircutting, and received a towel, soap, toothbrush, toothpaste, mat, and a blue uniform. Each source received a daily food ration worth VN$36.50, later increased to VN$49.00, which was equivalent to the daily ration of an RVNAF enlisted man. There were daily sick calls, a physician to care for them, and a dispensary with medics on duty 24 hours a day. The more seriously ill were hospitalized. The international Red Cross occasionally requested to visit or contact the PW, and the requests were granted. Reports made upon completion of these visits were very positive.

Prior to their selection for evacuation to CMIC the PW were subjected to tactical interrogation at the units. Evacuation of PW captured by the RVNAF operational units proceeded as shown in Chart 23.

PW captured by US Forces were moved as indicated in Chart 24.

In addition to the central CMIC in Saigon there were MR/Corps CMICs in Da Nang, Pleiku, Bien Hoa and Can Tho respectively. Interrogation coordination was effected at division level but the procedures were not as clearly defined as at corps level. At this latter level, an

---

[6] J-2, JGS Directive No 170-1- issued in 1969

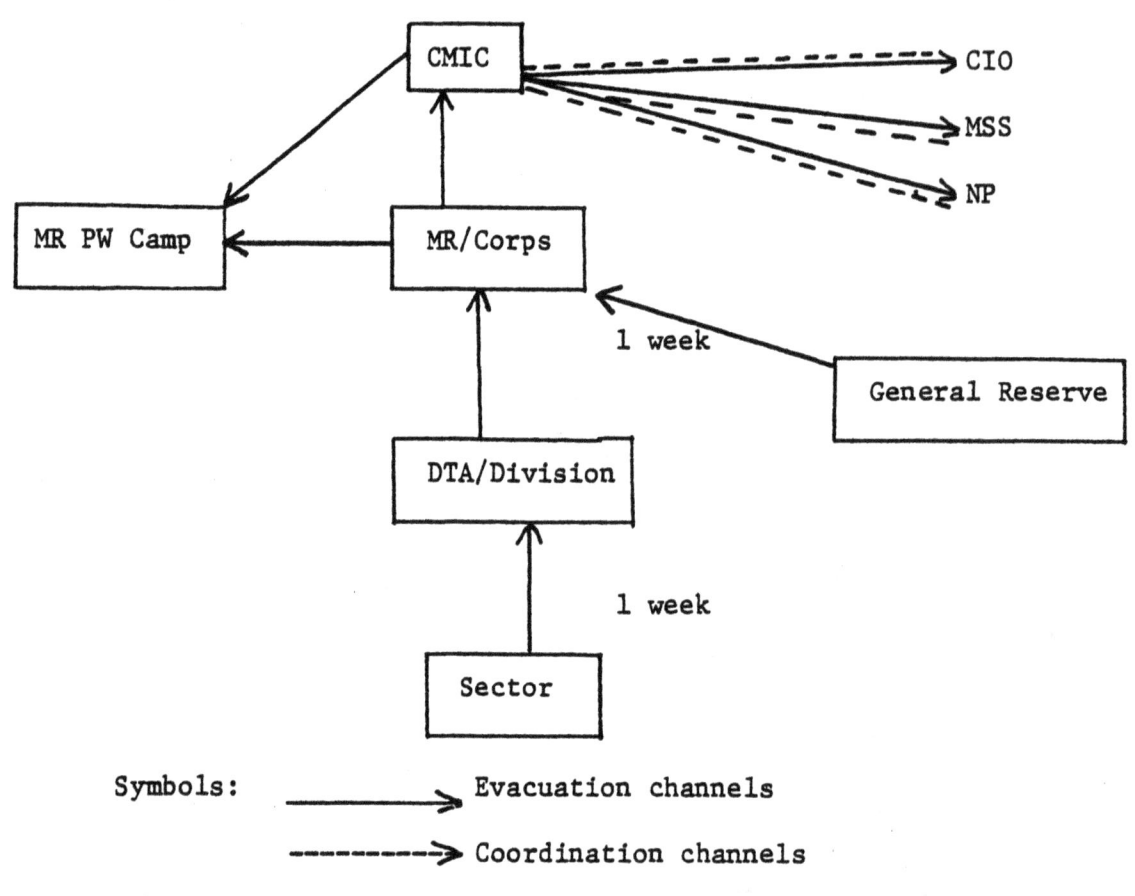

Chart 23 — RVNAF, POW Evacuation Channel

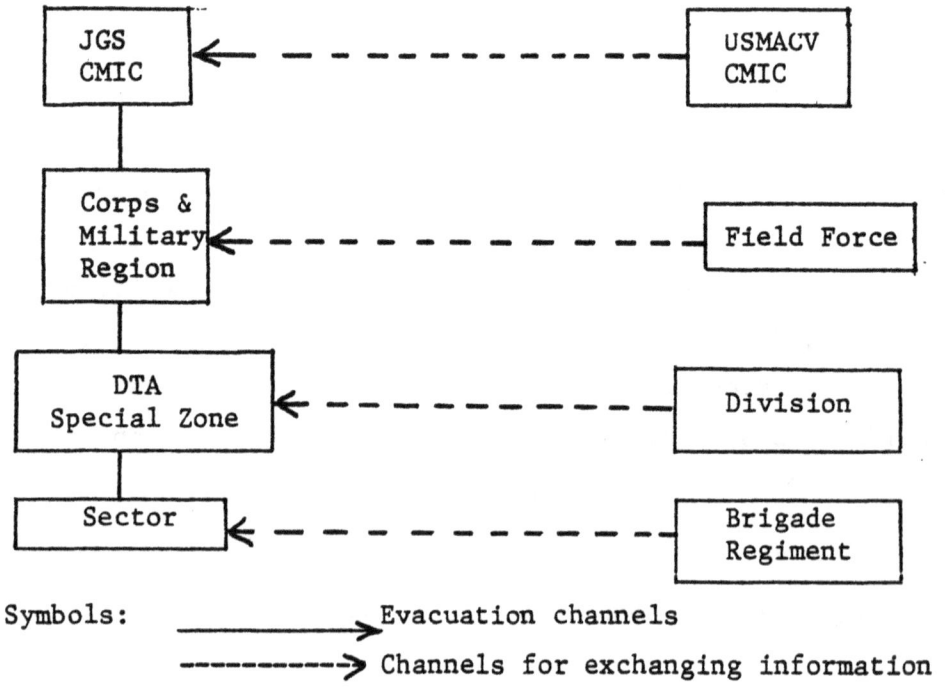

Chart 24 — US Forces, POW Evacuation Channel

agreement signed in April 1969 established the following coordination principles: commanders involved had equal rights to the PW; the operation of the center was Vietnamese responsibility; PW were not to be kept past six months unless specifically authorized by J-2, JGS and J-2, USMACV; logistics were a Vietnamese responsibility. In cases of shortage or lack of logistical supplies, the US side would help, upon joint agreement.

PW were kept at CMIC up to two months, then might be transferred to other national agencies such as National Interrogation Center/Central Intelligence Office (NIC/CIO), MSS or the National Police (NP), or be turned over to the PW camps of the military regions.

When speaking of interrogation matters, it was often believed, and more so by the PW, that they involved torture and inhumane punishment. These conditions existed only in the remote past. The Vietnam war was determined to be a war for the hearts and minds, a war of ideologies, and this concept extended to interrogation activities. The interrogator was trained to believe in the hearts-and-minds approach, and this belief was reinforced with each day on the job. Interrogation by psychological methods produced more and better results and brought the interrogator decent satisfaction and a sense of self-confidence. Communist troops and their cadre were extensively indoctrinated on RVN, society, the RVNAF, abuses, classes, savage torture, etc.

A Communist political cadre at provincial party committee level, captured on his way back from attending a regional-level discussion on the 1968 general attack, stated that he was firmly determined not to disclose any information and was prepared to cope with torture. This torture did not take place. The interrogator maintained an extremely decent attitude, and the subject was detained in a room with a window which allowed him to observe all the activities of the interrogation unit. Another surprise came to him when he noted the democratic

activities of the officers, noncommissioned officers and enlisted men of
the RVNAF, and the very close and non-discriminatory rapport between
them, particularly after work. The Communist attack right inside the
capital failed to cause these servicemen to panic and they continued
to perform their duties in a dedicated and cheerful manner, prompting
the cadre to ponder and to wonder if, after all, SVN did not have a
righteous cause. Even the presence of US advisers in the unit did not
provide him with an indication that there was something abnormal in
the relations between US and VN personnel or in their daily activities.
All these observations finally led him to decide to cooperate with the
interrogator.

Decent treatment came as a surprise to all PW and "hoi chanh". One
"hoi chanh" recalled he had turned himself in at a military base, bringing
along a K54 pistol. He expected to be harassed with questions for information of military value. He was surprised to find that the officer in
command treated him in a very friendly manner, asking about his family,
and about life in Communist ranks, as if they were two friends reunited
after a long separation and eager to learn about each other's families.
No mention was made of military information. The pistol he had brought
with him lay on the table, by his side, when it should have been put
away as a precaution.

Facing realities which totally contradicted prejudices gained
through indoctrination was the principal motivating force that prompted
interrogated personnel to cooperate. This cooperation became even more
sincere as the treatment of the source improved. On one occasion, a
high-ranking defector who had returned from regroupment to NVN indicated,
in the course of a conversation, that he missed his family very much.
With the lavish means available to the US side, the family was brought
in to be reunited with the source who never thought this could ever be
done.

Information provided by PW and "hoi chanh" was often of high value.
It would have been a real mistake to determine validity of information
solely on the basis of rank and position. This only applied to the US
and RVNAF people since they were subjected to need-to-know restrictions.

On the Communist side, the policy of group study and discussion of assignments enabled the individual private to gain some insight on strategic intentions and requirements behind the campaign to come.

Interrogation at the various levels and interrogation by the VN and US elements all produced results that were exchanged and consolidated. This allowed those involved to discard false information and make significant HUMINT contributions.

In interrogation, combined and coordinated activities showed that US efforts between 1965 and 1971 were directed at equally sharing the quest for information from PW and "hoi chanh". Beginning in mid-1971, as US Forces gradually withdrew from Vietnam, the number of US personnel assigned to the combined interrogation centers was reduced until there were only one or two left and the activities became more of a liaison than an operational nature.

Combined Materiel Exploitation Center (CMEC)

Of the four combined centers, CMEC was the last established. Prior to that, the VN element was a materiel exploitation section of the MI Center/J-2, JGS whose productivity in terms of in-depth exploitation of war trophies was negligible. Its primary concern with captured materiel was to use them as a basis for protests with the International Control Commission or for displays.

The Vietnam theater frequently saw the introduction of sophisticated arms and equipment from the Communist bloc. New weapons in particular, were used in every general attack to reinforce enemy troop confidence as well as to surprise the RVNAF with unexpected enemy firepower. In intelligence collection, the appearance of new types of arms and equipment at the frontline was always a telltale sign of a Communist general attack in the making. The Communists were cunning in that, despite being supplied with sophisticated materiel from abroad, they pursued their efforts to make some locally for propaganda and motivation purposes.

CMEC was organized as follows: *(Chart 25)*

Chart 25 — Organization, Combined Materiel Exploitation Center

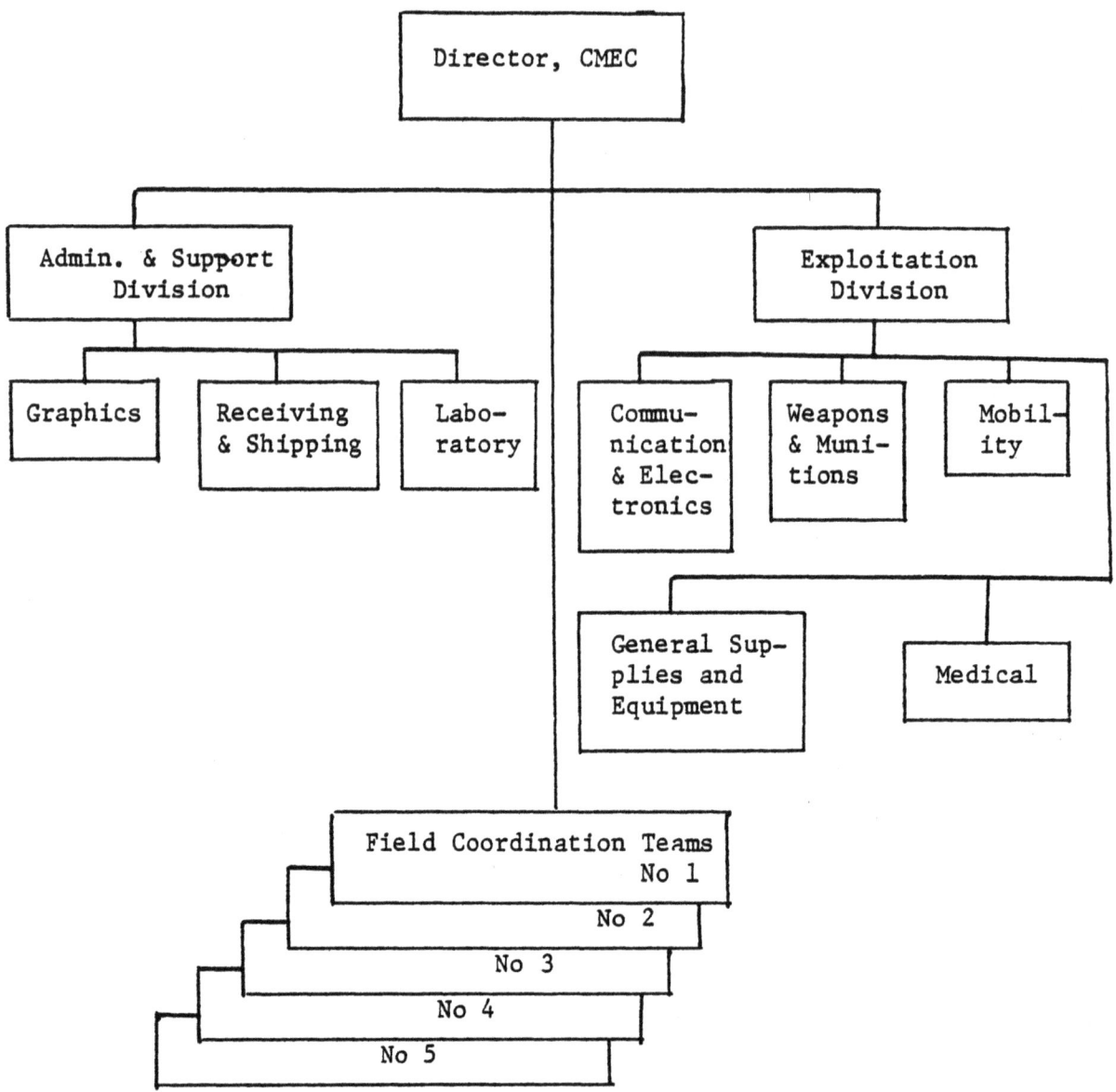

CMEC mission was to: 1. Test, evaluate, and categorize captured enemy materiel; 2. Disseminate technical intelligence information obtained and technical publications; 3. Motivate field units to turn in captured materiel and follow up on such activities; 4. Set up and maintain facilities to display captured enemy materiel; 5. Participate in interrogations of PW and ralliers and exploit of technical intelligence documents; 6. Dispatch field teams to visit combat units and provide them with technical guidance when requested.

US personnel assigned to CMEC numbered 93 while Vietnamese personnel numbered only 44. The Vietnamese element was basically organized like the US element except that its administrative and support division was strictly administrative in nature and its functions much simpler than those of the US element. Vietnamese specialists were detached from the various service branches: a medical doctor from the Medical Corps dealt with medical equipment; two Signal Corps officers worked with radio and electronic gear; two Ordnance Corps officers processed weapons; and a Quartermaster Corps officer handled quartermaster items. These representatives took the equipment to their respective organizations for testing purposes as CMEC did not have laboratories. The same procedure applied to the US side, and the usual rule was that only sophisticated arms were sent to the USA for examination and testing.

CMEC's most useful role was the publication of handbooks on Communist war materiel used or likely to be used in Vietnam. These handbooks helped tactical units identify and report captured materiel and equipment. In Vietnam however, the units often proved untruthful in their reporting of new Communist armament, particularly individual weapons identified by the handbooks as sophisticated. Many unit commander kept those trophies as souvenirs or gave them away as gifts to personalities in the administration. The best technical intelligence personnel could do was to photograph these items. Later, as the units were given authority to set up unit displays, many commanders found ways to retain numerous types of crew-served weapons that were captured for the first time.

Communist forces sometimes received arms from the Communist bloc that were not even featured in the handbooks. In 1972, when they used SA-7 heat-seeking missiles for the first time, these weapons were unknown to CMEC. Characteristics of the US Red-Eye missile had to be invoked when attempting to describe the SA-7. The first SA-7 missile to be captured, in Quang Tri Province, was turned over to the US, and so were subsequent catches in order for examination and testing to be thorough. Later, in faithful implementation of a section of the bipartite agreement which dealt with war trophies, a plastic replica of the SA-7 was made for display in lieu of the real thing.

Another weapon that the Communists used for the first time in Kontum in 1972, and caused serious psychological impact on RVNAF armored and infantry troops, was the SAGGER AT-3 missile, designed for use against tanks, boats or bunkers. At Tan Canh, Kontum, in MR-2, RVNAF armored units described the zigzagging flights of the projectiles in pursuit of armored vehicles and the subsequent destruction of the latter as in uncanny, deific battles of ancient mythology. Later the capabilities of the weapon were determined to be significant. This missile was rigged with wiring and the gunner had to steer it. Because of its jumbled wires it was first nicknamed "bach tuoc" (octopus). Firing from an exposed position while the battle was raging frequently made the gunner lose control and miss the targets. This prompted Communist troops to play with words and call the missile "bach truot" (ever-missing), a parody of "bach tuoc" (octopus).

The psychological effect that sophisticated arms and equipment of the Communist bloc initially made cannot be refuted. In this regard, enemy tanks and armored vehicles are not to be ignored. The RVNAF soldiers were used to fighting with tanks and armored vehicles supporting them from the rear. For a period of time they were rudely shocked when facing enemy tanks and armored vehicles for the first time. Later, as they received more advanced antitank weapons, gained more experience, and learned from CMEC of the vulnerabilities of each type of vehicle, the tactical units competed to destroy enemy tanks for rewards. Foremost of the tank-killer units were those defending An Loc.

Originally, CMEC was given authority to have the war trophies either sent to it or kept at the capturing units. Later this authority was passed on to the Central Logistical Command and CMEC was allowed to keep only one sample of each type. This limited CMEC performance and delayed the evacuation of new Communist equipment which came in increasingly greater numbers and types.

In summary, the Vietnamese military intelligence units had to rely on the US for detailed exploitation of technical intelligence. The lack of trained specialists and testing laboratories was an obstacle that was never overcome.

*Intelligence Cooperation And Coordination
At The Field Level*

While intelligence cooperation and coordination between US and RVN agencies at the four combined centers and at Collection Unit 101 were based on bilateral coordination, the cooperation at corps, divisions, sectors and sub-sectors was typically an adviser-advisee relationship. This was because US intelligence advisers to field units were part of the MACV advisory system. In reality, this relationship was more cooperative than advisory in nature.

At corps level, the senior intelligence adviser was a colonel or lieutenant-colonel, assisted by a deputy and other officers who performed the same duties as their Vietnamese counterparts in the corps G-2. In terms of coordination, the advisers to the corps G-2 supplied US-acquired intelligence data, particularly information produced by SPAR (Significant Problem Area Report), SLAR, Red Haze, aerial reconnaissance photos and agents. United States advisers also provided office supplies that the Vietnamese did not have funds for or could not find on the local market, arranged for aircraft or helicopters to fly their counterparts on various assignments, supplied equipment not provided for in the Vietnamese TOE, and helped obtain slots in overseas training course.

The corps G-2 supplied the intelligence advisers with information acquired by the VN side, PW or ralliers interrogation reports, refugee interviews, preliminary document exploitation reports and information reported by agents of the Vietnamese nets. This method of cooperation indicated that there was no direct coordination between the Vietnamese corps G-2 and the G-2 of the US Field Force. In most cases, communication was made through the US intelligence advisers. Intelligence cooperation and coordination at division level were confined to the same framework as at corps level.

At sector level, intelligence cooperation and coordination received special consideration because the heavy responsibility for coping with the VCI and local force units was far out of proportion to the meager collection resources available, especially since the one and only security/intelligence platoon was always engaged in assignments not relevant to intelligence. The sector S-2 staff of ten could not cope with all the requirements. Since sector personnel allocations came from the Regional Forces (RF) there was no way to reinforce sector and subsector intelligence staffs with Regular Army MI personnel. Sector S-2s were also occupied in miscellaneous duties assigned by the sector commanders and could not keep up with new intelligence organizations or directives from the JGS. Generally speaking, sector S-2 advisers had received only crash intelligence training prior to assignment and possessed no practical experiences in the field. As a result, in 1966 there was a requirement for both sector MI officers and their advisers to attend a special four-day training class. Each class had 20 students from ten sectors of the various MRs. The instructors were intelligence officers from J-2, USMACV and J-2, JGS as well as from the combined intelligence centers.

Intelligence at sector level was very complex because the concept of effectively coping with the enemy infrastructure by providing for a firmer friendly infrastructure had led to the establishment of too many organizations and committees at sector level. Sector intelligence committees included the Provincial Intelligence Coordination Committee, the Provincial Phung Hoang (Phoenix) Committee, and the Provincial Security Committee. In addition to advising and cooperating with the sector S-2, the sector intelligence adviser had to coordinate US intelligence activities in the various sub-sectors, receive reports and disseminate information to all places concerned, and provide intelligence support to US/FWMAF units operating in the sector's territory. Sector intelligence advisory teams started out with three men and later were increased to seven.

At sub-sector level there were only two intelligence advisers, both noncommissioned officers with the grades of E-7 and E-5 respectively. Sector and sub-sector intelligence advisers provided office supplies and equipment to the related S-2s, and funds to operate the volunteer agent program, to support the conduct of special operations.

Military Intelligence Detachments (MID)

Though Vietnamese liaison officers were assigned to US tactical units to help in public relations involving both the GVN administration and civilian population, intelligence needs warranted immediate assistance in exploiting combat intelligence information derived from documents, PW, and ralliers because US personnel were not familiar with the Vietnamese language. Originally, a joint concept was formulated that provided for an exchange of MIDs, i.e. Vietnamese MIDs were to be attached to US/FWMAF units and vice-versa. Later it was determined to be unrealistic to detach US/FWMAF MIDs to RVNAF units and only Vietnamese MIDs were detached to US/FWMAF corps (Field Forces), divisions, and separate brigades. Each was structured like an Airborne or VNMC (Vietnam Marine Corps) MID, with 30 men: 8 officers, 18 noncommissioned officers and 4 enlisted men. The detachment had a headquarters, an interrogation team, a document exploitation team, an order of battle team and an imagery interpretation team. The mission of the MID was to exploit on the spot intelligence information obtained by the US units for immediate tactical response. The MID later acted as intermediary for the US unit in contact with local authorities, Regular and Popular Forces (RF/PF) units, the National Police, the "Chieu Hoi" (Open Arms) services, etc.

Because of pressing needs, the MIDs could not have their full complement of men and their TOE was revised to include only 20 men organized into two essential teams: interrogation and document exploitation. An allocation of 360 men was approved for the activation of 18 MIDs. Priorities for assignments were determined by J-2, USMACV. Three of these detachments were assigned to FWMAF (two to Republic of Korea Forces and one to the Australian Task Force).

These MIDs were placed under operational control of the G-2s of the allied units they were assigned to and coordinated with these units' own MIDs. The concept of cooperation was justified because it responded to intelligence requirements, although not every G-2 was entirely satisfied with the MID accomplishments. The reason for this was that in the Vietnamese MIDs, except for the detachment commanders, all other personnel, officers and noncommissioned officers alike, were fresh out of military schools and basic intelligence training. They did not respond to the needs and were not familiar with the enemy situation. On the other hand, though selected for their English language skills, these very skills proved to be limited. Living in most cases in the same barracks and making the first contacts with a foreign unit proved to be difficult for both sides because of differences in customs, habits and language.

On the US side, counterintelligence (CI) was part of intelligence. This was not so on the VN side. Consequently, some US units insisted that the Vietnamese MID perform CI functions such as checking identification of Vietnamese civilians working in US military installations, investigating illegal activities, etc. To the Vietnamese this went beyond the scope of the MID's mission. These MIDs were subordinate to the MI Center of J-2, JGS but control was ineffective because inspections were conducted only once every six months. Later, the MIDs were placed under operational control of the corps G-2 and the MI Center was restricted to administrative and logistical support. The MID program was gradually terminated as US and FWMAF phased out of Vietnam.

Cooperation and Coordination in Human Intelligence

RVNAF Human Intelligence (HUMINT) units included: Unit 101 of J-2, JGS, the collection sections of corps and division G-2s, and the collection sub-sections of sector and sub-sector S-2s. The Vietnam Navy (VNN) had Unit 701 and the Vietnam Air Force (VNAF) had its own, undesignated, collection detachment. Human sources were the oldest and most basic form of intelligence collection but to the Vietnamese Armed Forces, it was not until 1962 that this concept began to materialize and develop. At this time the 300th Special Detachment was activated with a strength of 388 men. Its mission was to collect strategic intelligence on the Communists, but its operations were limited to SVN territory. From the very beginning it conducted bilateral operations with US elements.

A basic agreement was signed between MACV and the JGS, which defined this coordination in terms of the following basic points: 1. The Vietnamese Communists (VC) were the target of the collection effort;

2. No coordination would be effected with third countries nor would operations be conducted in third country territory; 3. The US would provide financial and material support; 4. Information collected was to be equally shared.

At that time the US intelligence unit coordinating with the Special Detachment was SMIAT (Special Military Intelligence Activities). The 300th had a headquarters in Saigon, a detachment in each MR and numerous teams operating in the provinces. Because of security requirements and the unit's personnel limitations, not every province had a team. The US side was organized similarly and coordination was as much advisory as operational. This fact was very important, because from 1962 to 1975 the activities of this Vietnamese collection agency reflected entirely the organizational concept, operational procedures and techniques of the US collection agency. This peculiarity was beneficial for coordination because both sides shared the same techniques and methods. However, it did not help develop collection concepts and methods consistent with the Vietnam theater.

Though effecting very close coordination in their collection efforts on common targets, each side gradually developed unilateral operations in response to its own needs. On the VN side for instance, the internal political situation in 1963 grew tense with the Buddhist movement opposing the government and thus generated new, unilateral collection needs. This was precisely why the 300th Special Detachment became too well known after the 1 November 1963 revolution. Therefore its designation was changed to the 924th Support Group and it was placed under operational control of the Chief of Staff, JGS, although technical supervision was provided by J-2, JGS.

In 1965, when US combat forces were committed in the Vietnam war, more intelligence information was needed for tactical operations and this collection unit was subsequently expanded. On the US side, Detachment 1 of the 500th MI Group was transferred to the 525th MI group and intelligence coordination was effected through the 149th Battalion of the 525th. After the Communist general offensive of 1968, the Vietnamization plan was put into effect and 924th Support Group was again changed to

Unit 101 under direct control of J-2, JGS. It gradually expanded on the basis of a TOE strength of 918 men. By early 1975, however, because of difficulties in training and personnel, the unit had only 799 men of whom 44% were officers, 34% noncommissioned officers and 22% enlisted men. Unit 101 was organized into a headquarters and six collection detachments. (*Chart 26*)

Chart 26 — Organization, Unit 101

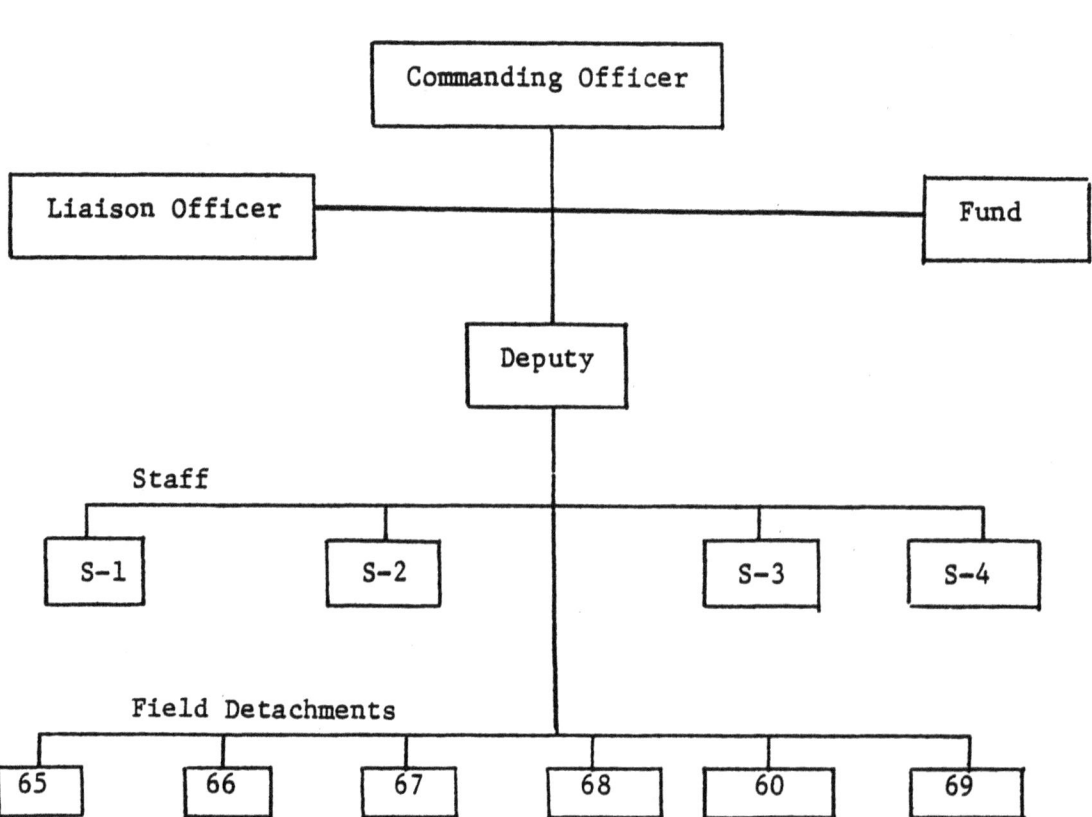

Detachments 65, 66, 67 and 68 were in charge of MR-1, MR-2, MR-3 and MR-4, and based in Da Nang, Dalat, Bien Hoa, and Can Tho, respectively. Detachment 69 was in charge of operations in the Capital Military District (CMD), border areas and third countries, while Detachment 60 was especially targeted against COSVN only.

The 525th MI Group, its counterpart, was composed of four detachments: the 571st MID in MR-1; the 572d MID in MR-2; the 573d MID in MR-3; and the 574th MID in MR-4.

No longer constrained to its original mission as the 924th Support Group, Unit 101 now reached into Cambodia to support RVNAF cross-border operations conducted in 1970. Unit 101 teams dispatched officers, under the cover of representatives of J-2, JGS and corps G-2s, to the Cambodian military region G-2s and to some important provinces of Cambodia to exchange information on the enemy situation and monitor the tactical situation.

In South Vietnam, because collection operations were conducted covertly, facilities and personnel were placed under civilian cover. Agent handlers were given civilian occupations compatible with their own skills and consistent with the environment in their respective target areas. These occupations included teaching in private schools, operating small businesses, selling hogs, driving cargo trucks, etc. Resources had to be provided to build the cover. The US provided operational funds which helped purchase civilian vehicles and motorcycles, rent safehouses, pay agents, and provide for other expenditures related to collection operations. Vietnamese funds, allocated by the Defense Ministry, paid for only 10% of the necessary expenditures. As a result, the US picked up the tab for the remaining 90%. The US also provided portable SSB radio transceivers for the internal communications system which linked the headquarters to the detachments and teams. In their professional field, US coordinators and case officers advised Vietnamese personnel in all phases of Field Operations Intelligence (FOI). In addition, US Mobile Training Teams (MTTs) organized FOI classes for collection personnel at the Vietnamese MI School, beginning in 1961. In later years the training took place at the US Army Intelligence School in Okinawa.

Though supported devotedly by the 525th MI Group in funds, resources, and technical advice the Vietnamese collection effort met with two major difficulties which seriously hampered its operations. The first one was not unique to Unit 101. As a matter of fact all other HUMINT collection organizations experienced the same problem. It involved cooperation from the sources and the civilian population.

In Vietnam a long standing question was: why was our side unable to set up a "people's intelligence" system i.e. use the populace in an intelligence capacity as the Communists did. The answer to this question was very simple except for an unwillingness to face the truth. One had to motivate the Vietnamese civilian to perform intelligence duties or to cooperate with intelligence agencies. The motivation on the Communist side was that failure to comply meant harsh punishment. However, on the RVN side incentives were hard to find, and there even was a motivating force which produced adverse effects. The people in SVN who lived under the nationalist regime were still very much influenced by Confucian ethics which asserts that reporting on someone else's activity is not chivalrous if the report brings harm to that person. Non-interference with another person's action might also have derived from the Confucian philosophy of "not doing unto others what one shalt not have others do unto oneself." This led the Vietnamese civilian to adopt the oft-condemned attitude of "not lifting a finger while the neighbor's house is burning." These views, added to prejudices against the activities of the old French "Deuxieme Bureau" in Vietnam, caused people to look down on those connected with security and intelligence, or those providing information to these agencies.

Prejudices against security and intelligence were gradually washed away with time, but collaboration continued to be ignored by the populace, and most agents cooperated for subsistence rather than for ideals. Even in this case the earned income hardly justified the risks encountered, particularly when going deep into enemy-controlled zones. The Communists were merciless against those they considered spies, to whom they meted out harsh punishment. Many people were assassinated and notes were found on their bodies accusing them of acting as agents for the SVN government, which in many cases was not true. This was why the bona fide agents program designed to induce popular collaboration in return for rewards also failed. The only agents available were mostly professionals who worked simultaneously for several agencies or doctored known information for their own reporting.

An agent once provided Unit 101 with information on enemy forces in an entire MR, complete with extremely accurate details on their cover designators, cover numbers, letter box numbers, organization charts, etc. The accuracy caused such bewilderment among intelligence officers that J-2, JGS had to check with Unit 101 to reascertain the reliability and capability of the source. Later, the source slipped up and was found to be in possession of a MR-prepared document on Communist OB which he had used to write reports on real units but imaginary activities. This is not to say there were no outstanding agents or those with extremely promising potential. However, where such sources were found, active competition developed among the collection agencies and the winner was always the one with the most means and power. Unit 101 frequently saw extremely good prospective sources unexpectedly terminate their services just as they were about to be officially recruited.

The second difficulty encountered in HUMINT was the state of general mobilization which caused all male citizens from 18 to 37 years of age to be conscripted. Personnel of the various intelligence nets of Unit 101 operating under cover were required to have papers certifying the legality of their draft status, draft exemption, or military discharge. As far as agents were concerned, failure to obtain draft deferment for them negated all the efforts to develop them as sources.

The agency which had authority to issue such documentation was the Mobilization Directorate. It refused to do so because it considered such action to be illegal, though the JGS and the Defense Ministry had both approved it for intelligence purposes. Finally, the Directorate approved draft deferment for no more than 30 agents a year and no more than three times each. To fulfill the need for legal documents for the agent handlers, Unit 101 had to resort to forging discharge papers. This, however, was legal forgery in that J-2, JGS and the Mobilization Directorate were given rosters identifying those to whom such papers had been issued.

In addition to the two major obstacles described earlier, there were other difficulties, for example, communications between the agent and his agent handler, and between the agent handler and the team. The good sources who operated in enemy/friendly boundary areas or had access to contested areas were frequently impeded by tactical operations. Uncompleted contacts had to be carried over according to plan, thus causing loss of time. There were no available technical means of communication.

Other difficulties originated from unit commanders, particularly those in command of sectors. They frequently had two conflicting attitudes. Either they suspected Unit 101 personnel of spying on them for J-2, JGS and reporting to the JGS on internal affairs of the sectors or they used them to meet their own needs for tactical intelligence. As strategic intelligence was difficult to acquire, the agent handlers were always willing to oblige by responding to tactical needs, disregarding strategic needs.

The two main difficulties encountered by Unit 101 were the same as those confronting the collection sections of corps and division MIDs, and to a certain extent were the common difficulties encountered by the various agencies in Vietnam in collecting intelligence through agent sources, though the extent to which they were hampered depended on the power of each agency. Generally speaking, though bilateral collection efforts helped resolve the problem of collection means and techniques, they failed to upgrade the quality of information acquired and collection through agent sources enjoyed but a modest position with regard to other collection techniques, even when the 525th MI Group was always there to support these activities during the period from 1965 to 1973. In 1972, this support was gradually reduced until after the Paris Agreement went into effect on 28 January 1973, when there was but a single representative of the 500th MI Group which was beginning to replace the 525th.

*Cooperation And Coordination in
Aerial Photo Reconnaissance*

During World War II, it was estimated that 80% of intelligence information acquired came from aerial photo reconnaissance. This percentage remained the same during the Korean conflict. In the Vietnam war, although no official statistics are available to this date, aerial photo reconnaissance probably accounted for 65 to 70% of the intelligence information acquired.

Unlike the cooperation and coordination in other fields such as combat intelligence or special collection, in aerial photo reconnaissance, the VN side's contribution was rather modest. This was because the US, with its air superiority and abundant assets, bore the brunt of the photo missions throughout the Vietnam war.

By 1960, VNAF had only two C-45 aircraft for air photo missions, both with extremely limited capabilities. In 1965, VNAF was able to organize a reconnaissance squadron and in 1967 this was increased to two squadrons. However, the total number of aircraft was only 13, of which there were three RC-47, one EC-47 and nine U-6A.[7] Aircraft such as the T-28 were modified to become RT-28 for photo missions over areas defended by enemy antiaircraft guns. Later this program was terminated because the equipment was too old and photos taken could not be used for mapping purposes. Not until after the Vietnamization plan had been implemented did the VNAF get to activate a squadron of twelve RC-47 (716th Squadron) and another squadron of six RF-5 (522d Squadron).

Meanwhile, during the same year, 1967, the US had the following reconnaissance aircraft operating in VN:[8]

US Air Force: 37 RF-4C, 13 RF-101, 3 RB-57, 34 EC-47.

US Army Aviation: 282 Bird Dog 01, 69 Mohawk OV-1, 20 Beaver U-6A.

US Marine Corps: 9 RF-4, 8 EF-10B.

7th Fleet: 27 AEW.

The above force continued to be increased. By 1968, for instance, there were 327 01 Bird Dog observation aircraft and 115 Mohawks. The Mohawks were first introduced into VN in September 1962 after the Vietnamese government had realized that Vietnamese RC-45 and RC-47 could only operate in the lowlands and coastal areas. Six Mohawk OV-1s were

---

[7] <u>Fact Book</u>, MACV J-3: August 1967, p. 39.

[8] Ibid., p.p. 23, 24, 36, 37, 46.

brought to Nha Trang and Qui Nhon airfields to support the air photo needs of II Corps. A Vietnamese observer participated in each mission. Reconnaissance targets were proposed by II Corps and submitted to the corps advisor for approval and determination of priority before they were forwarded to the 23d Special Warfare Aviation Detachment for execution.

In the first years of its use in VN, the Mohawk proved very effective because the enemy was not familiar with it or with its characteristics. With its high speed, this type of aircraft was able to approach a target undetected. The Mohawk OV-1A was equipped with a KA-30 camera installed under its fuselage for vertical photography and a KA-60 near the nosetip for panoramic photography with a field of view of $180°$. The KA-30 camera, with its 6 in. lens, produced photos scaled to between 1:3000 and 1:5000, which were very useful for ascertaining enemy targets and activities. Later, the Mohawk OV-1A was tasked to perform another mission, tactical support, because it was armed with rockets and cal..50 machineguns. II Corps requested this unconventional support in many emergency cases.

Once the photo flight was completed, US processing of the materials was very expeditious and results were immediately relayed to the requestors for appropriate action. Meanwhile, on the VN side, facilities were scarce. There was a lack of darkrooms, printers, processing paper, and chemicals. Gradually, the Vietnamese units became used to submitting their requests for air photo reconnaissance through US channels and practically ignored VNAF. From 1965 to 1969, the RVNAF were responsible only for supporting pacification and rural development; thus there was not much need for air photo reconnaissance. Besides, photos taken by the US side on its own were sufficient to meet the needs on the VN side. The Mohawk's coverage was limited but the United States Air Force had aircraft whose coverage was extensive. Combined US Army/US Air Force action ensured better results in aerial photography.

Later, to minimize personnel losses in the face of increasing enemy air defense capabilities, unmanned aircraft were used and their photos proved satisfactory to the users.

Besides aerial photos, of which VNAF was able to contribute but a few, two other air photo reconnaissance techniques were totally new to the Vietnamese: SLAR and Red Haze. Mohawk OV-1B aircraft were fitted with Motorola side looking airborne radars which recorded moving target indications generated by enemy troops as they moved on the rivers or along jungle trails. Later, SLAR was applied for the detection of truck convoys moving along LOCs. Mohawk OV1Cs applied infrared or Red Haze techniques in low-altitude flights to pick up heat energy generated by enemy activities, camps, troop concentrations or staging areas. Many films generated up to 400 or 500 returns. SLAR activity was coordinated with Shadow aircraft (Air Force gunship No 3) which could fly at speeds comparable to the Mohawk's for timely intervention, or with the artillery warning control center or helicopter gunships for tactical response. Results obtained from picking up energy emissions were not well received because it was difficult to identify the sources of energy: person or animal, or activities, etc. Rain and humidity also restricted collection activities. The RVNAF participated more in air reconnaissance than in air photography. The participation began in 1964 with the assignment of permanent observers to the US Army. These personnel conducted observation and made contact with RVNAF infantry units operating in the target areas. At that time the US had three platoons of O-1 Bird Dog observation aircraft, totalling 53 aircrafts. One platoon was based in Pleiku, one in Nha Trang and one in Can Tho. The participation became more active after 1969, when VNAF activated five L-19 observation squadrons, each with 25 aircraft. These squadrons were located as follows: the 110th in Da Nang; the 112th in Bien Hoa; the 114th in Nha Trang; the 116th in Can Tho; and the 118th in Pleiku.

Aircrafts were assigned on the basis of one per sector and two per division for observation, operational support, directing air and artillery strikes, supporting military convoys and maintaining liaison. Because of the varied duties involved, observation was usually given low priority. By cease-fire day, VNAF received an additional number of O-1 and O-2 aircraft which gave it three more squadrons: the 120th in Da Nang; the 122d in Can Tho; and the 124th in Bien Hoa.

In addition to conducting visual reconnaissance, the observers were trained to operate hand-held cameras, usually Japanese-made with 200-mm lenses for target pinpointing. The US side was also equipped with 4 x 5 Polaroid cameras and sometimes used Kodak Ektachrome infrared aerofilms, as at Ba Den mountain in Tay Ninh Province, to expose camouflaged items. This worked on the principle that metal absorbs infrared radiation, while living plants reflect it quite strongly due to the presence of chlorophyll. Genuine foliage may appear for instance as pale blue, but a bunker or other camouflaged objects will reveal itself by being shockingly pink. The shortcomings of this type of film were its cost and the complexity of processing techniques.

Another technique in air reconnaissance used unilaterally by the US was the airborne personnel detector (sniffer) also known as manpack personnel detector (MPD) which determined the presence of personnel concentrations by the detection of compounds excreted by the human body. To accomplish this, helicopters which carried the devices had to fly not more than 200 feet above the ground at speeds of 80 to 100 knots. The difficulties were a failure to identify man versus animal, exposure to hostile fire because of the low altitude, and the effect of weather conditions, rain, fog, dust on the results. This technique was usually applied to verify enemy troop concentrations reported by agents or aerial reconnaissance and was suitable for areas ascertained to be unpopulated.

Information from air photo reconnaissance was very reliable and the various units competed in asking for more, making it important to ascertain priorities and legitimacy of the requests. On the VN side requests for air photos were directed to the corps where priorities were determined. They were then forwarded to US advisers and J-2, JGS was notified. A Target Research and Analysis Center (TRAC) was set up at Tan Son Nhut and staffed with US and VN Army and Air Force personnel to oversee and satisfy air photo needs. Requests that VNAF was deemed able to fulfill were turned over to the VN side. This was particularly true for the areas in the Mekong Delta. Requests that matched photos available from previous US flights were satisfied immediately if the information derived from these photos was still considered to be valid.

Those photo requests that required new flights would be responded to upon completion of the flights and subsequent processing of the films, at which time the photos would be forwarded to the requestors through regular channels and information copies would be furnished to related agencies.

By cease-fire day the air photo program had fulfilled all the needs of the requesting units, with the US providing 97% of the coverage and VNAF credited with the remainder. The Vietnam Air Force's participation in visual reconnaissance was greater but this program was restricted by the weather, nocturnal conditions, terrain concealment, particularly in mountainous areas, and enemy antiaircraft firepower. The Vietnam Air Force's ability to fill the gaps caused by the withdrawal of effective US support following the Paris Agreement was minimal, particularly in the face of continued requests by the units which had become overly dependent on aerial photographs.

Signal Intelligence

In the RVNAF, J-7, JGS was responsible for the acquisition of signal intelligence (SIGINT). Prior to 1961, Signal Intelligence (SIGINT) was unknown in the RVNAF. However, the 1st Republic did give consideration to applying this technique in intelligence activities. The nucleus of a center for radio intercept was established in Saigon in 1955 under the RVNAF Telecommunications Command with a staff of approximately 80 military and civilian personnel who had had basic radio intercept experience with the French Army. This center had a branch in Da Nang. At that time, the mission was to monitor broadcast from Communist radio stations in Peking, Moscow and Hanoi, as well as free-world stations such as the BBC and the VOA.[9]

In 1961 when SIGINT materialized the unit which first came into being was designated 1st Signal Research and Exploitation Company and placed under technical supervision of the commander, ARVN Telecommunications Command. Another agency was established which took the name of "Special Technical Exploitation Agency" and became subordinate to the Chief of

---

[9] Information obtained from the BBC and VOA were used to crosscheck domestic news.

Staff, JGS.

After repeated political upheavals such as revolution and successive coups, the agency in charge of radio intercept at the CIO which in turn reported directly to the Chief of State and Commander-in Chief, was transferred to the JGS and J-7 thus came into being. The 1st Signal Research and Exploitation Company was deactivated and its components reorganized to become Unit 15.

Coordination was effected in the form of bi-weekly meetings to discuss operations, intelligence collection requirements, priorities, and assignments. With the increasing need, detachments were activated to provide direct support to Vietnamese infantry divisions. In late September 1967 the first three detachments were organized to support the 2d, 22d and 5th divisions respectively. Other detachments were subsequently formed for the remaining divisions and they became operational in 1968. Radio Direction Finding (RDF) stations were also established: in Da Nang to support MR-1; in Pleiku to support MR-2; in Song Mao (Phan Thiet) to support MR-2; in Vung Tau to support MR-3; in Can Tho to support MR-4; and in Con Son to support MR-4.

J-7, JGS personnel were trained in airborne radio direction finding (ARDF) from U-6A aircraft in early 1968. In 1970, as the Vietnamization program began, J-7 personnel were trained by the 694th Air Force Security Force in ARDF from EC-47 aircraft. Unit 17 was activated to meet the needs of airborne RDF from U-6A and EC-47 aircraft. EC-47 aircraft were rigged for both intercept and RDF and there were two intercept sections to one RDF section: improvements were made in RDF capability of the Vietnamese to prepare them to replace US units which were phasing out. This system was reinforced by replacing outdated equipment at the MR stations with more advanced equipment. RDF was also directed at urban targets but in this case equipment had to be borrowed from the US. J-7, JGS used 390 and 392-type radios for RDF and AN/PRD-15s for radio intercept. For ground intercept it received 80 radios against a TOE of 120. For short-range RDF it had AN/PRD-3s which were usable in the lowlands but not in hilly or mountainous area.

Between 1965 and 1968 the US was the sole provider of ARDF information. Between 1968 and 1970 the US provided 95% and the Vietnamese 5%. As regards MRDF information, the US acquired 50% and the Vietnamese 50%. GRDF information was credited on the basis of 65% to the US and 35% to the Vietnamese up to cease-fire day. The 718th Squadron, 33d Wing, 5th Air Division, VNAF, had 33 EC-47 for airborne RDF. Twenty three of these were based in Tan Son Nhut for missions in MRs 1 and 2. J-7, JGS gradually gained credit for up to 90% of ARDF and MRDF information acquired in country. Until cease-fire day the principal US Army unit was the 509th RR Group which consisted of the 146th Aviation Company (RR) in Can Tho, 138th Aviation Company (RR) and 224th Aviation Company (RR) in Da Nang, 175th RRFS in Saigon and 8th RRFS in Da Nang. A team of ten specialists from J-7, JGS was dispatched to coordinate with the US unit in Nakhon Phanom, Thailand, which was targeted against enemy activities along the Ho Chi Minh trail.

Signal intelligence proved to be a valuable source of information and was very well appreciated by tactical unit commanders since it provided early warning of enemy troop movements and allowed time to devise countermeasures. This confidence was reflected in the designation of ARDF information as A2 information and everyone but the intelligence specialists swore by A2 information but had no idea what ARDF was.[10]

---

[10] The RVN military intelligence evaluation system was the same used by the US Army. Letters A, B, C, D, E, F are used to indicate the relative reliability of the source while numbers 1, 2, 3, 4, 5, 6 are used to indicate the evaluation of the accuracy of the information itself.

Intelligence Training

The need to train intelligence and security personnel was not recognized until late in 1955. It began with the establishment of a school in Cholon to train officers and noncommissioned officers from the intelligence, security, and psychological warfare branches of the RVNAF. The school was named Cay Mai. Special classes were held for Civil Guard personnel. In 1957 an annex was established in Vung Tau to train the security/intelligence platoons and squads of the sectors and sub-sectors.

The Cay Mai school could accommodate 200 resident students and ten courses. There were 22 different training programs in security and intelligence. Intelligence courses consisted of: 1. Basic Territorial Intelligence Officer Course; 2. Intermediate Intelligence Officer Course; 3. Imagery Interpretation Officer Course; 4. Interrogation Officer Course; 5. OB Officer Course, and the FOI (Collection) Officer Course.

There were three security courses: 1. Basic Security Officer Course; 2. Intermediate Security Officer Course; 3. DAME/DASE Course.[11]

Noncommissioned officers (NCOs) were trained according to Central Training Command (CTC) instructions and upon completing their training were awarded certificates or diplomas. These were: 1. Certificate of Qualification in MI, first degree; 2. Certificate of Qualification in MI, second degree; 3. Diploma of MI Specialist, first degree; 4. Diploma of MI Specialist, second degree. The same certificate and diplomas were available for Security or Counter-Intelligence specialists.

Courses attended by NCO specialists included: Imagery Interpretation; Interrogation; Order of Battle; and Agent Handler.

From its very inception the Cay Mai School designed its own programs of instruction and prepared its own training materials based on available reference documents which covered both US and French intelligence techniques. United States documents were made available to the Training

---

[11] Defense against Methods of Entry and Defense against Sound Equipment.

Relation and Instruction Mission (TRIM) but they were not complete. In 1956 a US adviser was assigned to the school but his role was very general. He made recommendations on maintenance of barracks and arms, but in training his role was limited to discussing training aids and monitoring instruction and students' morale.

In September 1959 the first US-conducted intelligence course for VN officers was opened in Okinawa to last ten weeks. The second and other succeeding classes placed additional emphasis on training instructors. The Okinawa school then began to provide adequate security and intelligence training materials to Cay Mai. In the succeeding years Okinawa opened special courses such as DAME/DASE for MSS and FOI (Collection) for the 300th Special Detachment. Beginning in September 1960 mobile training teams (MTT) were sent to Cay Mai to instruct personnel of the 300th. Instruction in Okinawa and by the MTTs was conducted through Vietnamese interpreters. Later, however, Okinawa conducted Allied courses which VN officers could attend if they passed the English test. In 1965 intelligence training was stepped up as the US became directly involved in the VN war, and Vietnamese officers were sent to the Intelligence School at Fort Holabird, Md.

In 1968 it was determined that staff coordination between G-2s, G-3s, chiefs of staff, and commanders was not close enough because of a lack of knowledge of the mission and capabilities of intelligence officers. Special orientation courses were conducted for G-3s, chiefs of staff, and unit commanders. These courses were effective in changing the attitudes of the students, making them more inclined to cooperate and coordinate with intelligence personnel.

Intelligence training both at home and abroad had a shortcoming in that it was not consistent with realities of a wartime situation. Staff regulations and procedures were seldom required by the commanders or were followed with great reluctance because they were considered burdensome, dogmatic. To remedy this, intelligence students were sent on field-exercise assignments to the divisions and sectors but results left a lot to be desired because of time limitations. In lieu of classroom instruction, intelligence officers working at central agencies or at corps level were sent out to deliver briefings on current events and on their own duties and to visit various intelligence facilities to describe the capabilities of their own agencies. This was aimed at acquainting students with the specialized support available to them on their jobs. Students were also asked to write intelligence lessons as a means to make individual experiences known to other students.

United States advisers contributed to training by providing documents from Fort Holabird or Okinawa, or by participating in courses conducted by MTT instructors. The most noteworthy example of training coordination, however, remained in the training of US and Vietnamese intelligence officers at sector level by intelligence officers from J-2, USMACV and J-2, JGS.

Documents provided by the US were revised to include typical situations and field exercises based on factual incidents recorded in the Vietnam theater. Still, training documents failed to meet the need to train intelligence officers for an unconventional war.

CHARTER V

Military Intelligence Cooperation And Coordination
in Vietnam Following United States Military Disengagement

Defense Attache Office, Intelligence Branch

The Paris Agreement of 27 January 1973 called for withdrawal of all US forces from Vietnam except 50 servicemen assigned to the Defense Attache Office (DAO). This also applied to US intelligence organizations. They left, taking home their sophisticated equipment, lavish means, and numerous technicians. The US intelligence apparatus which remained in Vietnam after cease-fire day consisted of OSA and the DAO Intelligence Branch.

The DAO Intelligence Branch was an entirely new organization with extremely limited personnel allocations—by previous standards—of 10 military and 97 civilian personnel. Later, the number of military personnel was further reduced to three. The mission of the DAO Intelligence Branch was to collect, evaluate and disseminate information on North Vietnam and the Viet Cong in response to intelligence information requirements levied by the US Army Support Activities Group in Thailand, Commander in Chief Pacific in Hawaii, DIA, and other national intelligence agencies. The organization of the DAO Intelligence Branch is shown in the following chart. *(Chart 27)*

Chart 27 — Organization, DAO Intelligence Branch

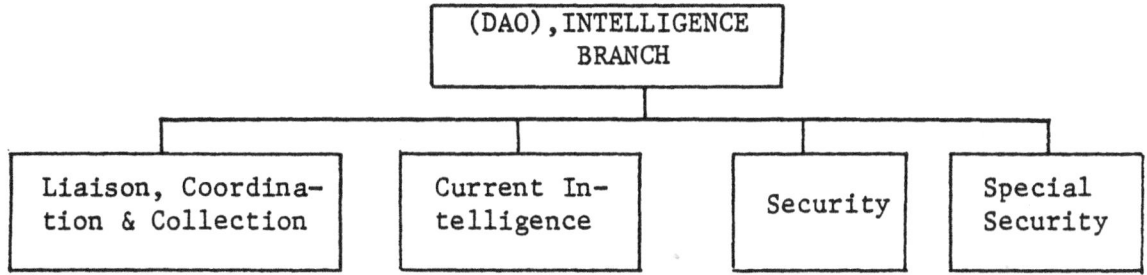

The Liaison, Coordination and Collection Section was the main element of the Intelligence Branch. Its principal effort was in liaison. To that effect it had four teams: Team 1 conducted liaison with Republic of Vietnam (RVN) intelligence agencies in Saigon and at the military regions; Team 2 conducted liaison with N-2, Vietnam Navy (N-2, VNN) and was reinforced with representatives of the 500th Military Intelligence Group from Thailand; Team 3 conducted liaison with A-2, Vietnam Air Force (A-2, VNAF) and was reinforced with representatives of the 7602 Air Force Intelligence Group; Team 4 conducted liaison with Unit 101 and was reinforced with representatives from the 500th MI Group. In its coordination capacity, this section coordinated with aerial reconnaissance units of the United States Air Force (USAF) in Thailand in relation to Photographic Intelligence (PHOTINT) needs. The Current Intelligence Section monitored the daily tactical and enemy situations and prepared daily intelligence reports. The Security Section was responsible for classified correspondence and documents forwarded to the RVN. The Special Security Section ensured the coordination of counterintelligence activities and requirements, personnel security clearances, and liaison with the US Embassy on counterintelligence and security matters. It also coordinated the activities of US military criminal interrogation teams in Vietnam.

Personnel of the DAO Intelligence Branch were newly assigned. Few had worked for J-2, USMACV. The basis for cooperation and coordination between the DAO Intelligence Branch and J-2, JGS was jointly agreed to be as follows: exchange, on a broad and timely basis, of intelligence requirements and data related to the threat against both parties (US and Vietnam) and therefore of common concern to both parties.

Intelligence data supplied by J-2, JGS to the DAO Intelligence Branch were intelligence data acquired within the scope of its responsibilities and pertaining to South Vietnamese territory. Intelligence data furnished by the DAO Intelligence Branch to J-2, JGS were informtion pertaining to the areas outside South Vietnam, information on North Vietnam and information related to infiltration from North Vietnam to South Vietnam.

Difficulties Encountered

Under the new situation, after US forces had left and the Paris Agreement went into effect, intelligence data could be classified in two categories: 1) Totally lost, or 2) Limited and reduced. Those data in the first category included: information obtained through SLAR (Side-Looking Airborne Radar), Red Haze and People Sniffer techniques, information derived from sensors; weather indicators from satellites. Data of the second category included: Aerial photographs of North Vietnam and Laos; information from in-country air photo reconnaissance, information from combat intelligence sources; information from agent sources;and special intelligence studies.

The substantial reduction of communications,liaison, transportation and support means made it more difficult to conduct intelligence operations. Intelligence training in Okinawa was discontinued. To fill this gap, in-country courses were planned for personnel of Unit 101 and VNN Unit 701, with the participation of US mobile training teams from Thailand, but only two courses were actually held. The liaison system of the DAO Intelligence Branch was unable to replace the intelligence system of J-2, USMACV in the function of crosschecking intelligence information, tactical information, etc., with the Vietnamese side. It was precisely at this time when intelligence was confronted with numerous obstacles and challenges that the need for intelligence information became more pressing and important, more imperative even, than during the war. The Paris Agreement brought no peace of mind to the leaders of South Vietnam. There was a continuing strategic intelligence requirement to determine the changes in North Vietnam's conduct of the war in the wake of the agreement, the state of rehabilitation of military and economic potentials in North Vietnam and Communist-controlled portions of South Vietnam, and the level of infiltration of personnel and logistics from the North to the South. Other less important but much needed information pertained to negotiating strategies at the four-and two-party commissions, the composition and activities of the Communist delegations, etc.

The standstill cease-fire had brought the Communists an advantage in that they now had buffer, leopard-spot zones. These were considered by the Communists to be access points to the zones effectively controlled by each side. The Communist objective was to prevent infiltration by RVN intelligence into their zones through these points while using the same points as bridgeheads for their own infiltration into nationalist zones to gather intelligence.

The Paris Agreement gave birth to a new political element, the Third Force, which encompassed the left-oriented political forces opposing the government. Civilian intelligence agencies and the Military Security Department (better known as MSS) virtually diverted their entire efforts to cope with this threat.

None of the armed forces intelligence agencies, J-2 or J-7, JGS, received any additional means to cope with their new difficulties. STRATDAT (Strategic Technical Directorate), too, was deprived of all the means that had given it mobility and it was reduced to reassigning its teams to the military regions to assist them in a tactical capacity.

The combined intelligence centers of the past were ordered merged into a single center designated Unit 306 of J-2, JGS. This reorganization created additional difficulties for J-2, JGS because the TOE was subsequently revised to reflect a reduction by one rank for all job titles while the missions required more effort than in the past. The organization of Unit 306 is shown in the following chart. *(Chart 28)*

Chart 28—Organization, Unit 306 - J-2, JGS

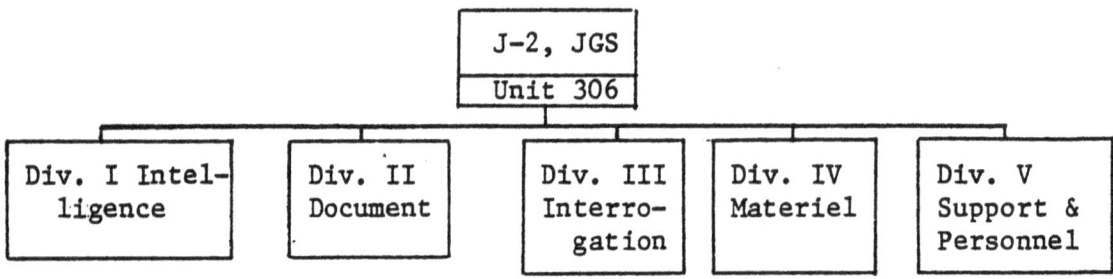

The Combined Intelligence Center, Vietnam (CICV), was reorganized to become the Intelligence Division or Division I; the Combined Documents Exploitation Center (CDEC) became the Documents Division or Division II; the Combined Military Interrogation Center (CMIC) became the Interrogation

Division or Division III; the Combined Materiel Exploitation Center (CMEC) became the Materiel Division or Division IV; and the Military Intelligence Center became the Support and Personnel Division or Division V.

Equipment formerly available at the combined intelligence centers was owned by the US side. Because this was costly, sophisticated equipment, it was not covered by MAP-funded TOE allocations. Moreover, the Vietnamese side did not anticipate that the day would come when the Vietnamese element would no longer have access to such equipment. When the US side prepared to pull out, J-2, JGS requested that some essential equipment be left behind. J-2, USMACV agreed in principle but ultimately the equipment could not be transferred to the Vietnamese side because there had been no advance planning for the authorization of such items. Some non-essential items such as filing cabinets, desks, and chairs were transferred to the Vietnamese by their respective US counterparts though they were not TOE-listed. However, this prompted the Logistical Command to order that all such items be turned in to storage depots. In order to keep them for Unit 306 personnel to use, US liaison officers had to resort to signing for them on a loan basis.

Liaison between JGS, military region/corps, division G-2s and sector S-2s ran into difficulties because intelligence liaison flights were no longer available. Documents and correspondence were forwarded through the military postal system. Except where special provisions were made, an average of three months elapsed between the day an enemy document was captured in the field and the day it was received at the Documents Division, whereas document evacuation used to be completed within a week. When the exploitation was completed, it was another two weeks before the results were disseminated to the unit. If the unit were a Regular Army force engaged in an operation in another area, the document exploitation report only reached the rear base, and there was no set time as to when it would reach the MI officer.

Prisoners of war and "hoi chanh" (defectors) were retained at local stations and the Interrogation Division sent teams out to interrogate them whereas they should have been evacuated to the central Interrogation Division as in the past.

Captured material was sent in only if it presented new characteristics, but how could any characteristic be identified as new when not all levels of intelligence were able to recognize the difference? Combat intelligence data acquired were substantially reduced. In 1973 for instance, the enemy targeted his attacks against isolated outposts near infiltration routes, and by concentrating large forces, was always assured of victory. Such battles yielded no PW or documents to help identify the enemy units involved. "Hoi Chanh" now came in smaller numbers and there were no high-ranking ones. The psychology was such that defections came when the fighting was fierce, when the enemy's tactical position was weak, and the RVN had the upper hand. In the seesaw situation of semi-war and semi-peace only the most determined defected and there was a high rate of false defections.

Fewer documents were captured, not only because there were fewer contacts with the enemy but also because the enemy had applied stricter secrecy control measures, forbidding his troops to carry documents during an operational mission. This prohibition occurred after the RVN had repeatedly used captured documents to substantiate its protests of Communist crimes and deliberate violations of the cease-fire.

Intelligence previously acquired through communications means was substantially reduced because the Communists had identified the communications intelligence reliance on overflights. To contain friendly air activities, an additional 20 Communist air defense regiments infiltrated after the cease-fire with sophisticated armament never before observed in the Vietnam theater. Among this new arsenal were SA-2 missiles; modified SA-7 heat-seeking missiles; radar-guided 100-mm, 57-mm, and 37-mm antiaircraft guns; and self-propelled, multiple-barreled antiaircraft artillery. The air defense perimeter expanded daily and proportionately reduced aircraft operational ranges. Typically in MR-3 enemy 37-mm antiaircraft guns were positioned in Ben Cat, Binh Duong, 15 miles northwest of Saigon. The antiaircraft missile which caused the strongest psychological impact was the modified SA-7 missile. Its effective altitude and speed had been increased, the altitude being increased from 9,000 ft. to 15,000 ft., forcing VNAF pilots to fly above 15,000 ft.

However, RC-47 and EC-47 aircraft could not fly above 10,000 ft. Moreover, photos taken by RF-5s flying above 4,500 or 5,000 ft. were not usable because of the type of cameras mounted on the aircraft. The cameras were the 70-mm KS-92. Photos from these cameras were to cover an area between 400 and 500 square meters and the photography was unusable for mosaics. Furthermore, no VNAF aircraft were equipped with radar lock-on-warning (LOW) equipment. Areas denied to aerial photo reconnaissance were MR-1, the tri-border area and the highlands of MR-2, and the northern part of MR-3. Missions over these areas were very difficult because VNAF had no long range rescue teams. On 22 September 1973, when the Communists launched their first armor-supported attack after the cease-fire against the Le Minh outpost 38 km west of Pleiku, photo aircraft were directed to record the number of enemy armored vehicles and their progress. This was to serve as a basis for a RVNAF tactical response and as evidence of blatant violations of the Paris Agreement. However, it was not until five days later that the flights were conducted. By that time there were no traces left of enemy armored or infantry units. In Quang Duc, MR-2, the same problem occurred when in early November 1973 the Communists attacked the border outposts of Bu Prang and Bu Dop. The requirement then was to determine the locations of enemy armored, anti-aircraft, and artillery positions so that the corps might make counterattack plans. Wrong coordinates and inclement weather were blamed for a delay that caused the air photo mission to be completed after the counterattacks had been launched.

Beginning on 1 September 1974, reductions in military aid caused fuel allocations and replacement parts to VNAF to drop to 65% of the year 1973. This, in turn, led to a drop of air photo reconnaissance performance to 52% of the previous year. Total flight time for RC-47s was reduced to 150 hours a month, for RF-5s to 45 hours a month. To meet an essential air photo reconnaissance need, J-2, JGS interceded with J-3, JGS to either borrow flight time from the following month or to reduce other flights, but this was virtually impossible. These situations occurred when the Communists launched large-scale attacks as in Ban Me Thuot. In other cases, air photo reconnaissance needs conflicted with the needs to fly tactical air or logistical support.

The Vietnam Air Force could not conduct night reconnaissance as it did not have sophisticated aircraft such as the RF-101 C Voodoo, RB-57F Canberra, RF-4C Phantom or OV-1 Mohawk. After Communist forces had overrun Ban Me Thuot the requirement was to detect enemy armored and vehicular movements from Ban Me Thuot toward MR-3 or the coastal areas of MR 2. Monitoring the lines of communication (LOC) was possible for a maximum of only eight hours a day, which meant enemy forces had 16 hours a day to move undetected.

United States-ARVN Intelligence Cooperation and Coordination In The Face of New Difficulties

In air photo reconnaissance VNAF could meet only 7 to 10% of the in-country requirements, which meant that 90% of these requirements were still dependent on USAF air photo reconnaissance capabilities called upon through the DAO Intelligence Branch.

Most US aircraft took off from Thailand. Reconnaissance flights were conducted over North Vietnam, Laos and South Vietnam by SR-71 and U-2s. RF-4s provided coverage of Cambodia and a 25 nautical mile-wide corridor along the Vietnamese-Cambodian border. Unmanned aircraft, or Buffalo Hunters, were also used in South Vietnam.

In order to ensure secrecy and avoid North Vietnamese protests, information obtained from SR-71 and U-2 missions was not passed to the RVN. Exceptions were made in only very special cases and with DIA approval. Photographs and information obtained by RF-4s were passed to the Vietnamese upon special request and with adequate justification of the need. Unmanned aircraft, or Buffalo Hunters, were the only source of information that the Vietnamese were totally entitled to. These aircraft were launched from DC-130s at an altitude of 20,000 ft but this was not allowed over Laos territory after June 1974. Thirty to forty flights were performed per month, especially over areas inaccessible to VNAF. Photos thus taken were very sharp and clear. The overflights were programmed four days in advance and occasionally mechanical problems did develop. In some areas Buffalo Hunters were used in a tactical reconnaissance capacity to provide information in support of battlefield requirements. This occurred, for instance, in July 1974 during the battles of Thuong Duc and Duc Duc in MR 1.

In mid-1974, Buffalo Hunter and RF-4 flight were stopped in Laos. When the situation in the RVN began to pick up in intensity, the US reinforced drone overflights with RF-4 missions in South Vietnam but such flights were conducted at very high altitudes to avoid complications which might develop should any be shot down.

Photos from Buffalo Hunter missions were originally delivered by aircraft to the Vietnamese in three days. Later this was reduced to a day. Prior to receiving the photographs the Vietnamese were given readouts by messages. The photos consisted of three duplicate positives, mission traces, select prints, and vu-graph slides. Of the three duplicate positives, one went to VNAF Imagery Interpretation Center, one to Division 1/Unit 306, and one to the military region concerned.

The two Vietnamese Army and Air Force Imagery Interpretation Centers usually re-interpreted and reprinted the duplicate positives for distribution to the areas concerned. Re-interpretation served a purpose. A photo, for instance, was interpreted by Nakhon Phanom (NKP) as showing NVA T-60 medium tanks on RVN territory. Verification of this information was of utmost significance as North Vietnam had not been known to have such tanks. Re-interpretation indicated these were only T-54 or T-59 tanks. Finally, another overflight was conducted over the target area and DIA interpreters identified the tanks as T-54s and T-59s. Additional prints made by the VNAF Imagery Interpretation Center were sent to the air divisions, but they did not reach them until three days later. The Imagery Interpretation Section of Division 1/306, for its part, used hotlines to relay readouts to the corps and divisions concerned. They also sent selected prints but these did not reach the recipients until a week later.

In urgent cases, a method commonly used for delivery was to carefully package the prints and take them to a civilian terminal. There they were entrusted to passengers on Air Vietnam's domestic flights who were deemed reliable such as high-ranking military officers on TDY or leave, or members of the clergy. Identification of these passengers, the flight number, flight time, etc., were then transmitted to the local agency which sent personnel out to meet the plane. This became the prime method used by RVN military intelligence to ensure expeditious delivery of documents.

The US and RVN held many discussions as to how to improve the photography process. In June 1974 they came up with an immediate solution and a long-range solution. The immediate solution called for replacing the obsolete KS-92 cameras with KS-121s for the four RF-5 aircraft. Testing showed that the KS-121 had twice the resolution and three times the accuracy, in addition to many other advantages. This program was to fulfill its objective within six to nine months of the signing of the camera purchase contract. The second solution provided for F-5Es to be used in aerial reconnaissance. These aircraft could be outfitted with KS-121s for photographing from low-to-medium altitudes, or with KA-95s for medium to high altitudes. Purchasing the KA-95s alone would have cost $7.5 million. The KA-95s and the KS-121s would have cost $13.5 million. If approved the program was not expected to fulfill its objective before mid-1977. However, till the very last day it remained in the stage of a project.

In late 1974 another effort was undertaken in the form of a project to equip C-130s with F 638-120 cameras to be borrowed from the Air Force Logistics Command. This did not materialize either because the cameras were not available.

As a substitute source of air photos, hand-held cameras received special consideration. However, VNAF hand-held cameras had only 200-mm lenses and the high altitudes of the flights were not conducive to sharp photos. A 600-mm lens would have been the minimum but even so, VNAF was not able to borrow more than one. The ideal lens would have been the F:11 1000-mm Yashica which did get proposed but for which no funds could be obtained.

The difficulties encountered by VNAF impacted seriously on the SIGINT program of J-7, JGS.

Though J-7, JGS had 33 EC-47 aircraft, one was destroyed by an attack by fire while at Tan Son Nhut airbase in late 1973 and two others were downed by SA-7s over northern Tay Ninh in May 1974. Of the remaining 30, a theoretical operational status of 50% or 15 aircraft a day was prescribed but in reality only 33 to 35% of the aircraft were operational on any one day because of lack of maintenance or personnel, or because the targets were located too deep in enemy territory. For example, of the ten EC-47s based in Da Nang, four should have been available for daily overflights. On many occasions, however, only two were serviceable. An effort was made to improve the EC-47 program by adding 7 more to raise the total force to 40 aircraft and the number of daily flights to 20 but this project never materialized. Actually, with the enemy's new air defense capabilities in the South, only RU/JU-21s could operate over enemy-controlled areas thanks to their altitude of up to 26,000 ft. and their speed of 180 knots versus an EC-47 altitude of 10,000 ft. and speed of 120 knots. Communist countermeasures were another obstacle to ARDF. Once an EC-47 entered a target zone, it took five to ten minutes to pick up radio signal and three lines of bearing (LOB) had to be obtained for a target fix. In the wake of the cease-fire the Communists frequently used 2- to 5-watt radios with very short ranges which, added to the rugged features of mountain and forest terrain, made intercept very difficult. In addition, they used FM voice communications which the EC-47 could not pick up as it was not equipped for DF/FM voice intercept. The Communists also used landlines whenever they could. A comparison in 1974 based strictly on the number of aircraft dedicated to ARDF would show that the capability for this type of mission had dropped to about 1/3 of the 1972 capability. Moreover, each flight was reduced from eight hours to five. Furthermore, a situation which received very little attention prevailed during the period from late 1973 onward. In the face of increasing costs of living, military pay remained stationary and therefore military personnel had to reduce their consumption of nutrients. As a result, their productivity dropped markedly after three flight hours.

Five ground stations at Phu Bai, Pleiku, Song Mao, Vung Tau and Can Tho constituted the backup for the ARDF program. The HFDFs, with their high frequency direction finders (HFDF), did not produce effective results; however, they were useful in locating target areas for ARDF coverage. These centers were equipped with AN/TRD-15s which were not as advanced as the AN/TRD-23s. There were only 80 such direction finders against 120 authorized, and by late 1974 only 50 were operational. To replace them would have required funding and a delay of a year from the date of order to date of delivery.

While PHOTINT encountered numerous obstacles resulting from US troop withdrawals, the obstacles were minimal in the area of HUMINT. Before leaving, the 525th Military Intelligence Group had transferred to Unit 101 and MSS all transferrable equipment, including 17 radio-teletypes. It had also trained 50 NCOs for five weeks to replace personnel of the 504th Signal Detachment in operating these radio sets. To improve Unit 101 intelligence reporting, an automatic data processing (ADP) program was set up which provided for the encoding of intelligence information reports (IIR). The 525th also trained a key puncher for two weeks and experimented with encoding Detachment 69's IIRs. However, the CICV computer had been removed and Unit 101 had to use the ADP facilities of JGS. Shortage of qualified personnel to run this program caused it to make no further progress. After the cease-fire the US representative was a member of the 500th MI Group's Special Activities in Thailand. This group continued to fund Unit 101's operations. Bilateral operations of the past were now conducted solely by Unit 101 personnel. However, from a technical point of view, these personnel had by then become extremely proficient and the results showed no negative effects of a change to unilateral operation. On the contrary, unilateral operations gave them opportunities to test new methods. Furthermore, the 525th MI Group left barracks and quarters which provided more housing for Unit 101 families, thereby boosting its personnel morale.

Generally speaking, the cease-fire entailed a substantial reduction of intelligence sources and collection means, particularly PHOTINT means. Those difficulties of a financial nature could not be resolved because funds were just not available. This was why efforts to overcome PHOTINT limitations could not succeed though many projects had been formulated. An objective of this plan was to create voice intercept teams at the Sector level. Sector S-2's were to be tasked to activate and control such teams. In addition to Divisional Communications Intelligence Detachments which had been operational for some time, there were created additional detachments for those divisions whose tactical or territorial responsibilities required more coverage such as the Airbone and the 23d Infantry Division. This effort, however, still failed to provide coverage of the entire territory and meet the needs of the sectors. In mid-1973, pilot sector intercept teams were set up in Binh Dinh, MR 2, and Quang Tin, MR 1. Personnel of these teams were selected from the sectors and their S-2 staffs and equipment consisted of AN/PRC-25s or captured enemy radios. Thanks to enemy codes previously captured in their local areas, these teams gradually succeeded in intercepting and decoding most radio communications between enemy Local Force units and in some cases between enemy Main Forces. This experiment was very successful and the equipment required no additional costs.

In late 1973 sector S-2s nationwide were directed to organize similar radio intercept teams after the experience of the above two sectors had been studied for good points and shortcomings. Not all sectors enjoyed similar successes, though, because such efforts depended on the sector commander's attitude toward organization not sanctioned by TOEs, his personal interest in radio intercept, and in case such a team was created, the ability of the team to break the enemy code. Overall, the efforts produced a significant volume of information which made them worthwhile considering the minimal investment in personnel and equipment. However, an internal problem developed from the J-7 belief that such intercept practices would eventually jeopardize J-7's own operations. J-7 thought that failure to give S-2 personnel specialized training would lead them to make mistakes which would expose their intercept operations to the enemy and thereby cause the enemy to take preventive measures. An agreement was finally reached which called for J-7 specialists to provide technical advice to sector radio intercept teams if deemed necessary, and information acquired by these teams would be passed to local J-7 technical detachments.

In the field of HUMINT, new measures were applied to Unit 101. First, to ensure adequate response to the unit's primary mission of collecting strategic intelligence, agents were screened to reduce the number of sources whose experience was limited to tactical intelligence. Those thus terminated were transferred to sectors or sub-sectors which had indicated a need for them. This measure helped economize personnel and funds for better support to strategic intelligence collection. Prior to reducing its agents, Unit 101 produced an estimated 1,500 IIRs monthly from its 92 intelligence nets. This massive production was precisely the reason analysts found it hardly possible to evaluate and follow up on the information reported. As a result of the new measure, the number of collection nets was reduced by an estimated 10% to 80 but there remained a substantial number of agents. Selection then took place in the form of immediate termination of those individuals found guilty of feeding the unit falsified information. The next step was to place the 101 collection detachments under the technical control and guidance of the corps G-2s. This was beneficial in terms of planning, employment and evaluation, and gave the detachments increased support from their respective corps G-2s. Unit 101 was tasked with tapping enemy landlines but never succeeded because the targets were usually located in fighting areas and, the unit did not have compact, concealable equipment to perform these operations.

Radioteletype equipment transferred from the 525th to Unit 101 were in turn loaned out to corps and division G-2s for their communications with J-2, JGS and Unit 101 in Saigon. From the very beginning J-2 did not have a specialized communications system such as the ones enjoyed by MSS and J-7. Repeated proposals for establishing a specialized communications system for the Military Intelligence Branch were turned down because, it was claimed, equipment was not available. Information transmitted through common-user communications channels usually experienced a delay of at least 48 hours. To ensure expeditious exchange of information, J-6, JGS and the Signal Department provided special support to help J-2, JGS establish hot lines for direct communications with corps G-2s and the G-2s of divisions whose areas of responsibility were experiencing increased tactical pressure. Field-grade officers from J-2 were detached to corps and division G-2s to expedite the routing of information over this communication system. Intelligence and tactical information reports were thus dispatched immediately after they had been made available.

Conclusions

Prior to the cease-fire, intelligence information acquired by the various units was usually sent by US advisers through secure US communications channels to USMACV which in turn passed it to J-2, JGS. This was faster than using regular Vietnamese channels. After the cease-fire, the DAO Intelligence Branch had representatives at corps level only. These were assigned as staff members of the US consulate general in each military region.

At JGS and DAO HQ, coordination was extremely good because it was based on practical considerations, openness, and mutual trust. Credit for successful cooperation must be given to Colonel William E. LeGro DAO Chief, Intelligence Branch, a true professional with broad experience and a very dedicated man. Daily meetings between the two sides were held to exchange information, discuss the situation, coordinate requirements, and divide responsibilities, particularly in the area of PHOTINT. Though data were picked up by J-7, the interpretation of Communist unit relationships and subordination required assistance from the US side because J-7 could not relate call signs to specific Communist units, particularly those in North Vietnam or those recently infiltrated from North Vietnam. Daily and weekly intelligence summaries were exchanged regularly between J-2, JGS and the DAO Intelligence Branch. Every month the DAO Intelligence Branch conducted situation briefings which were of special interest to the Vietnamese side, particularly in terms of information on North Vietnam and infiltration-related activities. Because it did not have enough personnel, the DAO Intelligence Branch limited its own activities to current intelligence and situation estimates and did not compile intelligence studies. In contrast, J-2, JGS made it a special effort to conduct studies on the enemy and was noted for its achievements in the areas of: Communist military doctrine; Communist strategic and tactical courses of action; artillery; communications; engineers; armor; messenger services; sappers; and Communist base areas.

In summary, the cease-fire saw the US side drastically reduce field collection activities since direct needs no longer existed. DAO intelligence requirements had to compete for priority with intelligence requirements in other areas of Southeast Asia. On the Vietnamese side, PHOTINT was substantially reduced but this was compensated in part by increased efforts in COMINT. Quantitative reduction of combat intelligence was offset by qualitative improvements and revamping of collection agent networks. Close coordination between Vietnamese and US intelligence agencies also helped intelligence respond effectively to the needs of the situation from the cease-fire to the very last day.

CHAPTER VI

Successes and Failures of ARVN Intelligence

The 1968 General Offensive

When the Communists launched their General Offensive against cities across South Vietnam in 1968, including Saigon and Hue, almost everybody agreed that it was a total surprise. The general populace of South Vietnam felt that the intelligence establishment had failed to discover the enemy scheme. Moreover, casting the blame on intelligence was partially justified. Any military offensive must be preceded by preparations. There was no reason why an offensive of such proportions should have entirely escaped the prying eyes and ears of every intelligence agent. Strange as it may seem, no one reproved US intelligence for this common failure, but they did reprove the United States. One widespread popular Vietnamese belief at that time was that the United States had entered into a tacit agreement with the Communists to let them proceed with a military action designed to bring about a quick political solution for the war.

On the RVN side, no timely warnings were issued nor was there any indication that an enemy action was imminent. Two days before the outbreak of the offensive, there was a decision to reduce the Tet truce from 48 to 36 hours and to confine 50% of troops to barracks. However, at the time the Communists began their attacks, on the second day of Tet, most ARVN garrison units were left with only a scant 10 to 20% of their combat strength. The majority of the troops were absent to celebrate Tet with their families. President Thieu himself was not in Saigon; he was quietly celebrating Tet in My Tho, home of his wife's family. Intelligence had failed; there was no question about it. What concerned many people in retrospect was to what extent intelligence had failed, and how the Communists had gone about preparing for their general offensive.

To put the event into its proper perspective, an examination of the military situation in 1967 is deemed necessary. This was a period of relative stability; the security picture displayed throughout rural areas was truly bright. Our two-pronged strategy of "pacification and search-and-destroy" inflicted important losses on the enemy. On the battlefield, major engagements took place only in border areas such as south of the DMZ, west of the Central Highlands, and the northeast of MR-3. The first indicator of a general offensive was an enemy document captured from the CT-5 Division in March 1967 which revealed a planned attack against Saigon. This plan of attack was so primitive and so ingenuous that intelligence experts simply disregarded it as utopian. Then, some time in early October, the RVN intelligence establishment learned about the content of Resolution No. 13 issued by North Vietnam's Labor Party Central Committee. The resolution called for large-scale offensive attacks designed to bring about victory within a short time. At about the same time, another captured enemy document belonging to the Armor Section of COSVN, code-named Detachment 16, mentioned an enemy effort to train his troops in sapper techniques and the use of captured ARVN tanks. Then late in November, another captured document dated 1 September 1967 and bearing the title, "New Mission, New Tasks" revealed among other things that the new objectives now coveted were to terminate the American presence in Vietnam and a coalition government. The document also disclosed that the conduct of the offensive was basically a triple effort: military, political, and proselyting action, to be launched in conjunction with a general popular uprising, hence its code-name TCK-TKN (abbreviations used in the document for general offensive—general uprising). Two other captured documents again pointed specifically toward a general offensive. The first one, a document of the B-3 Front headquarters captured in Dakto (MR-2) in October 1967 spoke about large-scale preparations being made for the 1968 Winter-Spring Campaign. The second document, captured in Quang Tin, during the same month was most specific of all. It said in effect: "It is about time we proceeded with the general offensive and general uprising. By utilizing military units in coordination with the uprising movement of the popular mass, we will attack all provincial capitals and district towns and eventually liberate the capital."

Thus during 1967, the number of captured documents was substantial and indicated a large military move. In addition to the documents specified above, there were several other piecemeal documents mentioning combat tactics in cities, a kind of tactic heretofore never subjected to discussion or training by the enemy.

Aside from documents, our intelligence also learned about an enemy effort to reorganize his territorial command and control, particularly in his MR-4 or Saigon — Cholon MR and his Tri Thien Hue MR. As of September 1967, the enemy MR-4 was reorganized into five sub-regions centered on Saigon which in turn was divided into five areas or sectors. At that time the significance of this enemy reorganization effort was unclear. Only after the offensive was launched did we know that it was part of the attack plan. Each of the five sub-regions was responsible for the offensive effort against a related target area of Saigon.

On 17 November 1967, the National Liberation Front of South Vietnam proposed a seven-day truce for the Tet holidays which began in late January 1968. This was advanced at the same time with the three-day truce proposed for Christmas and New Year. The truce proposal was immediately interpreted by our intelligence officers as an enemy move to take advantage of the truce to increase his logistic movements prior to a major offensive. With all the intelligence data gathered, and in the light of the documents captured, it was evident that the enemy was preparing for a major offensive campaign. Our intelligence apparatus correctly estimated this move but its attention was directed toward the areas usually considered strategically important such as Khe Sanh. The probability of Khe Sanh becoming a decisive contest objective like Dien Bien Phu in 1954 was foremost in the minds of our intelligence analysts. Little attention, if any, was given to the cities as probable objectives. The timing of the enemy offensive was also estimated as more likely to occur sometime after Tet than before.

In early January 1968, another enemy document was captured in II CTZ. This was Combat Order No. 1 detailing a plan of attack on Pleiku city some time before Tet.

On 28 January 1968, during a raid conducted in Qui Nhon city, the local MSS arrested 11 Communist cadres of the city local force together with two pre-recorded tapes. The tapes contained a proclamation inciting the population to rise up against the government and announcing that in addition to the occupation of Binh Dinh province, the "Vietnamese forces struggling for Peace and Unification" were also in control of Saigon, Hue and Da Nang. The captured cadres declared that Communist forces were going to launch an attack against Qui Nhon city and certain others during the Tet period.

On the same day, G-2 of III Corps discovered the concentration of an enemy force consisting of 1 artillery and 2 infantry regiments in an area north of Bien Hoa. Then the next day, 29 January, the local population of Ho Nai district, Bien Hoa province, reported the appearance of a Communist unit in an area adjacent to the district headquarters itself. During the night, guards on duty at III Corps Headquarters discovered an enemy armed reconnaissance team and shot down one team member at the gate.

In Can Tho, Communist sappers disguised as tourists were apprehended by the police while they were looking for rooms in a hotel.

At 2100 hours on 30 January 1968, troops of a RF battalion manning positions on the defense belt of Saigon captured an enemy soldier armed with an AK-47 rifle. He disclosed that Communist forces were going to attack Saigon city, Tan Son Nhut airport, the Joint General Staff, and the Saigon radio station at 0300 hours on 31 January. Then at 2130 hours, another Communist soldier was captured at Phu Nhuan (in Saigon) with two AK-47's of the collapsible stock model.

At exactly 0300 hours on 31 January 1968, or the second day of Tet (Year of the Monkey, lunar calendar), the enemy general offensive broke out.

Those were the intelligence data collected in a chronological sequence that pertained to the 1968 general offensive. Through these data alone, the enemy scheme of a general offensive was evident.

Other data of significance could have proved helpful in intelligence analysis and situation estimates during that time, but they were overlooked or not given proper attention. There was for example the appearance of new Communist weapons such as the modern AK-47 rifle and RPG-2 (B-40) rocket launcher. The existence of such weapons was regarded by our intelligence experts as part of a normal modernization process and not particularly significant. Then a rapid succession of enemy attacks against district towns in III and IV CTZs, to include an attack on the city of My Tho, failed to raise any suspicion of an abnormal effort by the enemy. The attack on Loc Ninh district town in Binh Long province, north of Saigon, on 29 October 1967 was particularly significant since it was conducted by forces of the CT-9 Division, reinforced by 2 regiments of the CT-7 Division and artillery units. The enemy succeeded, despite heavy losses, in occupying this district town which they held for some time. The significance of these enemy actions was somehow lost to our intelligence experts. Only sometime after the Tet general offensive had begun did it dawn on them that all these attacks were conducted with the purpose of testing the effectiveness of combat tactics used against cities and towns and probing the reactions of the United States and the RVN.

The "Happy Tet" poem by Ho Chi Minh that Radio Hanoi repeatedly broadcast for some time before Tet was also a significant indicator that failed to draw the attention of our intelligence experts. For one thing, it had become a habit of the North Vietnam leader to address Happy Tet wishes to the North Vietnamese population every year. For another, words of exhortation to victory were nothing new in Communist propaganda jargon. What our intelligence experts failed to detect was the meaning that something new would happen this coming Tet and that it was going to be entirely different from previous years. The significance of Ho's short poem as a signal for preparations and attack was later confirmed by several enemy prisoners and returnees.

In brief, the information on hand was clear enough. There could be no mistake about its implication and meaning. It is much easier in retrospect to see the enemy general offensive coming out loud and clear against city targets. What made our intelligence experts ignore the enemy plan was simply that they were all convinced, out of prejudice and pride, that the enemy did not possess the capability, and that it would be sheer foolishness for the enemy to attempt to attack our cities. Such reasoning is understandable. Clearly, it is in line with the military intelligence theory that only capabilities are real and valid for estimate purposes; intentions are vague at best, hence not valid. It was precisely because of this theory that our intelligence experts overlooked the most basic thing in the analysis procedure, a synthesis of all pertinent data, in this case of the data in hand on offensives against cities. Such a synthesis could have been used to see if the threat of a general offensive was real or how probable it was. At the very least, there would have been requirements for additional intelligence data or some advance warnings to the military leadership.

However, our military leaders would not have believed such a probability if they had been warned. Given the optimistic mood prevailing in domestic and American politics at the time, they were all elated about military gains and generally held the view that a military victory would materalize in the not too distant future. The intelligence establishment was heavily influenced by such optimistic prospects and its tendency to echo the official line was understandable. The important lesson under such circumstances is that the intelligence community should make every effort to provide a highly professional estimate based on all available information even though this estimate might be unpopular and irritate some leaders.

As a matter of fact, there did exist some intelligence analysts who were really concerned about information available. However, they persisted in thinking in a Phase I, II, III manner. During 1967 the general tendency of enemy activities was still confined to Phase I of Communist strategy which was essentially defensive. To pass onto the Phase III, which was the general offensive phase, they thought that the enemy had to proceed through Phase II which was a holding phase characterized by limited contested actions. But our error was the assumption that the enemy military effort at the end of 1967 was still in Phase I. In reality, judging by the mobile form of warfare which the enemy had been conducting for some time, he had already passed on to Phase II, although this transition had been gradual.

A major shortcoming of Vietnamese intelligence during this pre-Tet period, which contributed to its failure to predict the Tet offensive, was the total lack of coordination among its multifarious agencies. Each intelligence seemed to be interested only in its own activities as an independent organization. The exchange of information was formal, if any, and generally untimely. No one agency had real authority in intelligence or was qualified to serve as a clearing house uniquely responsible for intelligence production. The coordination between RVN and US intelligence agencies was also slack and piecemeal. Forty-eight hours before the general offensive began, US forces were placed on general alert. It was apparent that US intelligence was concerned and took no chances. On the RVN side, ARVN Corps Commands were also issued a warning by JGS as to the possibility of an enemy offensive but apparently the warning came too late for any effective preparations. It was in fact issued on New Year Day, barely sixteen hours before the outbreak of the first attack.

The 1968 Tet general offensive was a sobering event for the Vietnamese intelligence establishment. Many of its deficiencies were exposed and it was able to learn many invaluable lessons. First, it was learned that in an ideological war such as the Vietnamese conflict, political considerations almost always outweighed tactical considerations. Experience shows that even though the enemy might sometimes lack the military capabilities for an offensive, he still went ahead with this offensive against all odds if there was a certain political goal to be achieved. One lesson was that the search for enemy intentions was also important. Second, it was learned that the enemy always tried to achieve the element of tactical surprise for each new major effort by the employment of new weapons or weapon systems. The tactic to be used was also usually tested prior to launching the offensive. Another invaluable lesson learned by the intelligence officer was: he should be truthful, unbiased, and should never try to please his superiors by interpreting facts under a light they favored or in the way they wished.

The first phase of the 1968 general offensive also helped the RVN intelligence establishment to learn more about the enemy. Unprecedented numbers of prisoners, returnees, and important captured documents contributed toward deepening our knowledge on the enemy's strategy and policies. As a result, we knew well in advance every detail about the follow-up phase of his offensive, even the exact time of the first attack, which began on 5 May 1968. This was due to our agent sources within enemy ranks. In addition to information on the enemy campaign, these sources also divulged the difficulties that COSVN was facing, particularly the deteriorating morale of Communist units. At the same time, high ranking returnees contributed much invaluable information on the enemy's internal situation.

The general offensive of 1968 resulted in a very significant military defeat for the enemy. He had thought that he could achieve a quick military victory by going all out against our major cities and population centers. He had hoped that the population would rise up and give him a hand, but none of these things had happened. At the cost of thousands of lives, he must have realized that his strategy did not work. Within just a few months after the defeat, COSVN felt compelled to issue in rapid succession three major policy documents, Resolution No. 8, Addendum to Resolution No. 8, and Resolution No. 9, justifying the military defeat and explaining the need for a change in strategy, all in self-serving propagandistic style. If anything, these documents showed to what extent the morale of enemy troops had been shattered and revealed the disarray of his units. But the political gains the enemy obtained through his general offensive apparently led to the disengagement of US forces and the initiation of the Vietnamization program. Operations which revealed progress in Vietnamization, such as the cross-border incursions into Cambodia in 1970 and into lower Laos in 1971, were among the many causes that compelled the enemy to launch his general offensive of Summer 1972.

The 1972 Easter Offensive

In early December 1971, information concerning a Communist general offensive during 1972 was already being obtained and recorded. In contrast to the previous experience of 1968, the first information gathered on the enemy preparations in North Vietnam was detected and made available to me by the J-2 of MACV. It was learned that North Vietnamese general reserve divisions, after a prolonged campaign in lower Laos during 1971, were redirected to North Vietnam where they went through a process of replenishment and refitting and were preparing to move south. From a strategic viewpoint, the probability of an enemy general offensive during 1972 made sense since it was a presidential election year in the United States. The enemy apparently anticipated the internal difficulties that the US was going to face during the election year. He surmised that these difficulties would give him favorable opportunities. During 1971 foreign aid to North Vietnam had increased substantially and its level was only a little less than during 1967. Based on lessons learned during 1968, this increase in foreign aid level was unmistakably an indication of a general offensive. Battles fought in lower Laos early in 1971 confirmed the fact that Communist forces had received quantities of deadly new weapons such as artillery field guns and howitzers of 100-mm, 130-mm and 152-mm, T-34 and T-54 tanks, SA-2 anti-air missiles, etc. With the new deployment and disposition of NVA general reserve divisions in South Vietnam, it was estimated that the general offensive would take place in three specific areas: Tri Thien — Hue in MR-1, Kontum — Pleiku in MR-2 and Tay Ninh in MR-3. It was estimated, that the enemy's tactical approach would be concentrated on a few key objectives in each military region instead of encompassing all objectives throughout the country. The timing for the offensive was estimated to be some time during March 1972.

Such was, in general terms, the intelligence estimate concerning the enemy 1972 general offensive, which was issued in mid-January 1972 as a result of an ever increasing flow of data. The exact time frame for this offensive was still under debate at that time. It was estimated that

March would be the best time as far as the enemy was concerned because during the dry season, which had begun in October the previous year, enemy supplies were moved in great quantities into South Vietnam. By the end of February, it was estimated, these supplies would have reached COSVN and been distributed to units under its control in MR-3 and MR-4. Since the 1968 memory was still fresh, the assumption was that the enemy would chose not to strike during the Tet holidays but probably before or after.

Late in February 1972, President Thieu paid a visit to ARVN major units, during which he presented his Happy Tet greetings to the troops. The places that he visited almost coincided with the probable objectives of the enemy offensive. It appeared as if his itinerary had been selected on purpose: Dong Ha and Hue in MR-1, Dakto, Tan Canh, Le Minh and Binh Dinh in MR-2. The visit was also intended to provide the president an opportunity to review the military situation with his field commanders in the face of the coming general offensive and particularly to assess the concern of our troops regarding the use of 130-mm artillery by the enemy against the area south of the DMZ. But enemy tanks and their probable use in the offensive did not give rise to any appreciable concern among our field commanders. Apparently they thought that, with the US tremendous airpower, enemy tanks would be sitting ducks.

On 19 February 1972, information was obtained concerning instructions passed from High Command Hanoi to Headquarters B-3 Front. Subsequently, some of these instructions were passed on by this headquarters to its subordinate divisions and provinces. The indications were clear enough and led both US and the RVN intelligence authorities to the conclusions that the enemy was going to launch his general offensive immediately after the truce, probably on the 5th day of Tet. In Vietnamese intelligence eyes, this date was of particular significance since it was the day selected by Emperor Quang Trung to launch his famous military march north to defeat the Chiang in 1788.

As a result, a general alert was issued to units throughout the country. But the enemy changed his plans and chose not to strike on that date. It was unclear to the RVN intelligence as to why there was such a countermand order. It was possible, however, to surmise that the postponement had some connection with President Nixon's visit to mainland China from 21 to 28 February 1972. It was probable that China asked for such a postponement because it did not want any misstep to spoil the nascent US-China relationship.

Late in March 1972, information was obtained by J-7 of the JGS that 29 March was to be the D-day of the general offensive. This information was disseminated to all ARVN units as a measure of precaution.

The 1972 Summer Offensive, as it became known to our side, broke out at first in the DMZ area on 30 March 1972. Enemy 130-mm artillery pieces positioned north of the DMZ concentrated their fire on all ARVN outposts in the DMZ area. In a subsequent action, NVA general reserve units moved across the Ben Hai river with the support of tanks. The direction of attack during the enemy offensive in MR-1 was a surprise to our field command. As a matter of fact, we had failed to predict that the enemy would cross the DMZ and mount a frontal attack against Gio Linh, Cam Lo and other outposts. It had been our assumption that the enemy attack would be from the west instead of the north because crossing the DMZ would be a blatant violation of the Geneva Accords. The enemy firepower and forceful, all-out drive across the DMZ so overwhelmed our advance positions that they were unable to report accurately the situation to the Headquarters of the 3d Division and I Corps. As it turned out, up to three days after it was launched, the enemy general offensive in MR-1 still failed to arouse any major concern in Saigon.

The situation became serious when Communist forces infiltrated into MR-3 from Cambodia and overran Loc Ninh on 4 April. Intelligence data collected from a returnee and communication sources had pointed toward Binh Long province as a major target area, but our own attention was directed more toward Tay Ninh than Loc Ninh (a northernmost district town of Binh Long province) because of Tay Ninh's political importance. The enemy chose to attack Binh Long with two divisions, the CT-5 and CT-9, with the support of tanks and with the CT-7 Division establishing blocking positions on QL-13 between Chon Thanh and An Loc. The appearance of Communist tanks on the Binh Long front was claimed by the III Corps commander to be a complete surprise. The tanks were instrumental in the quick overrunning of Loc Ninh district town and the encirclement of An Loc, provincial capital of Binh Long province. Information on enemy tanks, however, had been reported by agent sources during the ARVN operation at Krek and Chup in Cambodia as early as in December 1971. Those reports disclosed that there was a concentration of about 30 tanks, including PT-76s, T-34s and T-54s in the area of the Chup plantation. Reports made at that time by the Cambodian local population to G-2, Republic of Khmer Forces General Staff also indicated the same thing. But still our aerial photo reconnaissance failed to produce any positive evidence. These reports on enemy tanks had been disseminated three times to the III Corps Commander and his subordinate division commanders. His claim of surprise was therefore unfounded. When enemy tanks moved toward An Loc, two new types among them were discovered: Chicom-make T-59s and some other models of the Russian made BTR.

In MR-2, the enemy general offensive had already begun during March, by drives against military strongpoints in the Truong Son mountain range northwest of Kontum. The enemy main force conducting those attacks was the 320th and NT-2 Divisions, whose presence had been detected by American sources. Two ARVN Airborne brigades, deployed as reinforcement for II Corps, had been engaged by enemy forces several times but it was not ascertained as to whether these forces were part of the 320th Division. Finally the II Corps commander promised to give a big reward to whichever unit succeeded in capturing enemy prisoners needed to corroborate intelligence reports and identify enemy forces. One day later, an Airborne battalion captured five enemy troops of the 320th Division and the next day another four prisoners of the same division. The enemy pressure was particularly heavy at Dakto and Tan Canh where the 22d ARVN Infantry Division Headquarters was located. On 21 April, based on intelligence reports, the enemy intention to attack the division headquarters became evident. In the light of synthetized data on enemy movements, the Division G-2 warned of an imminent tank-supported attack against the division headquarters, probably during the next two or three days. But this enemy capability was rejected by the II Corps commander and his American adviser. On 23 April, enemy PT-76 tanks moved in to attack the 22d Division headquarters and overran it during the day.

During the first three months of the general offensive which broke out almost simultaneously on three separate fronts, it was difficult to know which front was the enemy main effort. On all three fronts, intelligence collection was provided effectively by information derived from all sources available, such as aerial photos, communications intercept, and radio direction finding, in addition to combat intelligence and agent sources. In fact, US — RVNAF intelligence forces were so effective during this time that the movement of the 271st Regiment was accurately followed from the DMZ area to Tay Ninh. After the 271st Regiment was engaged by our forces in Tay Ninh, its identity and other particulars were confirmed by prisoners and documents captured.

The loss of Quang Tri city on 1 May 1972 and the heavy casualties suffered by forces of the 3d Division while retreating on what became known as the "Boulevard of Horror" toward Hue aggravated the situation and endangered this city. The question pondered by intelligence experts at that time was when Hue would be attacked. It had become evident that should the enemy choose to attack Hue immediately, this city stood no chance of holding out, given the shattered morale of ARVN troops and the local population. The enemy's failure to advance onto Hue after Quang Tri was regarded by many from hindsight as one of his major blunders, for he had squandered an invaluable opportunity to overrun this city. The simple truth was that he had run out of his capabilities after taking Quang Tri, although he was fully aware of the situation in Hue and willing to take advantage of it. Through reports made by enemy units to higher commands, it was learned that two regiments of the NVA 304th Division were almost totally annihilated.

During the months that followed, battles continued to rage with fierceness despite a decrease in their number. In the meantime, at the conference table in Paris, the positions held by the US and North Vietnam were still light years away from each other. Based on a synthesis of intelligence data in mid-July 1972 J-2, JGS nevertheless predicted quite accurately that a cease-fire was in the making and would probably materialize sometime during November 1972. The cease-fire, it was also foreseen, would be a stand-still arrangement leading to a situation of "leopard skin" troop disposition and calling for the creation of a national council of reconciliation and concord, the transitional step toward an eventual coalition government. The fact that a cease-fire was in the making became evident in the light of stepped up orders issued by the enemy to make a census of RVNAF prisoners, and to search for detailed information on his own personnel that were detained by the RVN, including names. Information on the date of the cease-fire became clearer in early October 1972, and up to one month before it actually became effective, our intelligence had gathered much data on an enemy scheme to take advantage of the cease-fire.

The cease-fire of 28 January 1973 was a new page in the history of the Vietnam war, and brought about new challenges for the RVN.

The Post-Cease-Fire Period

Whatever the viewpoint, the Paris Agreement of 28 January 1973 came about as a real turning-point of the war in Vietnam. It brought about a temporary and uncertain peace. But how long would this peace last and how soon would the war resume and under what form? Was it going to be a coventional general offensive of the 1972 type or was it to be a combined military-political effort in which military pressure was used as a leverage to force the RVN to comply with political solutions conceived and advanced by the Communists? Those were the questions that arose because resumption of war was foreseen as inevitable, regardless of its form. But the vital question that preoccupied the RVN was the matter of time: When?

The first information that helped confirm the eventuality of war resumption was provided by our own prisoners, who had been released by

North Vietnam and gathered the information on their way south. In North Vietnam, they reported, the mandatory military service was still as effective as ever and North Vietnamese cadres never believed that there would be true peace. The official party line was particularly clear as to the meaning of peace and the Paris Agreement. As it was explained by Van Tien Dung and To Huu during their visits to Communist units in South Vietnam in March 1973, and later reported by enemy prisoners and returnees, the Paris Agreement was but a pause, a stop-over rest on the long journey toward conquering the south. The idea of a stopover rest stemmed from a practical policy espoused by Truong Chinh which, as has been mentioned in Chapter I, was aimed at buying time for North Vietnam to reorganize and refit its own forces while continuing to attrite the adversary forces by military action.

As a matter of fact, two plans were implemented simultaneously by the Communists during that time. The first plan pertained to the implementation of the Paris Agreement whereby, based on and taking advantage of the legalistic aspect of the Agreement, the Communists would take up a political struggle to achieve political gains. This amounted to demanding twelve basic freedom rights for the people of South Vietnam, to include the right of movement. To achieve this goal, the Communists felt they should demonstrate to the Vietnamese people, particularly the South Vietnamese populace, the attractiveness of life under their regime. Among other things, they believed they ought to show that Communist living conditions under a Communist regime were adequately comfortable and not in any way inferior to those found in South Vietnam. As a result, Dong Ha, formerly a RVN district town, was transformed into a modern city intended both as an unofficial capital for the PRG and a model of Communist-run cities. It mushroomed overnight with pre-fabricated buildings, was provided with electricity and running water, and was even adorned with a public transportation system of some 30 brand new buses. The first aerial photo taken of Dong Ha, which revealed the presence of these buses, took our intelligence experts by surprise because even in Hanoi, the capital of North Vietnam, there were no buses of this type. Our conjecture at first was that the buses

AERIAL VIEW OF DONG HA – POST CEASE-FIRE PERIOD
BUSES SEEN ALONG STREETS IN UPPER RIGHT QUARTERS

were needed to meet increasing demands in logistics transportation.
But subsequent information obtained from Dong Ha indicated otherwise.
The buses were used to transport civilian passengers, which was something highly unusual but required to make up a showcase of Communist
modern living. The significance of the whole show became evident when
we learned about a Communist plan to induce people to return to their
home villages in the areas under their control and to attract those
living under government control to go over to their side. In the Dong
Ha market place, Red Chinese consumer goods were plentiful and conspicuously displayed.

At the same time, North Vietnam also introduced teachers, public
health workers and the administrative cadre into enemy-controlled areas
in order to assist in running those places. In MR-3, according to
agent sources, about 5,000 Vietnamese living in Cambodia had been coaxed
by the Communists to repatriate and settle in an area near Tay Ninh;
this information was later confirmed by enemy prisoners. For a long time
the NLF of South Vietnam had contemplated Tay Ninh as the future capital
for a Communist-controlled nation, because geographically it was adjacent
to War Zone C and the Cambodian border and politically, it was an important area where the Cao Dai temple was located. The enemy's plan of
"returning people to their home villages" was initiated at about the
same time with the "Land and Population Grab" plan which was designed to
wrest more control away from the RVN government. Those were the objectives
contained in Directive No. 2/73 that COSVN issued about one week before
cease-fire day. One month after the Paris Agreement went into effect,
COSVN issued another directive, No. 3/73, whose aim was to reassert the
five plans and objectives of struggle earmarked for the post cease-fire
period: military struggle, political struggle, proselyting of RVNAF
troops, development of combat forces and expansions of territory, and
legalistic implementation of the Paris Agreement. Through this directive,
the Communists still considered political struggle as the main effort
but they also strove to achieve a military balance in their favor by
developing a combat force larger and more powerful than the RVNAF.

Directive No. 3/73 was known to us only partially, however. Most of
the information came from various agent sources and piecemeal documents.
We came into possession of the complete text of the directive only after
a raid conducted by the Sector of Binh Thuan into an enemy base in May
1973.

During this period, two enemy troop movements took place simultaneously. On the one hand, general reserve units such as the 304th, 308th and
312th Divisions withdrew into North Vietnam to undergo refitting. On the
other hand, troop infiltrations continued their movement into South Vietnam, intended as local replacements and replenishments. In logistics,
the enemy initiated a campaign called "logistic general offensive" to
increase movement of supplies into South Vietnam, particularly into the
northern area of MR-1. Intelligence sources indicated that the first
campaign lasted 45 days. Later, aerial photos taken to confirm those
reports revealed that the amount of supplies brought south was so great
that much had to be stored in the open. Apparently additional warehouses
had not been built in time to store the increased influx of supplies.

The Joint Communique signed in Paris on 13 June 1973 did not bring
about any concrete results. Neither side was willing to make concessions,
and only paid lip service to enforcing a true cease-fire. Internationally,
meanwhile, several events of importance occurred, the most significant of
which, as far as the RVN was concerned, was the termination of US involvement in Cambodia. Domestically, some opposition movements came into the
open and were particularly active, such as the national reconciliation
movement, the anti-corruption movement, the famine relief movement, etc.
All these events spurred COSVN into issuing Directive No. 4 in September
1973. The entire text of this document was provided by an agent working
with the enemy. Its genuineness was recognized after being collated with
other sources. The purpose of COSVN Directive No. 4 was "to provide
guidance for military and political cadres, people's organizations and
party members in mobilizing the popular mass for a three-front struggle
against the South Vietnamese government, with particular attention given
to the violent force of the popular mass."

Also during this time, the Sector of Lam Dong succeeded in enlisting the collaboration of an enemy provincial political commissar. This political commissar, who later returned to our side, gave us a most important revelation: the Communists were preparing a "strategic-raid" type offensive in MR-1 whose objectives were Hue and Da Nang. North Vietnam's Air Force, it was disclosed, would also be employed during this offensive. The purpose of the enemy plan was to strike a forceful military blow to achieve some accomplished facts and exert pressure for political demands related to the implementation of the Paris Agreement. By chance, an aerial photo taken over Laos revealed a reduced model of an airfield constructed on the ground complete with airplanes parked in revetments, landing strips, and control tower. Our intelligence experts tried to match this model with configurations of airfields in Vietnam, Laos and Cambodian, and discovered that the airfield model represented exactly the structural configuration of Da Nang airfield. As to the enemy's plan to employ the North Vietnamese Air Force in an offensive in South Vietnam, it was learned as early as during the first week of the 1972 Summer Offensive that North Vietnam had plans to conduct air raids against Carroll base and Quang Tri city despite the absolute air superiority enjoyed by both the US and the RVN Air Force over South Vietnamese battlefields. The enemy strategic raid plan was later made public by the RVN government in an effort both to denounce the Communist scheme of making a mockery of the Paris Agreement and to forestall an enemy military action that could result in grave consequences.

At the end of 1973, several Communist leaders openly hinted at a strategy shift in South Vietnam. The new Communist strategy, it was disclosed, purported to push hard with military activities and escalate attacks in terms of target importance and forces committed. Communist forces would concentrate now on more important targets such as district towns and subsector headquarters instead of isolated outposts, and would increase the size of their attacks to regimental level and above with combined use of artillery, armor, and anti-aircraft weapons. This strategy was affirmed by Resolution No. 21 of the North Vietnamese Labor Party as a result of a session held in October 1973. Based on this guidance, COSVN developed Resolution No. 12 of its own, whose existence became known to us in early 1974 but its entire text was not available until March. According to this resolution, the Communists admitted that never before in the war had their military forces in South Vietnam been so strong and were in fact stronger than the RVNAF. The resolution also indicated that military activities to be conducted in the future would all be large scale actions but they would be consistent with a policy of flexibility, or skillful coordination between military and political-diplomatic efforts. In other words, the Communists contended that military actions should result in political and diplomatic gains.

North Vietnam's assessment of its military might was not entirely subjective or self-serving. On the contrary, it reflected quite accurately the balance of forces between the two warring sides. For, in addition to replacing losses incurred during the 1972 Summer Offensive, the enemy also succeeded in increasing substantially his military potential, particularly in terms of anti-aircraft weapons, armor and artillery. At Khe Sanh, for example, SAM-2 anti-aircraft missiles were installed as soon as the cease-fire went into effect. Other radar-controlled anti-aircraft weapons, such as 37-mm and 57-mm guns, were deployed as far south as in MR-3. *(Map 3)*. There were more than 400 enemy tanks and armored vehicles after replacements were received. *(Map 4)* Heavy artillery, such as 130-mm and 122-mm fieldguns, was introduced into the three-border area in MR-2 and north of MR-3 in great quantities. *(Map 5)* Despite serious limitations in aerial photo reconnaissance, our intelligence was able to detect enemy tanks, either camouflaged under thatch roofs or while moving, and able to detect the movements of 130-mm artillery guns from outside the border into MR-3. This information constituted evidence of tremendous infiltrations and logistical buildup during the post-cease-fire period.

Information provided by the US Defense Attache Office revealed that Logistics Corps 559 and three of its subordinate units Logistics Divisions 470, 471 and 473, formerly operating on Laotian territory along the old Ho Chi Minh trail, had moved inside South Vietnam to construct roads and transport supplies along the newly opened Truong Son corridor. Other

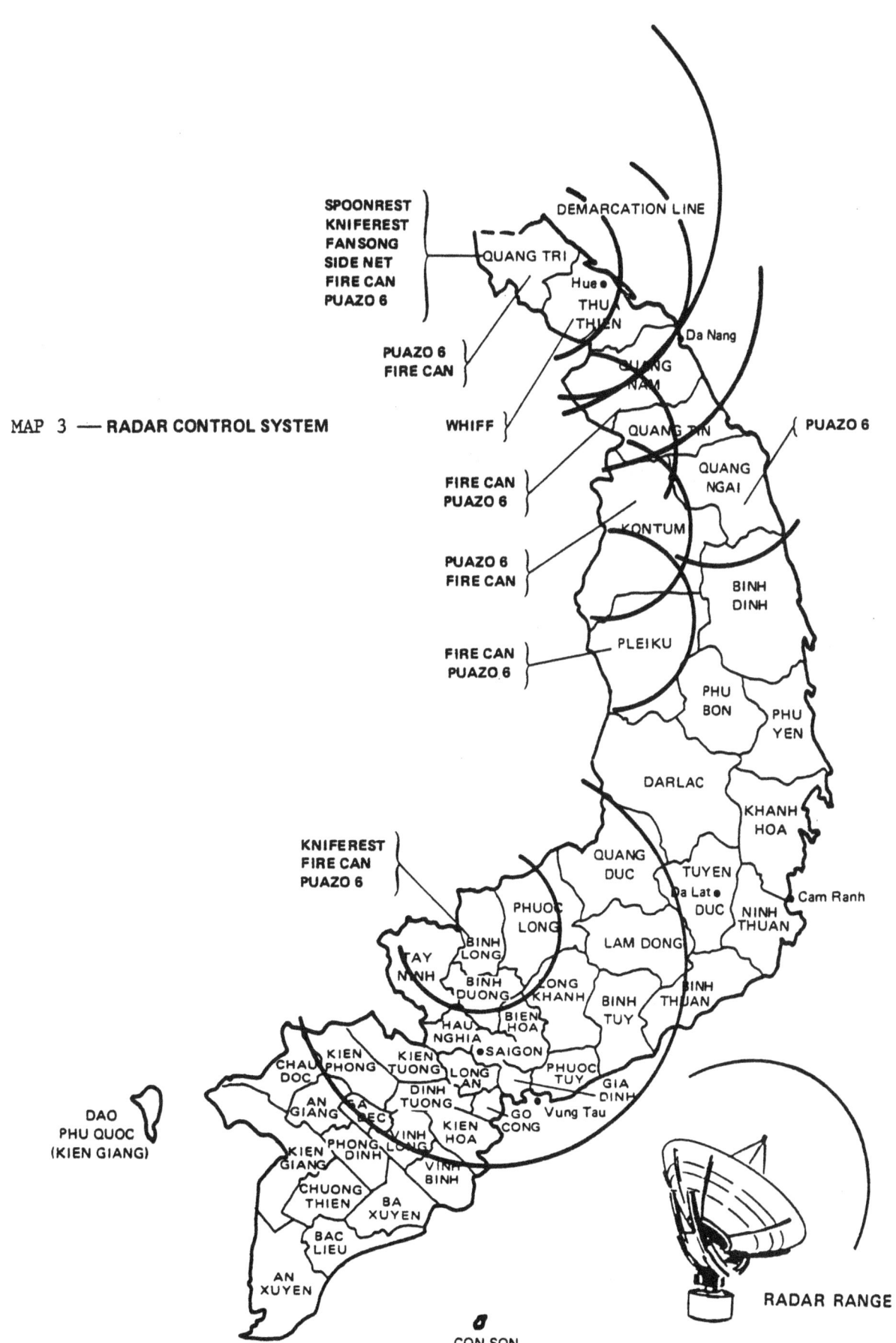

MAP 3 — RADAR CONTROL SYSTEM

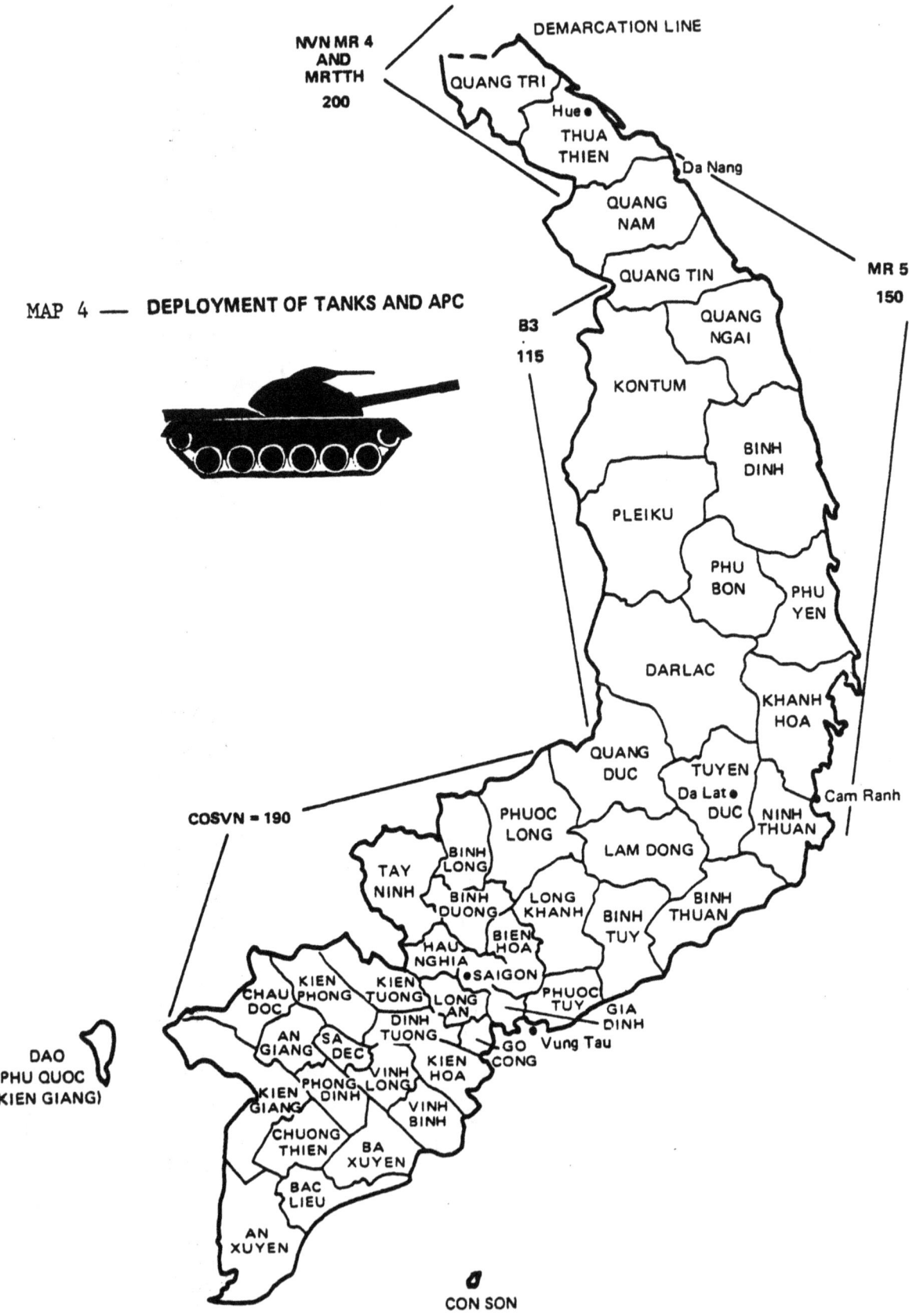

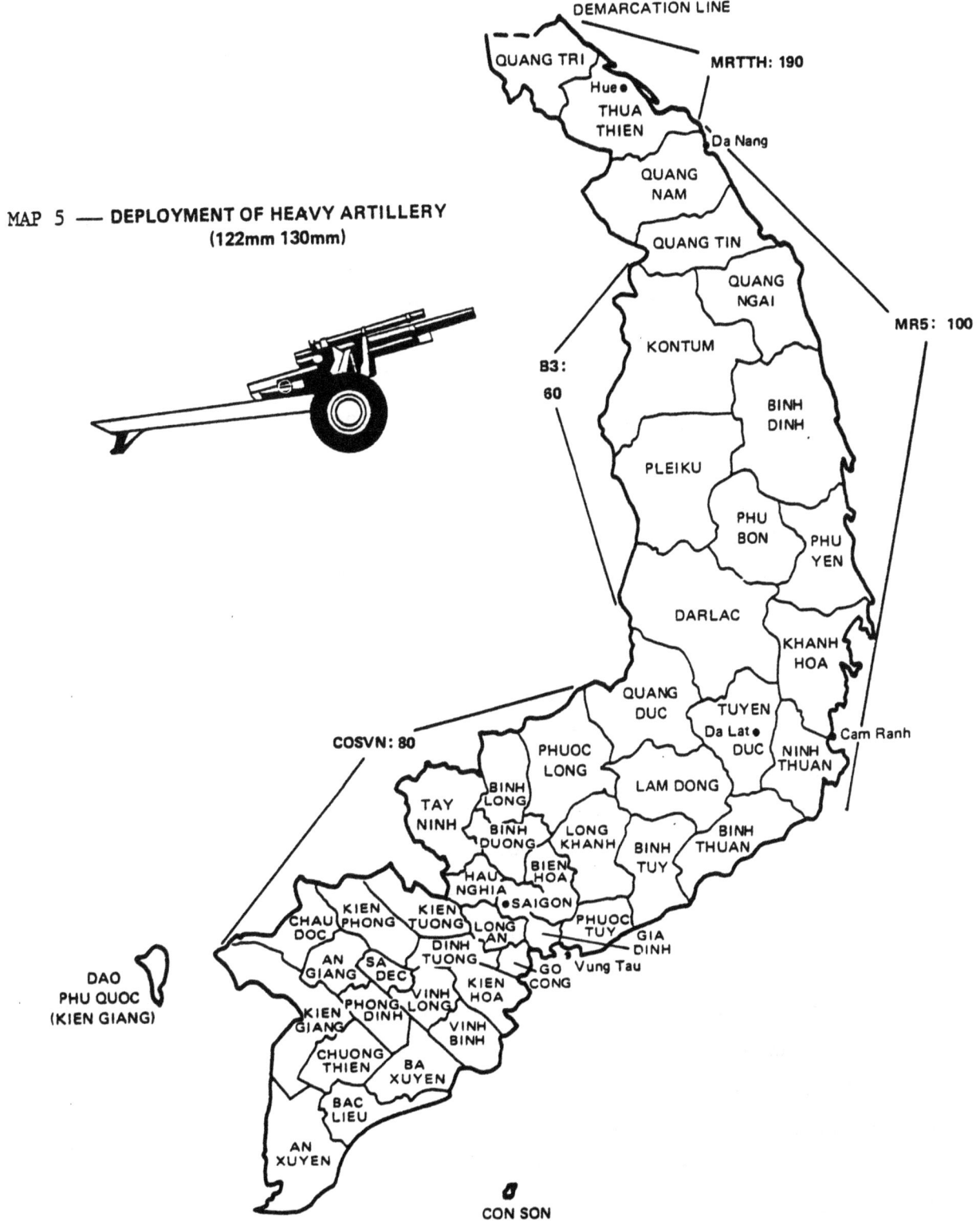

Logistical Divisions of Corps 559 meanwhile still continued operating outside South Vietnam, Division 472 in lower Laos, and Division 571 at Ban Karai and Mu Gia Pass. The Truong Son corridor, or new Route 14, was now extended from North to South Vietnam and major targets of enemy attacks all lay in those areas bearing upon the extension work on this new road system. *(Map 6)* In addition, the enemy installed two separate fuel pipeline systems, one leading from North Vietnam across the DMZ into MR-1 and terminating in Quang Nam province, and the other running south from Laos into South Vietnam along the Cambodian border and reaching into Quang Duc province in MR-3. *(Map 7)* Data gathered on the characteristics of these pipelines were carefully studied by our intelligence experts who found that they carried diesel oil. This fact was confirmed by the end of 1974 when a long-range reconnaissance team was sent into Quang Duc province to destroy part of the pipeline system.

Implementing Resolution No. 21 of North Vietnam's Labor Party and Resolution No. 12 of COSVN, enemy forces attacked and overran their first target of importance, the Dakpek district town in Kontum Province, which was in effect the first district town lost to the enemy since the cease-fire. The enemy attack took place on 17 May 1974, and was an instant success. The lack of forceful reaction on the part of ARVN forces appeared to stimulate and encourage the enemy to overrun in rapid succession a series of other district towns. The most significant enemy action was his attack on the Thuong Duc district town in Quang Nam province in July 1974. This attack was significant not so much because of the economic and demographic importance of the target area, which included the Nong Son coal mine and a population of 20,000, but primarily because of a new tactic employed by the enemy, a form of conventional, combined-arms mobile warfare. The enemy unit conducting this attack was the NVA 304th (-) Division which had been directly deployed from Quang Tri and joined forces with the 29/324B Regiment which had moved north from Dakpek in Kontum Province. The combined movements of these two units came about as a complete surprise for the local field command because, in contrast with the previous period, we were unable to detect them. In addition to these

MAP 6 — NEW ROUTE 14 OR TRUONG SON CORRIDOR

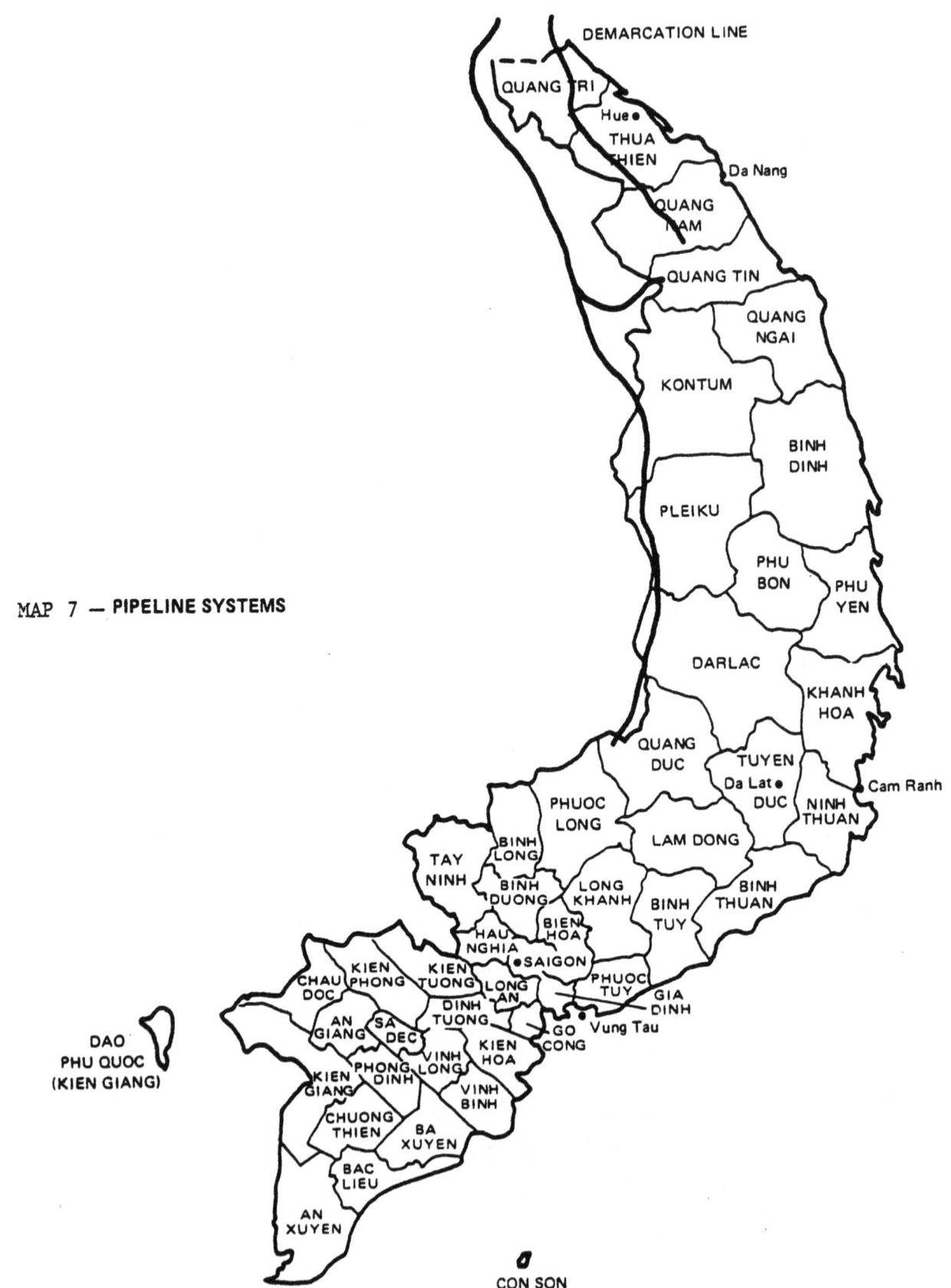

MAP 7 — PIPELINE SYSTEMS

COMMUNIST RADIO EQUIPMENT

SOVIET PORTABLE FLAME THROWER – MODEL LPO

SOVIET 23-mm AUTOMATIC ANTI-AIRCRAFT GUN — ZU-23

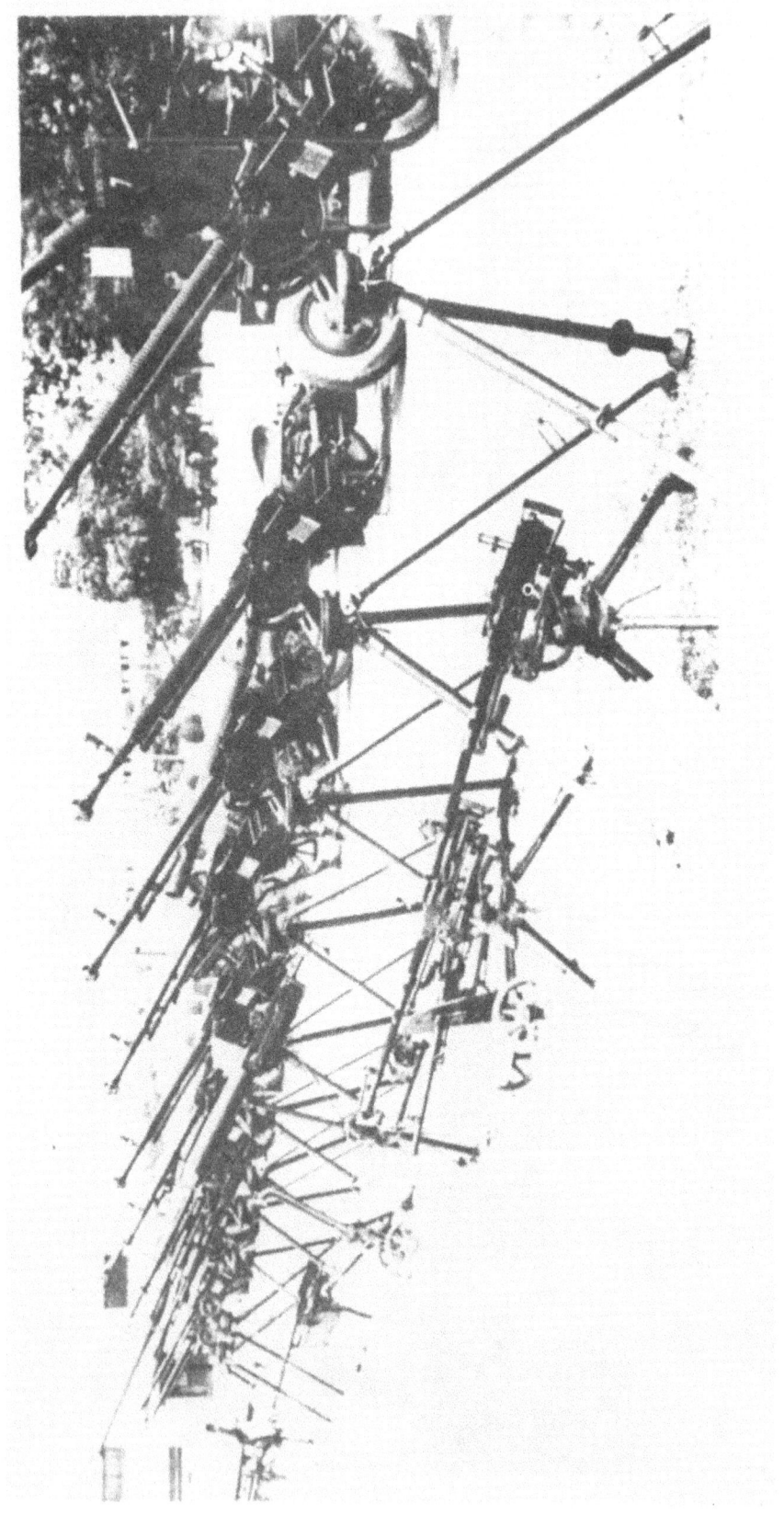

CALIBER .30, .50 ANTI-AIRCRAFT MACHINE GUNS

SOVIET 57-mm ANTI-AIRCRAFT GUNS — MODEL S-60

SOVIET 130-mm FIELD GUN M-46 (Left)
SOVIET 122-mm FIELD GUN M-1931/37 (Center)
SOVIET 122-mm HOWITZER M-1938 (M-30) (Right)

SOVIET ARMORED PERSONNEL CARRIERS

CHICOM – T-59 TANK

SA-7 ANTI-AIRCRAFT MISSILE (Background) and "SAGGER" ANTI-TANK MISSILE AT3 (Foreground)

infantry formations, the enemy employed one artillery regiment and one armor regiment. Intelligence failed however to provide accurately the enemy's order of battle during this attack and the movement of these forces to Quang Nam was a complete surprise to the local field command.

The new mobile, combined-arms tactic was recorded as the first instance of its employment by the enemy on a South Vietnamese battlefield. In the eyes of Vietnamese intelligence experts, it was reminiscent of a lesson learned previously from the enemy's practice of testing a tactic before actually using it in a major offensive. This mobile tactic was also characteristic of the maneuvering concept espoused by Van Tien Dung, NVA Chief of Staff. It obviously bore his personal mark. As a result, it was surmised that he, instead of Vo Nguyen Giap, would be tasked to direct a future general offensive effort in South Vietnam.

In October 1974, a returnee who belonged to a reconnaissance unit of the CT-7 Division, disclosed that the enemy was planning to attack the district towns of Phuoc Long Province which lay along QL-14 such as Don Luan, Duc Phong, and even the provincial capital itself. He also revealed that the CT-7 Division was tasked to conduct this offensive campaign with the support of tanks and artillery. This information proved correct and reliable, being later confirmed by communications intercept and agent sources. It was also consistent with the enemy's advocated strategy of escalating his military effort from attacks against isolated outposts to attacks against district towns and then provincial capitals. The enemy launched his initial efforts against Don Luan and Duc Phong on 14 December 1974 and finally overran the Phuoc Long provincial capital on 6 January 1975.

The 1975 General Offensive

The enemy's preparation to reinfiltrate his general reserve divisions from the North into South Vietnam was first made available to JGS by DAO. It was revealed in November 1974 that the NVA 316th Division, after its withdrawal from the Plain of Jars in Laos and after undergoing

refitting and indoctrination in North Vietnam's MR-4, was the first
one ordered to move into South Vietnam. Another NVA division, the
341st, which had been disbanded since 1968, was now reactivated and
received the same orders. The NVA 312th, 338th and 320th Divisions
followed suit at a later time. New recruit training centers in North
Vietnam, especially those in MR-4, which had the specific mission of
training troops as replacements and were capable of accommodating 18
recruit battalions at any time, were ordered to cut down their training programs to two weeks just as had been done during the 1968 period.
In logistics activities, there were increased movements of supplies
and personnel into South Vietnam at the outset of the 1974 - 1975 dry
season which began in October. Long convoys, sometimes numbering more
than 200 vehicles, were sighted moving along the new infiltration route
which began in North Vietnam, extended along QL-9 into lower Laos via
Khe Sanh, then veered south toward the tri-border area in MR-2, and
from there toward COSVN headquarters. In addition, other vehicle movements
were also seen bringing men and supplies from the A Shau, A Luoi area
into Quang Nam, Quang Tin and Quang Ngai provinces in MR-1 and into
northern Binh Dinh province in MR-2.

Gradually, indications of a general offensive in the offing
became complete and evident. There was also a marked increase in enemy
proselyting actions directed toward RVNAF troops. The MSS in effect
succeeded in neutralizing an important enemy proselyting organization
operating in Saigon. Among enemy cadres apprehended, there were those
responsible for military dependents in the Saigon-Cholon area and those
specifically responsible for the general reserve units, the Airborne
Division, the Rangers and the Armor Corps. The year-end estimate of the
situation in 1974, issued by J-2, JGS observed that the Communists had
the capabilities to launch a general offensive of a scale and intensity
comparable to those of the 1972 Summer Offensive and that this offensive
could be sustained for as long as 18 months. The scope of the general
offensive, it was forecast, would be a compromise between the 1968 and
1972 campaigns, that is an effort encompassing both frontline offensives
and attacks against cities and provincial capitals. The most appropriate

time frame for this effort was estimated 25 March 1975 onward.

Not everybody believed this prediction. While there was general agreement on the facts presented, a few people were of the opinion that during 1975 there would be attacks of a major scale but short of a general offensive. These individuals thought the general offensive would probably take place in 1976, a US presidential election year. The RVN military intelligence nevertheless stuck to the estimate that 1975 would be the year, especially after several additional enemy documents advocated the need to launch decisive attacks against major cities such as Hue, Da Nang, Saigon and Can Tho. The enemy reasoned that once these important cities were taken, others would follow suit.

By now in the Mekong Delta, an intelligence synthesis indicated that the enemy's main effort was to attack and occupy Moc Hoa, provincial capital of Kien Tuong, open an infiltration corridor leading from outside the Cambodian border into his base in the Plain of Reeds, and interdict movement on QL-4 between Saigon and Can Tho. But the CT-5 Division, which was to carry out this scheme, was defeated by the ARVN 7th and 9th Infantry Divisions.

With an aim to coordinate its general military effort, COSVN made plans to attack Tay Ninh city with the CT-9 Division and elements of the CT-5 Division, to be augmented in time by newly infiltrated units. This piece of intelligence was provided by an enemy agent and duly confirmed by other sources. Politically, Tay Ninh was an important province because it was the seat of the Cao Dai sect and militarily it was a key buffer zone between the Cambodian border and War Zone C and the Iron Triangle. It had been coveted by the enemy for a long time. To counteract this enemy move, III Corps deployed the entire 25th Infantry Division, reinforced by one infantry regiment, the 81st Airborne Ranger Group, and an armor brigade into Tay Ninh. The engagement broke out on 10 March 1975 and led to the loss of a string of outposts located along the western bank of the East Vam Co river, west of Tay Ninh province. But the 6th Regiment of the enemy CT-5 Division suffered heavy losses during this battle. Southeast of Tay Ninh, Tri Tam district town and the Michelin plantation were also attacked and overrun by the CT-9 Division. The CT-9

Division then joined forces with three local battalions in a subsequent move to cut off QL-22 and interdict traffic between Tay Ninh and Saigon. The CT-9 Division failed in this effort, however, and QL-22 was finally cleared by friendly forces. North of Tay Ninh, enemy pressure was particularly threatening after Ba Den mountain had been occupied. The enemy then moved his artillery pieces into mountain caves which had been transformed into invulnerable firing positions by his engineers. Tay Ninh city was thus directly threatened by enemy artillery fire. The mounting enemy pressure was such that the Cao Dai Church was compelled to issue a statement declaring that its Temple was a neutral zone and asking both sides to stop military actions in this area.

The enemy's main effort, however, was directed toward MR-2. Since early February 1975, contact had been lost with the NVA 320th Division which usually operated in the Duc Co area west of Pleiku. While efforts were being made to search for the whereabouts of this major enemy unit, an enemy cadre division was preparing to move south to launch an attack against Ban Me Thuot, to interdict QL-14 at the joint boundary of Pleiku and Ban Me Thuot provinces by attacking the district town of Thuan Man, and to mount ambushes at the Buon Blech Pass to interdict our relief efforts from Pleiku. The returnee also disclosed that this attack would be supported by tanks and artillery and that the 320th Division was under strict orders to conceal its movement toward Ban Me Thuot. Among other things reported by this returnee, it was learned that enemy troops and cadres were not informed of the geographical names of transit locations and that movements were to be made only during hours of darkness. The 320th Division also exercised complete radio silence while moving.

After the loss of Ban Me Thuot, an enemy prisoner disclosed an interesting detail concerning the enemy's attempt at deceiving our intelligence effort. To keep its movement secret, the 320th Division left behind its command radio station at Duc Co which continued to transmit while the division was slipping away. In fact, this deception served no useful purpose. For a long time our EC-47 airplanes had not dared to venture in this area because of heavy enemy anti-aircraft fire. The objective thus selected by the enemy for this offensive—Ban Me Thuot—turned out to be

an entirely new one since his usual objectives in MR-2 were Kontum and
Pleiku. Despite efforts by several reconnaissance units injected in
the area between Pleiku and Ban Me Thuot to look for the 320th Division,
its whereabouts was still unknown. But through many interrogation
sessions, our returnee proved to be sincere. As a result, G-2, II Corps
concluded in his estimate that Ban Me Thuot was going to be the target
of the new enemy offensive. At about this time, in Binh Dinh province,
intelligence sources of the 22d Infantry Division revealed that the entire enemy NT-3 (Gold Star) Division was concentrating its forces in an
attempt to interdict QL-19 at Binh Khe and An Tuc and that this effort
might last up to 3 months. Other sources from Nha Trang reported that
QL-21 would be interdicted between Nha Trang and Ban Me Thuot. All these
data clearly pointed toward an enemy plan of offensive whose initial move
was to cut off all lines of communication around Ban Me Thuot in order to
isolate it before conducting the main attack.

This was the intelligence estimate presented to the II Corps commander, but for some reason he did not believe the enemy would attack Ban Me Thuot. The defense of Ban Me Thuot was nevertheless reinforced by the 53d Infantry Regiment and the Tactical Command Post of the 23d Infantry Division. The city, up to that time, had been defended only by territorial forces. In the meantime, our intelligence lost track of the NVA 316th Division whose presence in North Vietnam had been reported. Our guess was that this division was moving south. A warning was then issued to all Corps and Division commands to watch for the 316th Division but all efforts failed to locate this elusive unit. Late in February 1975, intelligence sources in Binh Dinh province reported continuing movement of the NVA 3d Division toward QL-19 and on 3 March, it was confirmed that this axis of communication was being interdicted. The 22d Division reacted immediately by deploying two regiments to Binh Khe and An Tuc. Although friendly troops held firm their positions at these two places, they were unable to clear QL-19. At the same time, the enemy 95-B Regiment attacked QL-19 at Le Trung, making the interdiction of this vital road more serious. At Khanh Duong, the enemy 25-B Regiment established blocking positions on QL-14 and effectively cut off all traffic from Ban Me Thuot to Nha Trang. On

7 March, during an engagement with enemy forces at Duc Lap, southeast of Ban Me Thuot, our troops captured a document which revealed the presence of the F-10 Division in this area. So this division, too had moved away from the Kontum area into the vicinity of Ban Me Thuot. Another captured document, which was the enemy plan of attack against the city, disclosed that the main effort would be driven from the southwest; it was to be preceded by sapper penetrations, artillery preparatory fire and an initial assault by tanks. On 8 March Thuon Nam district town was attacked; QL-14 was thus interdicted midway between Pleiku and Ban Me Thuot, exactly as reported previously by the returnee. By this time, it had become evident that Ban Me Thuot would be the objective of the enemy offensive.

Preparations for defense were going on feverishly in Ban Me Thuot as of 9 March. The city braced itself for the attack because red alert orders had been issued. Garrison units established positions on tall buildings in the city and were issued additional anti-tank ammunition. At 0330 on the morning of 10 March 1975, enemy tanks began to move into Ban Me Thuot. But according to an enemy document captured later in Ban Me Thuot, the attack took place at least two days earlier than planned. The enemy had advanced the attack date because he knew his plan had been leaked. He rushed the attack before our forces had a chance to consolidate their defenses. As the battle unfolded, it was learned that the 320th Division attacked the city and the Phuong Duc airfield from the north. The F-10 Division moved in from the southwest while the 316th Division stayed back as reserve and did not participate in the attack until 11 March. Enemy prisoners captured from the 316th Division disclosed that their unit had moved from North Vietnam by trucks using the Ho Chi Minh trail in Laotian territory and only crossed into South Vietnam at Duc Lap in Quang Duc province in order to avoid detection by our intelligence. Orders given to the 316th Division were strict: its movement was to be kept absolutely secret, no radio contact between elements was allowed and on arrival at destination no contact was permitted even with local Communist authorities.

The enemy's basic objective when launching his offensive in the
Central Highlands of MR-2 in early March 1975, as developed from a
captured enemy document, was to occupy two out of its three provinces
by the end of the dry season. Then at the onset of the rainy season,
he would stop his military activities and offer to negotiate with the
RVN government. In all probability, he would demand the establishment
of the National Council of Reconciliation and Concord and perhaps a
coalition government as well. If the RVN should refuse this demand,
then he would have the justification to resume the offensive. In any
case, the offensive was intended to force the RVN government into making
political concessions. Since the Central Highlands was composed of only
three provinces (Kontum, Pleiku, Darlac) according to Communist territorial organization, the next target of enemy attack after Ban Me Thuot
was expected to be Pleiku.

The RVN decision to withdraw from Kontum and Pleiku must have been
a total surprise for the enemy. As a matter of fact, a report from the
B-3 Front on 18 March disclosed that the enemy was completely stunned by
this move. Almost immediately, the enemy field command at Ban Me Thuot
ordered the 320th Division to move quickly to intercept or pursue II
Corps forces, which had been withdrawing from Pleiku toward Phu Yen along
Interprovincial Route 7B.

When the II Corps convoy was stalled at Song Ba because of the lack
of river-crossing facilities, the 320th Division had already caught up
and engaged it in a battle at Phu Tuc. Enemy soldiers captured here confirmed that they belonged to the 320th Division. From Song Ba to Phu Yen,
the II Corps convoy was delayed again by enemy blocking positions and
mortar fire at Cung Son and it suffered extremely heavy losses. It was
a Communist local force, a battalion of Phu Yen province, that intercepted the ARVN convoy here. But ARVN Ranger troops inflicted heavy
losses on this blocking force. According to an enemy soldier captured
there, only 10 men of his unit were left after the battle.

At Ban Me Thuot, the F-10 Division was ordered to deploy its entire
forces by trucks to Phuoc An on 18 March. Phuoc An was a staging point
for the ARVN 23d Division (-) in an effort to reoccupy Ban Me Thuot.

After overrunning Phuoc An, the F-10 Division proceeded to Khanh Duong with the support of an armor squadron to attack the ARVN 3d Airborne Brigade. Its 105-mm and 122-mm artillery pieces were also towed along by trucks. Then at Khanh Duong, units of the F-10 Division took turns attacking the 3d Airborne Brigade. The 316th Division meanwhile was assigned to defend Ban Me Thuot and repel expected ARVN counterattacks. On Route 19, to the north, the enemy 968th Division and the 95-B Regiment were deployed to reinforce the NT-3 Division, and attacked the ARVN 22d Division at Binh Khe and northern Binh Dinh. Despite fierce resistance and gallantry in combat, both the 22d Division and the 3d Airborne Brigade were unable to contain the enemy divisions. Binh Dinh was lost to the enemy on 31 March and Nha Trang was evacuated on 1 April 1975. The disposition of enemy units following these actions was reported as follows: the 968th and 3d Divisions at Binh Dinh, the 320th Division at Phu Yen and the F-10 Division at Nha Trang where the NVA field command for the Central Highlands was also located.

After success had been assured at Ban Me Thuot, the enemy immediately increased action in MR-1. He moved the 325th Division from Quang Tri into the southwest of Hue with an aim to interdict Route 1 at Phu Loc. His 324-B Division meanwhile kept its pressure on the west of Hue. Although the enemy move was known in advance, I Corps was unable to contain it and QL-1 was effectively interdicted at Phu Loc on 22 March.

At Quang Tin, intelligence disclosed on 22 March that the enemy 711th Division was deploying its units toward Tam Ky, the provincial capital. Tam Ky was attacked and overrun on 24 March. By that time, most ARVN units in MR-1 had withdrawn toward Da Nang. On 28 March, the enemy ordered his units to attack Da Nang. As it became known to us, the enemy plan of attack called for heavy shelling of Da Nang airbase, Non Nuoc airfield, and I Corps Headquarters to begin at 0730 in the morning of 29 March. Then infiltrated enemy sappers would attack friendly positions within the city before regular infantry units moved in. Da Nang was lost to the enemy on 29 March 1975.

What remained now of MR-1 and MR-2 territory was just two provinces: Ninh Thuan and Binh Thuan. Both of these provinces were integrated into MR-3 to facilitate command and control. By then, some political opinions still expressed the hope that after their surprise victories, the Communists might pause and make a political move to obtain a desired solution. But available intelligence indicated otherwise. An intercepted message for example made clear that the Communists had decided to go all out for a total military victory. All Communist units were ordered to take advantage of initial gains to progress swiftly toward final victory. During that time intelligence revealed that the NVA 312th Division had moved from North Vietnam into the A Shau valley and was proceeding south toward MR-3. Another artillery unit, equipped with sixty 130-mm field guns was also detected in the tri-border area, preparing to move into MR-3. At the same time, aerial photos showed that SAM-2 anti-aircraft missiles were being deployed in the tri-border area. Later, on 19 April, these SAM-2 missiles were moved toward the boundary of MR-2 and MR-3 and finally were detected moving on QL-14 toward their final destination in War Zone D.

In MR-3, the presence of the 341st Division was detected in the vicinity of Chon Thanh, north of Saigon. One of its regiments was first detected by communications intelligence in late March 1975. Later, seven enemy prisoners confirmed the presence of this unit in the area. The CT-7 Division by this time had moved out of its usual area of operation at Phu Giao to conduct attacks against the district town of Dinh Quan on QL-20. Traffic between Saigon and Dalat was effectively interdicted after Dinh Quan was lost. Although this move had been detected two weeks earlier, ARVN forces were unable to stop the enemy. After overrunning Dinh Quan and moving into Dalat, the CT-7 was ordered back to reinforce the 6th and 341st Divisions in their attacks against Xuan Loc. The battle for this provincial capital began on 9 April and both the 6th and 341st Divisions suffered heavy losses.

After the loss of Phan Rang and Phan Thiet on 14 and 18 April respectively, the ARVN 18th Division and the 2d Airborne Brigade were forced to evacuate Xuan Loc on 20 April and move to Ba Ria. During this time, NVA 1st and 2d Corps and their subordinate divisions which had so far been operating in MR-1 and MR-2 were rapidly moving south into MR-3 in an effort to encircle Saigon from the north and southeast. South of Saigon, in the vicinity of Long An, three enemy divisions, the 5th, 6th and 8th were concentrating their forces under the control of a newly created corps command, designated Corps 232. To the west of Saigon, the CT-9 Division was deployed into Hau Nghia province where it joined forces with the 316th Sapper Regiment and prepared to attack Phu Lam and Cho Lon. The 316th Division meanwhile was poised somewhere between Trang Bang and Cu Chi with the apparent mission of interdicting QL-1 in this area.

In Saigon, however, political circles were still desperately clinging to the hopes that a political modus-vivendi and a cease-fire could be achieved at the last minute. They did not know that Hanoi had decided to take Saigon by 19 May, anniversary of Ho Chi Minh's birthday, that information was provided by an enemy agent on 17 April. The enemy final offensive, according to this source, was code-named the "Ho Chi Minh Campaign" and its final objective, Saigon, had already been renamed as Ho Chi Minh City.

In addition to tanks and artillery support, the Communists were also planning to employ airpower in their final push against Saigon, particularly to bomb Tan Son Nhut airbase, the Joint General Staff compound, and the Independence Palace. These reports on the enemy plan to use airpower over Saigon coincided with intelligence previously obtained in Da Nang which indicated that the Communists were conducting crash training courses for their pilots in the handling of A-37 and F-5 bombers. VNAF pilots captured by the enemy were being used as instructors. Another report revealed that the enemy had instructed his sapper units not to destroy bridges leading into Saigon and to leave public utilities in Saigon intact.

On 24 April an enemy plan to interdict QL-15 between Saigon and Vung Tau was obtained through prisoner and other intelligence sources. One captured enemy document observed that if Saigon and Can Tho were lost, other cities in MR-3 and MR-4 would also fall.

On 26 April, the enemy began attacking Long Thanh and Ba Ria and severed road communication by QL-15. Bien Hoa was also under attack.

On 27 April, an enemy artillery unit was ordered to locate firing positions from which to shell Tan Son Nhut airbase, the JGS compound, and the Independence Palace. A few days earlier an enemy sapper from the 316th Sapper Regiment was captured as he was looking for a house to rent near Gate No. 4 of the JGS compound. During interrogation he declared that he was an artillery forward observer sent into Saigon with the mission of directing fire on the JGS.

In the afternoon of 28 April, Tan Son Nhut airbase was attacked by three A-37 bombers which had taken off from Phan Rang.

In the morning of 29 April, the Communists began to shell Tan Son Nhut, the JGS and other places in Saigon. At the same time, enemy infantry units also launched probing attacks in the suburbs of Saigon. At 1000 hours the following day, 30 April 1975, orders for the RVNAF to surrender were proclaimed on Radio Saigon.

A nation had ceased to exist; an armed force had been defeated. Sharing in this national tragic event, intelligence had also been defeated. At least, that was what the leader of the Republic of Vietnam concluded when he scribbled a personal observation on a report submitted to him by the National Intelligence Coordination Committee in mid-April 1975:

> "Intelligence, beware of information planted by the Communists. They strike Ban Me Thout when you said Pleiku. And you said Tay Ninh while they attacked Phuoc Long."

AIR ATTACK ON TAN SON NHUT AIR BASE
APRIL 28, 1975
F5A DESTROYED

CHAPTER VII

Communist Intelligence

North Vietnam's Intelligence, Theory and Practice

During a war, Communist leaders usually write military articles in which they analyze the conduct of the war and comment on the strategies and tactics employed during each phase of the war. The purpose of these articles is almost always self-serving. It serves either to justify an action taken or to outline a new policy. Intelligence techniques, however, have never been discussed. In the very few instances where it is mentioned at all, intelligence is either treated as an implicit element of knowledge or broadly evaluated in terms of its effectiveness or usefulness during a certain war period.

Mao Tse Tung implied such a knowledge when he discussed the basic rules of guerrilla warfare. He wrote:

> "Since May 1928, however a basic principle, simple in character, with regard to guerrilla warfare was already set forth in keeping with the conditions of the time, namely a formula in sixteen key words:
>
> > Enemy advances, we retreat.
> > Enemy halts, we harass.
> > Enemy tires, we attack.
> > Enemy retreats, we pursue.
>
> This military principle in a sixteen-word formula had been accepted by the Party."[1]

In his book entitled "Our Protracted Resistance War Will Win" and published in 1946, Truong Chinh, a theorician and Politbureau member of

---

[1] Mao Tse Tung, <u>Selected Works</u>, Vol. I, 1926-1936 (International Publishers, New York: 1954) p. 212.

North Vietnam's Labor (Communist) Party, briefly criticized intelligence work in the Viet Minh Army in these words:

> "There are many ways of winning the initiative (one among them is): to clearly know the enemy's situation in order to be able to concentrate our regular troops rapidly and move our reserve forces swiftly to the required areas to act in good time. At present our forces are not only poor in intelligence work but also slow in moving and regrouping."[2]

In 1967, another high-ranking North Vietnamese military authority, Truong Son, wrote an article on "Lessons Learned from the NLF Victories" in which he advocated that, among the five lessons learned from military victories, the first one was Intelligence. Said he:

> "Only by understanding the enemy's strategic determination and correctly anticipating the laws and capabilities of enemy action can we rightly build our own strategic determination and our fighting pattern."

Truong Son also elaborated:

> "In the summer of 1966, the South Vietnam NLF Central Committee and various other echelons concentrated their efforts on studying matters concerning the enemy's front such as: during the dry season, what is the enemy's strategic intention, how many troops will he have, what are the capabilities of these troops, and where are they going to be used? What are their laws of action and so forth?"

The idea of intelligence as the first lesson to be learned in a war is shared by Van Tien Dung, North Vietnam Army's Chief of Staff. In an article on "Some Great Experiences of the People's War" published during this period, he wrote that he had learned the need to "correctly evaluate the enemy's strategic schemes and operational capabilities, develop a steadfast determination to achieve success, and make careful and positive preparations to cope with the enemy quickly and resolutely."

---

[2] Truong Chinh, *Primer for Revolt* (Frederick A. Praeger, New York, London: 1963) p. 187.

The first and last remarks ever made on intelligence by North Vietnamese leaders during the long period of 21 years spanning two wars from 1946 to 1967 thus indicate that Communist intelligence had come of age and was to be an effective tool during the conquest of the South.

Intelligence, generally speaking, is a process encompassing a number of basic principles that have become universal. But intelligence as it is actually organized and operated involves certain conceptual particularities and operational characteristics that vary according to the political philosophy and administrative structure of each country.

Being a Communist nation at heart, North Vietnam apparently derives its intelligence theory from Communist philosophical premises—in particular those of Marx and Engels—on the universality of contradiction as a rule. Engels in effect theorized that: "life consists just precisely in this—that a living thing is at each moment itself and yet something else. Life is therefore also a contradiction which is present in things and processes themselves, and which constantly originates and solves itself; and as soon as the contradiction ceases, life, too, comes to an end, and death steps in."[3]

Lenin later translated this conceptual premise into concrete examples that he used to demonstrate contradiction in almost all disciplines of human knowledge. In mathematics, for example, he found it in addition and subtraction, differential and integral; in mechanics, he found it in action and reaction; in physics, positive and negative; in chemistry, the combination and dissociation of atoms; and in social sciences, most particularly, class struggle.

From this purely theoretical philosophy, Mao went a step further

---

[3]Mao Tse Tung, Selected Works, Vol Two, 1937 - 1938 (International Publishers, New York: 1954), pp. 19, 20.

when he made it a basis for his war theories with a view to single out
the decisive factors on which each warring party would rely to gain
victory. According to Mao, war depends basically on man and weapons
or man and technology, but man is always the decisive factor that wins
a war. As a result, the Communists usually rely on human whereas the
United States and other antagonists of the Communist bloc—as if in
keeping with the rule of contradiction itself—choose to depend primarily on the power of weapons and technology when fighting a war.

It was on the basis of this human predominance axiom that during
the war North Vietnam built its intelligence largely patterned after
Red China, and to lesser extent, Soviet Russia. Based more on human
than technological resources, North Vietnam's intelligence system was
conceived within the conceptual framework of a people's war and came
to be known as People's Intelligence. As part of a people's war,
People's Intelligence also derived from it its two basic characters:
all-people and total, which implied that intelligence was the duty of
each citizen and should be carried out in every branch and every sector
or activity.

Just as the theory of people's war materialized in a unified effort to prosecute the war through the leading role played by the Party
and the State, it was also built into the intelligence system which,
under the same unified command concept, was placed under the direct
control of the highest Communist authority—North Vietnam's Politbureau.
War, to the Communist, is just a continuation of politics, and its
nature, essentially a political act. Likewise, as North Vietnam saw
it, there was no distinction between military intelligence and political
intelligence. Situation assessments or estimates, therefore, were
highly synthetized works that took into account every consideration,
every aspect of the war. Structurally there was no discrimination
either, since in North Vietnam there existed no separate military and
political collection agencies as was the case in South Vietnam. In
the same vein, North Vietnam made no distinction between domestic and

foreign intelligence or between tactical and strategic intelligence.

North Vietnam Intelligence Agency

Thus, North Vietnam's intelligence had been thoroughly guided by Communist philosophy, and people's war theory in particular, in addition to purely professional basic principles. Normally, theories and principles make no profound difference as to their intrinsic values or merits. What really matters is the extent to which these theories and principles are observed and put to practical use. In this respect, North Vietnam seemed to make considerable effort to narrow the gap between theory and practice.

The most visible manifestation of these efforts can be found in the establishment of the Central Research Agency (CRA) which has been North Vietnam's top intelligence agency for many years. During the war, the Central Reserarch Agency not only served the North Vietnamese Army High Command and the Ministry of National Defense but also the government council or cabinet. In many instances when important decisions had to be made, the CRA also provided instrumental intelligence estimates directly to the reduced Politbureau which consisted of the State President, the Party Secretary, the President of the National Assembly, the Prime Minister and the Defense Minister. In fact, the CRA was only responsible for military intelligence. Civilian intelligence was the responsibility of the Public Security Ministry whose structural ramification encompassed every echelon of the administrative hierarchy, down to villages. The missions of the Public Security Ministry included enforcement of security and order, collection of information, investigation, surveillance and apprehension of criminals and those elements or movements who opposed the Party and the State.

The Central Research Agency was organized into six staff divisions: Administration, Technical, Communications, Training, Protection, and Collection in addition to a Cryptographic Section. The Administration division was responsible for the status of intelligence personnel, prepared individual biographic records, and recommended appointments, assignments, promotions and sanctions. The Technical division collected all types of identification papers and documents, stamp and signature samples, established false identification papers for penetration agents, produced chemical inks for special document writing, and provided all materiel and equipment required by agents. The Communications division operated radio communications systems between the CRA and its subordinate agencies, other strategic intelligence services, and its emissaries operating in South Vietnam. The Training division conducted in-country intelligence courses or arranged for special agent training in Soviet Russia and Red China. Selected students also included CRA cadre courses varied in length, from six months to two years. The Protection division was responsible for counterintelligence activities; it prevented and investigated traitors, infiltrated agents, saboteurs, and kept a close watch on suspects or elements tainted by a bad record. The Collection division was organized into many sections, each section being responsible for a North Vietnamese military region. Most important, however, were the sections responsible for South Vietnam, Laos and Cambodia, which were called Battlefield C, B, and A Sections respectively. The Central Study Office also kept track of international developments, focusing particularly on countries that were directly or indirectly involved in the Vietnam war such as the United States, France, Thailand, South Korea, etc. The importance that North Vietnam attached to intelligence on the United States was evidenced by the creation of a separate section responsible for America.

Meeting intelligence requirements generated by the war in Vietnam was clearly the mission of North Vietnam's Central Research Agency. With this mission, CRA directly controlled all intelligence activities, including those in South Vietnam, Laos and Cambodia. In addition to collection networks which were generally local in character, CRA also controlled certain special intelligence nets which were operated by special "emissaries" from North Vietnam and focused on long-range objectives. While information collected by these special nets might be provided in support of local needs, North Vietnamese special emissaries who operated them were not under the control of local intelligence organizations. They made up instead a separate organization whose territorial-based structure was divided into: COSVN, MR Tri-Thien - Hue, MR 5, MR 6 and B3 Front. *(Map 8)* The military intelligence organization in each MR or Front directly subordinated to NVA High Command was similar to that of COSVN which in effect enjoyed the same relationship status with regard to North Vietnam. *(Chart 29)*

COSVN Intelligence Organization

Contrary to what its name may have implied, COSVN did not exercise control over all Communist intelligence activities in South Vietnam. Its control, based on Communist territorial organization, was limited to an area roughly the equivalent of RVN MR 3 and MR 4. The rest of South Vietnam came under the separate responsibility of the enemy B3 Front, MR 5, MR 6, MR 10 and the MR Thi-Thien - Hue.

COSVN's responsibility, however, also encompassed those Communist-controlled areas on Cambodian territory such as Krek, Svay Rieng, Prey Veng and Kompong Cham, etc.

Intelligence activities under control of COSVN's Permanent Committee (Labor Party Central Committee's delegates in South Vietnam) included security and military intelligence. Security activities were organized at every echelon of the Party hierarchy: COSVN, Military Region, Province, District, Village and Hamlet. As to military intelligence, while its activities generally followed along the same line, its organization also included tactical components of the military hierarchy, from Corps to Company. Basically, security functioned under the control of the Party at each level of its hierarchy while military intelligence was part of the staff organization at each tactical echelon.

COSVN's instrument to operate and supervise security activities

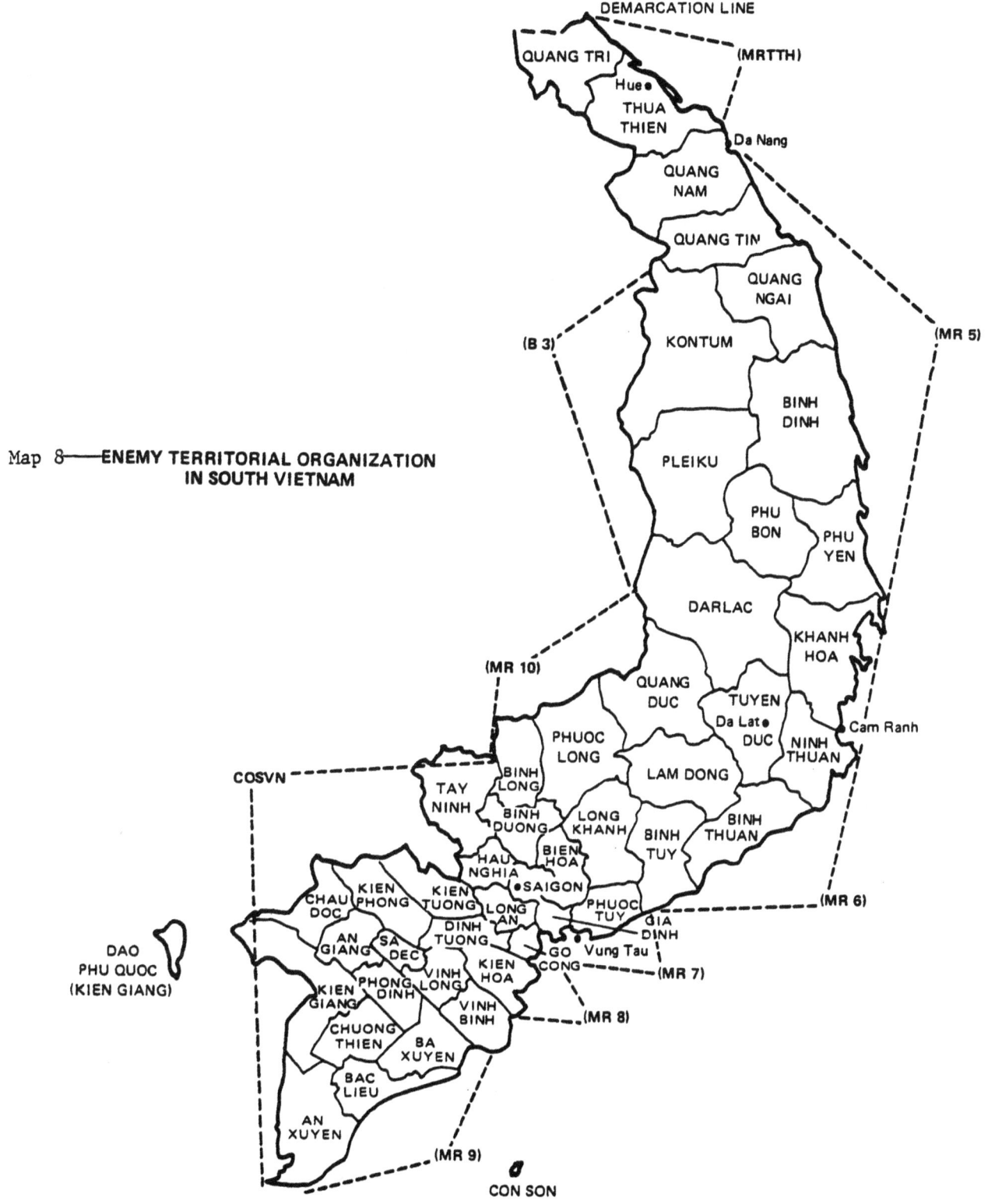

Map 8—**ENEMY TERRITORIAL ORGANIZATION IN SOUTH VIETNAM**

Chart 29 — Enemy Military Command Organization

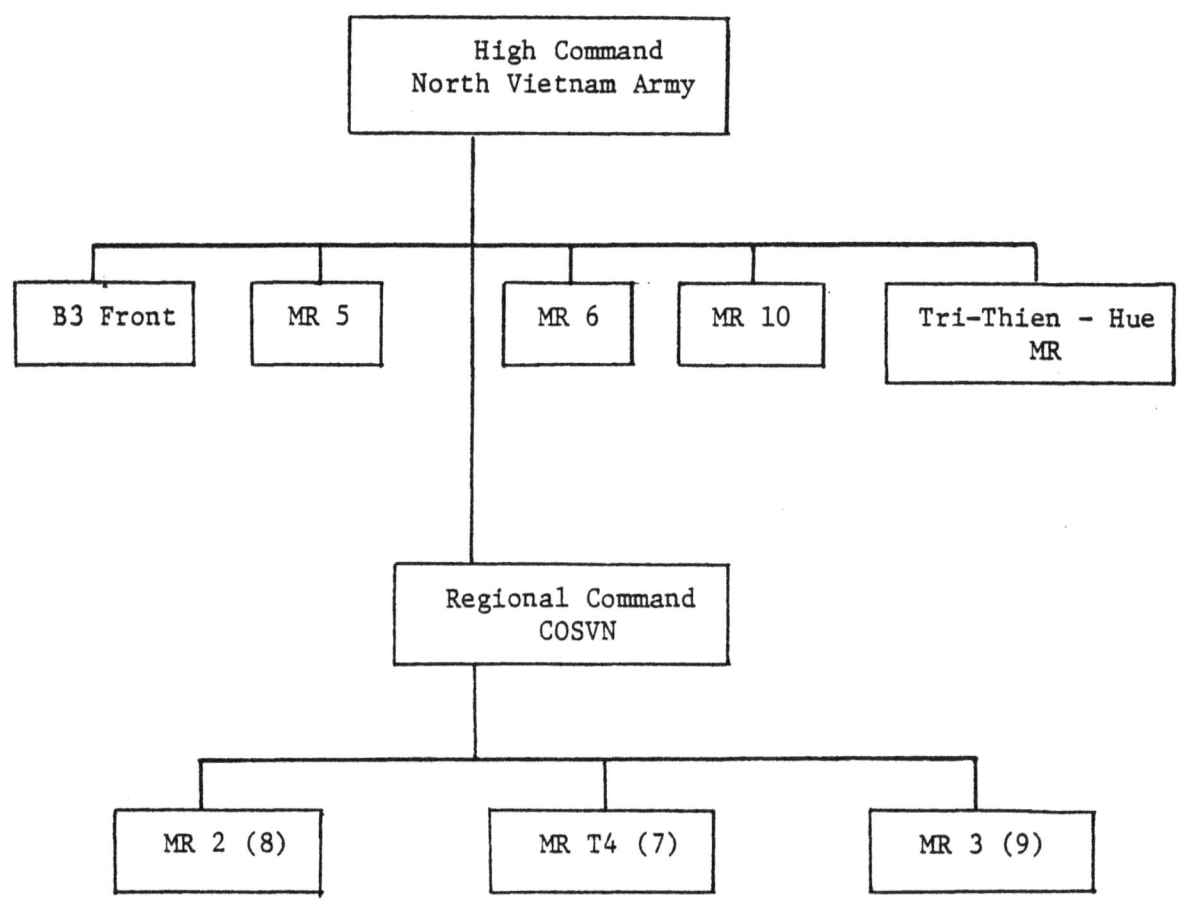

was the Security Agency. Its mission was to ensure internal security, keep watch over the thoughts and acts of all cadre and to prevent and discover RVN penetration agents. In addition, the Security Agency also provided security for headquarters and installations, protection for high-ranking COSVN and NLF cadre, and directed spy and counter-spy activities in RVN-controlled areas.

COSVN's Security Agency was organized into three sections: Internal Reconnaissance, External Reconnaissance and Protection.

1. Internal Reconnaissance Section:

The mission of this section was to maintain and ensure security in Communist-controlled areas in South Vietnam as well as in Cambodia. The section was empowered to arrest and detain suspects, civilian and military alike, interrogate, investigate, and establish reports. It operated a detention camp for security convicts (code-named K-25) and was supported by a security unit (code-named K-35). This unit studied personnel records, granted security clearance, kept a close watch over military and civilian cadre, and prevented the penetration of RVN agents. In general, the Internal Reconnaissance Section enjoyed large investigative powers and had the prerogatives to install its personnel in every organization to serve as its eyes and ears.

2. External Reconnaissance Section:

The mission of this section was to collect information through spy activities, recruit and train planted agents, train and re-train collection personnel, provide special espionage tools and weapons for agents, direct assassination plots and obtain security reports.

3. Protection Section:

This section was responsible for providing peripheral protection for headquarters and installations by using patrols, insuring protection for high-ranking cadre and constructing shelters. It conducted training for bodyguards assigned to protect high-ranking cadre during displacements through dangerous zones. It also deployed security personnel to help secure infiltration accesses into Communist-controlled areas along infiltration corridors and the Cambodian border, prevent sabotages and investigate penetration efforts by RVN agents. For the performance of its tasks the Protection Section was assigned to the (COSVN) Protection Regiment No 180 which consisted of two battalions, D-1 and D-2.

The D-1 battalion was assigned the responsibility of protecting COSVN high-ranking cadre, and providing security for headquarters and its base camp and installations. The D2 battalion was responsible for peripheral security.

Outside and under COSVN, security sections were established at every echelon of Party hierarchy. While the responsibilities of these security sections remained identical, their sizes and effectiveness varied greatly depending on the war situation and the extent of Communist control in each area. In general, at the village level, the security cell was tasked to organize and direct such security activities as manning guard posts, checking entry and exit movements, identifying strangers, arresting suspects or criminals, conducting preliminary investigations, and keeping watch over "reactionaries." Another responsibility of the village security cell was to deter and unearth crimes either by the populace or village government officials. In certain pre-determined cases or when authorized by a higher echelon, the security cell was permitted to carry out surreptitious executions or assassinations. Its assassination subcell was usually tasked for these ignoble jobs. A village security chief was generally appointed by the Party hierarchy and usually selected from among the members of the Village Party Committee. He was assigned two assistants if the village consisted of several hamlets. A hamlet was assigned two elected security agents by the village security chief if the hamlet was made up of several households. The village security cell was both subordinated to the Village Administrative Committee and the District Security Section whose mission was to organize and provide guidance to village security cells and resolve problems raised by or beyond the power and capability of village security chiefs.

At the district level, security activities had more of a professional character. They included establishing political and military order of battle records and keeping surveillance files on suspects, nationalist local parties or associations, religious organizations and leaders, and GVN employees or their relatives. Every month, the district security section prepared a situation report on friendly and enemy activities. With regard to the enemy (RVN), the monthly report specified which types of activities—political or military—had been more intense during the month and analyzed the objective, scope, intensity and characteristics of each. Reports on friendly activities included information on the populace's behavior and reactions to enemy activities, actions taken by the local Communist government with regard to the enemy and the populace, Communist military activities during the month in terms of frequency, form, results, advantages and disadvantages, and a recapitulation of political activities during the month. As far as the Communists were concerned, information on political activities consisted of such data as the results of enemy proselyting actions. Typical examples include: how many enemy troops had deserted, how many more had been contacted; the frequency of indoctrination sessions held, what subjects had been studied; and, in terms of political struggle, how many direct confrontations had been initiated, how many demonstrations had been organized, how many protest motions had been forwarded, etc.

In its responsibility to protect the local district government, the security section had the duty to coordinate security protection plans with military units operating in the area. When there were top echelon Communist organizations in the area, such a security plan usually divided the area into three distinct zones with different control measures applied to each. In the outer zone, checks were made on movements of strangers. The intermediate zone was a zone of restricted movements to strangers, in which every displacement or activity of the local population was placed under tight control. The inner zone was of limited access which was allowed only to people with official business.

In summary, the Communist security system was designed to carry out both defensive activities such as security, protection, order and offensive activities such as espionage. Its objectives included not only the enemy but also the population and Communist cadre and troops. Due to the predominant role played by the Party, in general, enemy security activities were closely coordinated with military intelligence for whose activities they also provided effective support.

COSVN's military intelligence instrument, the Military Intelligence Agency—code-named B-2—was subordinated to its military command, which was called "Regional Command". The Military Intelligence Agency, COSVN (MIACOSVN) was responsible for collecting information pertaining to the organization, operation, policies and plans of the RVN military, political, economic, administrative, diplomatic, activities and others. MIACOSVN supervised and provided guidance on intelligence activities performed by military units, to include espionage.

MIACOSVN was organized into eleven staff sections and was supported by a communications battalion. The staff sections were: Enemy Situation Study, Cadre and Organization, Ground Reconnaissance, Technical Reconnaissance, People's Intelligence Nets, Espionage, Law Enforcement, Techniques and Tracks, Rear Services, Training, and Crypto.

1. Enemy Situation Study Section.

This section was responsible for keeping track of developments in the RVN and allied military forces, political and economic activities, establishing and disseminating reports to user organizations.

Information and data collected by military intelligence organizations at all echelons were routed to this section which analyzed and interpreted them and developed intelligence estimates and reports. The Enemy Situation Study Section also received copies of information exchanged between COSVN and Military Regions or disseminated by North Vietnam's Central Research Agency.

2. Cadre and Organization Section.

This section was responsible for keeping personnel records, evaluating personnel qualifications, recommending jobs and assignments, receiving and assigning intelligence personnel infiltrated from North Vietnam, recommending promotions and sanctions, keeping track of the security status in units and areas under Communist control, and organizing military intelligence conferences.

3. Ground Reconnaissance Section.

This section was responsible for conducting reconnaissance of the enemy's military organization, dispositions, and equipment for defense in addition to collecting information on order of battle. To carry out this mission, the section was assigned one or two organic battalions, called Ground Reconnaissance (GR) Battalions. The D46 Ground Reconnaissance Battalion, for example, had a strength varying from 300 to 400 men and was organized into 3 companies and 1 section (Section 7). This section consisted of 3 GR detachments of 17 men each, whose specific mission was to collect information from areas such as Suoi Vang, Cau Khoi, Suoi Da and the Trang Sup airfield in Tay Ninh province. The Ground Reconnaissance Section directed and controlled the activities of 10 GR detachments which were deployed at Cu Chi (Hau Nghia province), Phu Hoa (Binh Duong province), Ben Cat (Binh Duong province), An Loc and Loc Ninh (Binh Long province), Boi Loi (Tay Ninh province), Ba Ra (Phuoc Long province), Phuoc Tuy, Bien Hoa and Long Khanh. Each detachment was commanded by a cadre having a rank ranging from deputy company to deputy battalion commander.

4. Technical Reconnaissance Section.

This section had been expanded considerably since 1965. Its mission was to intercep enemy radio communications to collect information as well as to conduct ICD (Imitative Communications Deception) and jam enemy radio systems. In its initial stage of organization, the Technical Reconnaissance (TR) Section activated a TR battalion, code-named D4, which was organized into 5 companies totalling approximately 300 men. With this strength, the section was able to organize 30 TR teams, all deployed in the RVN MR 3. Each team had a varying strength depending on the importance of the target area. According to its report of September 1966, the D4 battalion was able to exploit 7745 messages out of a total of 7793 intercepted. The TR teams were equipped with radio sets captured from the RVN and allied forces such as AN/PRC-10, AN/PRC-25, AN/PRC-6, AN/GRC-9, SCR-300, AN/VRC-3, SCR-694, etc. and supplied by Red China, such as models 71B and 102E, or even procured from the local market and modified to receive FM bands.

5. People's Intelligence Nets Section.

This section organized and provided guidance to people's intelligence nets in Communist-controlled and contested areas.

6. Espionage Section.

This section managed and kept track of espionage activities, provided guidance and direction to agents, and studied and reviewed intelligence reports sent in by spies and agents.

7. Law Enforcement Section.

This section detained, interrogated and investigated suspects and established reports. It also handled high-ranking RVN prisoners or those who were apt to provide important information, and provided information support to the Internal and External Reconnaissance Sections. Under the section's control there was a prisoner detention camp, code-named K55, which consisted of three wards, Nos. 1, 2, and 3. Prisoners and detainees were classified and treated in different manners according to their willingness to cooperate. Those who were die-hard or deemed dangerous were detained in underground cells of ward No. 3.

8. Techniques and Tracks Section.

This Section processed negatives and printed photos taken by Unit K45. It also produced false identification papers and documents intended for use in GVN-controlled areas or in Cambodia, collected documents and photos for a reference library, conducted investigations on lost documents and weapons, and endeavored to detect traitors.

9. Rear Services Section.

This section provided rear services for the Military Intelligence Agency and its subordinate organizations and units, to include food service and materiel support. It was organized into several subsections: procurement, truck transportation, bicycle transportation, quartermasters, production, etc.

10. Training Section.

This section prepared and published training materials, organized intelligence courses for all levels, established indoctrination programs, provided instructors and assisted in re-training personnel of the External Reconnaissance Section. Under the section's control, there was the K25 School which provided training only for low-level cadre, from deputy squad leaders down. Cadre of higher ranks, from squad leaders to company commanders were trained separately. Instructors were usually selected among cadre of various sections. Courses of instruction varied in length from three to six months. However, those cadre who were selected to undergo training in North Vietnam usually went through two years or longer courses, during which classroom training was given in Hanoi but practical work took place in Hai Phong.

11. Crypto Section.

This section's responsibility was to encode and decode messages exchanged between Reconnaissance Sections and their subordinate companies or detachments, or among various sections of MIACOSVN.

12. MIA Communications Battalion.

The MIA Communications Battalion was organized into three radio companies, one express messenger company, one repair unit and one training school. Twice daily, the battalion communicated with subordinate MI units to receive and transmit information. Equipment used by the battalion were all 15-watt Red Chinese or Russian supplied radio sets. The express messenger company was 50-man strong and equipped with 10 Honda motorcycles. In addition to dispatching high precedence correspondence, this company was also tasked to transport high-ranking military intelligence cadre or visitors from the duty guardpost to MIA headquarters and back. Another responsibility of this unit was to detail men to entry points to take delivery of newspapers published in Saigon.

In addition to its eleven staff sections and the communications battalion, MIA also operated a dispensary and a separate recovery center. The organization and operation of MID revealed certain characteristics of its own. First, its subordinate units underwent constant changes, either merging with each other or being disbanded as dictated by the circumstances. Second, every unit and its staff sections were assigned several different code-names and code-numbers. Third, MIA usually suffered from a shortage of specialists and had to rely on North Vietnam infiltrated personnel for certain key positions. Fourth, MIA enjoyed no prerogatives over strategic intelligence units detached from North Vietnam. Finally, new sections could be created as requirements arose. For example, during the period from 1968 to 1971, there was the Prisoner Exploitation Section, especially created to handle RVN prisoners of war. But this section was later disbanded and its personnel absorbed in the Law Enforcement Section. After the cease-fire, to meet the needs for prisoner exchanges, a Prisoner Section was created with the mission to study and recommend lists of prisoners susceptible to be released, determine which prisoners to be withheld and suggest which areas would be appropriate for the exchange of prisoners.

Compared to military intelligence organizations serving other military regions or the B3 Front for example, COSVN's MIA organization did not present any significant difference save for an additional subordinate MI agency to handle the Saigon - Gia Dinh - Cholon area which the Communists regarded as the nerve center of the RVN-US war apparatus. Particular importance was attached to this MI agency because it was responsible for an area where strategic decisions were made and directives issued and where internal differences or conflicts, as far as the RVN was concerned, usually broke out most intensively.

Sources and Dispatching Methods

Communist intelligence employed certain sources and dispatching methods which were radically different from those used by the US and the RVN. This difference materialized in reconnaissance and messenger units, and most importantly, in the Communist people's intelligence system.

1. Reconnaissance Units.

Reconnaissance was the name the Communists gave to intelligence units organized especially to serve a battlefield prior to and during a campaign. Generally of company size, reconnaissance units were organized into three-man cells assigned to operate with combat units from company to division level. Prior to launching a military campaign, reconnaissance cells were sent into the objective area to conduct a research on terrain and the situation. Elements of situation research included: enemy, local population, and probable impact of a military action on the political situation. Concerning the enemy, research efforts focused on his order of battle, strength, forces, organization, equipment, disposition, defenses, morale, habits, commanders and reinforcements. Concerning the local population, the research task was to find out the attitude of the people toward the Communists, toward the RVN, the kind of popular support that might be expected, and the probable impact of the campaign on the populace. Reconnaissance on terrain was aimed at collecting the same information that every tactical commander needed to know to plan and coordinate his fire and maneuver with accuracy and to make a judicious use of firepower on each type of target.

Reconnaissance as it was practiced by the Communists was guided by certain basic principles. First, it should be specific and based on sensory perception, or as the Communists put it, what could be "seen by the eyes and touched by the hands." Second, reconnaissance should be performed many times, by many different elements to double-check and cross-check all information gathered. A last-minute reconnaissance should always be conducted one or two days prior to launching the attack in order to preclude the unexpected. And if the attack was important enough, the commander of the unit conducting it was required to personally reconnoiter the terrain at least once. Data collected through reconnaissance would be reported on a scaled-down sand table constructed by the attacking unit for the purpose of planning and rehearsing actions by participating elements in minute detail.

Methods of collecting information through reconnaissance included observation from mobile or fixed positions which were generally established near enemy garrisons and along axes of communication; probes made among the local population; contacts with local party and government representatives who were usually supported by local sources such as people's agents nets, security agents and enemy informants; and abduction of enemy troops and seizure of documents if required. There were still other forms of reconnaissance which either employed military intelligence personnel disguised as local inhabitants or the local inhabitants themselves who lived near or within the target area and served as planted agents. During an offensive campaign, reconnaissance cells operated in conjunction with combat troops on the battlefield. Their mission was to keep track of developments in the enemy situation, his movements, reinforcements and supply activities, and to assess the results of shellings, attacks or raids. Reconnaissance units also assisted in the routing of information and messages by establishing field telephone lines between the command post and combat units. More recent tasks performed by reconnaissance cells included combined activities with artillery forward observers to assist them in adjusting fire on targets.

The various tasks performed by reconnaissance units were considered of utmost importance by the Communists who were usually convinced that half of the success in any attack depended on their completion. As a result, reconnaissance personnel were very carefully selected and usually regarded as crack troops. The effectiveness of reconnaissance units prompted the Communists to activate special-action units which came to be known as "Sappers." The initial mission given to Sapper units was reconnaissance; at a later stage, they were employed in sabotage missions. Sapper units were rapidly expanded and upgraded beginning in 1969. From company-size units operating individually, Sappers were later organized into battalions and finally regiments, all under control of a separate Sapper Command. If Sapper units drew much attention from ARVN and US forces during the war, it was only because of their conspicuous and sometimes spectacular exploits which seemed to overshine the more obscure, but nonetheless just as effective, accomplishments achieved by reconnaissance units. Because of its tactical nature, such reconnaissance work was called "ground reconnaissance" to make it distinct from another type of reconnaissance called "technical reconnaissance."

Technical reconnaissance units were in fact communications intelligence units whose mission was to collect information through radio communications intercept. Communist intercept activities, as a matter of fact, became more extensive during the period of US participation, beginning in 1965. For their operation, technical reconnaissance units used mostly captured US-made radio equipment, augmented by Red Chinese and sometimes home-made radio sets which were in fact circuit-modified commercial FM receivers procured on the local market and appropriately given local trademark labels such as Ap Bac, Saigon 1, Saigon 2, etc., after modifications. In general, these units operated in the vicinities of RVN or US unit headquarters for clearer reception of radio communications. Although their activation lagged behind ground reconnaissance units, technical reconnaissance units proved to be efficient and vital as providers of accurate intelligence for the Communists.

2. The Messenger Systems.

The enemy's basic deficiencies in signal communications and his fear of intercept led him to rely more on messengers for the dispatching of intelligence reports and official mail. Messengers made up an extensive and intricate system. They were usually selected among the local population because of their better knowledge of terrain and weather and their special ability to find alternate routes to bypass ambushes and troop maneuvers. Communist messengers were, therefore, highly familiar with our military activities; they knew where our patrols usually operated, the type of targets on which our artillery usually fired, and where our mines and obstacles were placed. There were two kinds of messengers: legal and illegal, depending on whether they lived and worked legally in GVN-controlled areas. In addition to their routine task of dispatching intelligence reports and official mail, messengers also doubled as intelligence agents. They were thus required, while on messenger routes, to report on everything they had observed concerning the enemy, the populace, the crops, the weather, road conditions, etc. Another task performed by messengers was to serve as guides for visitors, infiltration groups and supply parties.

The so-called "Ho Chi Minh Trail" -- sometimes dubbed "The Old Man's Route" by the Communists -- was initially a messenger route which resulted from painful and persistent pioneering efforts by the Viet Minh in their quest for a safe transportation and dispatching route from North to South during their "Resistance War in South Vietnam" episode, back in early 1946. This route, which meandered along tortuous mountain trails on the eastern slope of the Truong Son chain, was later expanded into a large infiltration corridor made up of both longitudinal and latitudinal local messenger routes connecting successive zones with each other. In each zone, there were established liaison way stations manned by local messengers who served as guides. Several way stations were manned by local messengers who served as guides. Several way stations were grouped under a "binh tram" (military post) which controlled messenger activities and routes within a defined zone. Linked together, local messenger stations and routes made up an integrated and intricate communication system which effectively ensured a continuous flow of men and supplies and whose appearance could be likened to a giant cobweb. In addition to the Ho Chi Minh Trail, there were other messenger routes which connected Communist bases and sanctuaries together. From the Cambodian border leading inside the Mekong Delta for example, there were three routes called Ia, Ib and Ic. The Ia and Ib routes were located in Kien Tuong province, while the Ic route was located in Kien Giang province.

    3. The People's Intelligence System.

Although reconnaissance and messengers were important elements of the Communist intelligence structure, its outstanding feature was the popular-based collection organization called the people's intelligence system. The concept of people's intelligence can be traced back to the Russian Revolution of 1917.

Fundamentally, people's intelligence means that every citizen participates in intelligence in order to safeguard his (or her) own welfare and the welfare of his family and community. The basic objective to be achieved in people's intelligence is to know everything that can be known about the enemy while concealing from him and denying him knowledge about us. The Communists usually likened the enemy to an actor performing on stage under floodlight before an audience. His every gesture, every utterance can be perceived by hundreds of eyes and ears, yet he cannot make out anyone from the audience who, like the people, blend themselves with the dark background.

To enlist participation of the people in intelligence work, the Communists in Vietnam likened informing and reporting to a civil duty bound on every citizen. Any refusal to cooperate, negligence or failure to report automatically made the defendant a reactionary or an accomplice of the enemy, which were crimes punishable by severe sanctions. It was this threat of severe punishment that forced everyone living under the Communist regime or in a contested area to cooperate in intelligence work.

To effectively check every citizen's thought and actions and ensure his cooperation, the Communists imposed on the citizenry a double control system, based on community or administrative divisions on the one hand and on trade, professional or civic organizations on the other. First, no household could function individually under a Communist regime. Every three or five households were to make up a household group in which each household was responsible for keeping watch over the others and reporting on them. Theoretically, each three to five-household unit was under control of a chief who was selected among household heads and assisted by three assistants, for economic and financial affairs, education and cultural affairs, and public health and social affairs, respectively. In reality, however, this type of organization was applicable only to larger communal units grouping ten or twelve households. Whatever the size and organization for control, the purpose of each household group was always to check on the activities and attitudes of its member households in terms of security and information gathering. The character of family gatherings, the identity and purpose of each visitor, for example, were all subjects for detailed reporting. Above the household group level, there were similar organizations based on household groups, streets and blocks.

The second type of control was apparently more important and more effective since it was based on trade, professional or civil organizations of which every citizen had to be a member. For example, farmers were required to be members of the Farmers Association; workers automatically became affiliated to the Workers Association, etc. For each trade, each profession, there always existed some kind of association whose membership was mandatory. In addition, there were also civic organizations that grouped children, youth, women and senior citizens under attractively named associations, such as the Youngster and Junior Vanguards, the Salvation Youth, etc. No one, in effect, could escape regimentation. It was these organizations that usually exerted a dominant influence upon the individual, much more so than the family. As a member of an association, the individual was constantly exposed to political indoctrination and civic education which taught him, among other things, that reporting was one of the basic and important civic duties.

The people's intelligence system thus reached down to every household and encompassed the entire social stratification. Its basic method of information gathering was reporting. In the areas completely under Communist control, reporting was directed toward counterintelligence and unusual happenings while in contested areas, it covered both intelligence collection and counterintelligence. The method of reporting was made simple enough for everyone to participate while tending to his usual business. A roadside bicycle mechanic, for example, could provide a daily report on the volume of military traffic, the types of military cargo transported, the direction of their movements, etc. A farmer tilling his land or a child looking after his buffalo in the vicinity of an airfield could give an account of how many aircraft had landed and taken off during the day and even their types. A woman merchant in a market place could provide such military information as troop strength, operational preparations, new units, etc., through doing her daily business. Within a household group, almost anyone could inform on unusual activities of others, the duration of their absence, contacts made with strangers, and so on.

Those people whose normal business required them to go back and forth regularly between Communist and GVN-controlled areas were usually tasked to dispatch information or documents or to procure items of military necessity. The Communists were especially interested in those people whose relatives worked for the GVN. Depending on the degree of relationship, these people could be used to press or blackmail their relatives into cooperation by providing information of interest to the Communists. Those who had special abilities in intelligence work would be selected to undergo training in order to be employed in a higher collection field, for example, as undercover agents, by posing as bar girls, waitresses, clerks in those business premises in close proximity to military bases, airfields, ports, etc. In general, women, children and old people were more likely induced into intelligence work than young men because draft-age youths were usually subjected to identification checks. When there were indications that US forces would participate in the Vietnam war, the Communists initiated a program of agent training whereby women were taught English and prepared to apply for jobs in American agencies and organizations. To give them credence and a good cover, the Communists subsequently managed to have them attend GVN-run English classes.

With time and experience, popular sources and informants were apt to graduate into full-fledged intelligence cadre at the service of military intelligence agencies. When thus promoted, they no longer belonged to the people's intelligence system which, in effect, functioned only at lower levels and in those areas under contest or Communist control. Not everybody, however, could become informants in the people's intelligence system. The Communists made certain exceptions and excluded from their service certain categories of people, in particular: 1. those who worked for the GVN or served in the RVNAF and the National Police; 2. those who were pro-GVN; 3. those who were active in religious organizations; 4. those who bore a hatred toward Communism for personal reasons; 5. those who had been convicted or indicted by Communists; 6. those former Communist personnel who had been detained and released by the GVN after cooperating with it; 7. and finally, ralliers.[4]

Despite these exceptions, informants working for the Communists were numerous and ubiquitous. They were generally able to gather information on our activities on a country-wide basis. Among their methods of operation, the most universal and effective was through familial connections.

---

[4] The purpose of listing these seven categories of persona non grata, according to Communist documents, was to eliminate the possibility of RVN-planted agents volunteering for Communist intelligence service. The Communists nevertheless focused on inducing GVN and RVNAF cadres into their spy network every time they felt they could be certain of success in each individual case.

Successes and Failures of Enemy Intelligence

In 1958, a lieutenant working for G-1, General Staff was found AWOL. He was responsible for processing ARVN strength reports. An investigation discovered that when he fled North Vietnam with other refugees in 1954, he left his family behind. With vital documents on ARVN strength in his possession, he had apparently returned to Hanoi.

In 1962, a young and brillant signal officer earmarked for an assignment in COMINT was extradited from the United States where he was attending a computer course related to decryptment work. He was arrested as soon as he arrived at Tan Son Nhut. It was discovered that he had been induced to operate as a planted agent in South Vietnam since his school days in Hanoi. While living in Saigon, he was watched over by a Communist cadre, his own stepfather, who also happened to be an ARVN warrant officer. Also arrested with him was his brother-in-law, a Communist agent, who was serving as an ARVN lieutenant and English instructor at the ARVN Language School.

During an operation in 1963, ARVN forces seized from the enemy a copy of the entire RVN Economic and Strategic Hamlet Plan. This plan was drafted in 1961 by economists Vu Quoc Thuc and Staley and disseminated to several governmental agencies. An investigation failed to determine when and where the document had been stolen.

During the 1968 Tet offensive, a note booklet was discovered on the corpse of a Communist intelligence cadre in Hue. In this booklet there was a long list of important RVN personalities, complete with their addresses, professions, vehicles, habits, etc. Even minor details were found carefully noted, if deemed relevant. On a certain official, it was noted, for example, that he always carried a pistol for self-defense but the pistol was usually put away in the glove compartment of his car.

In 1970, operational forces in MR-3 captured from the enemy a copy of the JGS Combined Campaign Plan (AB-144) in which important directives were given to Corps for the implementation of the GVN pacification and rural development program. After an investigation, it was found that the plan

had been sold by a major working at J-3, JGS for 250,000 piasters, of
which he had received 100,000. He claimed that he needed the money to
buy a house for his family. Again, in 1970, a Communist cadre disclosed that he was completely conversant with the RVN-US negotiating
platform and objectives in the Paris talks thanks to a source close to
a member of the RVN delegation.

One of the most important and public-rousing espionage cases was
the Huynh Van Trong affair, unearthed in 1971. He was a trusted aide
working in the Office of the Presidential Political Assistant. To
help his penetration, a Communist cadre recommended him to a Catholic
bishop who enjoyed a good relationship with President Thieu. Operating
under a pre-conceived plan, he provided much accurate intelligence data
on the Communists and soon earned complete trust from his superiors.
In his capacity, he was tasked to write situation analyses and estimates.

In December 1973, Communist sappers in coordination with planted
agents succeeded in blowing up the Shell fuel storage plant at Nha Be,
causing 80% destruction to the fuel stocks. This was done while the
world was being caught in the grips of an energy crisis.

In 1974, a rallier revealed that in Kien Giang province, the
Communists were able to intercept and break through 90% of the contents
of messages exchanged between the Sector and its Subsectors. This feat,
he said, was attributable to the effectiveness of Communist Technical
Reconnaissance units.

Again in 1974, a "legal" Communist messenger was apprehended at Cu
Chi. He was a peddler of plastic toys, and some microfilms were found
concealed in his merchandise. Among the microfilms seized, there was a
photocopy of a report by the Joint Senate-Lower House Defense Committee
filed after an inspection tour in MR-2. The report contained detailed
information on the friendly situation, enemy capabilities and policy and
the difficulties and requirements of MR-2. Another microfilm revealed a
photocopy of the enemy order of battle strength in South Vietnam. The
investigation on the Senate-Lower House report did not bring about any
results because of constraints imposed by congressional immunity. But it
was discovered, in the case of the enemy OB strength, that this document

NHA BE POL STORAGE DESTROYED BY SAPPERS – 2 DECEMBER 1973

had been loaned to a major working at the Central Intelligence Office by his friend, a lieutenant belonging to the OB section of Unit 306, J-2, JGS. Using his friendship, the major had asked to borrow the document for reference purposes, claiming that it would take him a long time to go through official loan procedures. He went into hiding one day after the "legal" messenger was arrested.

The above examples are but a few selected among other instances of enemy intelligence exploits. They indicate that the enemy was apt to employ every approach, every technique to collect intelligence data that were required for his strategic and tactical needs. Among his collection methods, the most widely used was found to be the familial connection approach. Quang Ngai province offered the most typical case of this approach. During 1973, an enemy notebook was captured which contained a long list of Communist "legal" agents among whom, there were several civil servants and servicemen. An investigation revealed that in most cases, these civil servants and servicemen had been pressed into Communist service by their close relatives.

Despite its extensiveness, the enemy collection effort was still plagued with tactical deficiencies and strategic errors. During the 1968 Tet offensive, for example, when attacking Quang Ngai provincial capital by surprise, the Communists had estimated that they could seize this city with relative ease. As a result, they began their attack at 0400 hours. Two hours later, ARVN forces of the 2d Infantry Division initiated a counterattack and drove the enemy out of the city, capturing in the process several prisoners. After interrogation, the prisoners revealed that their intelligence estimate for the attack indicated that the ARVN 2d Infantry Division was only armed with M-1 rifles and carbines. They admitted they did not expect so much automatic fire from ARVN forces, which caught them entirely by surprise. This was an instance of enemy failure to collect accurate intelligence data prior to an attack. One day prior to the enemy offensive, the 2d Infantry Division had received emergency shipments of M-16 rifles, for the first time.

In 1970, when ARVN forces made preparations to launch a cross-border offensive operation into Cambodia, an enemy document was captured which happened to be the CT-9 Division's intelligence estimate, dated one day before the operation's D-day. The enemy division estimated that ARVN forces would not dare to strike into Cambodia for fear of world-wide political and diplomatic repercussions.

In early 1967, the North Vietnamese leadership, and Vo Nguyen Giap in particular, concluded that the US would make a landing in North Vietnam. As a consequence he initiated a plan, which was approved by Hanoi's Politbureau, to organize a people's militia force to face an eventual US ground offensive. The activation of this colossal militia force was met by stiff opposition by some other North Vietnamese leaders because it created two major difficulties. First, North Vietnam ran the risk of drastic curtailment in economic production, its manpower being absorbed into non-productive national defense tasks. Second, the armed militia might be dangerous to the regime's security in case they became disenchanted with the war effort. Still, Vo Nguyen Giap was irretractable as to his prediction of a US landing, which apparently obsessed him and spurred him into taking some pre-emptive counteraction. This was how the 1968 general offensive came about, undoubtedly a result of Giap's estimate. He also predicted that this general offensive would be crowned with certain success because, according to his estimate, it was supported by a general popular uprising. Events had proved him wrong.

Another major intelligence blunder committed by North Vietnam was its failure to assess correctly the nature and extent of US reactions as it decided to blockade Hai Phong and fly B-52 bombing missions over both Hanoi and Hai Phong in late 1972. Hanoi's estimate at that time did not include these possibilities.

In early 1975, North Vietnam estimated that in case of a general offensive in South Vietnam, the US probably did not have the capabilities for a ground intervention by Army forces, but it still had the capabilities for intervention with the US Air Force. As a matter of fact, Hanoi's resolution asserted that no matter what will happen, we must be armed by a spirit that does not fear an American re-intervention.

An Evaluation of Enemy Intelligence

During the Vietnam war, it was evident that the Communists attached much importance to intelligence which they regarded as one of the major causes for success or defeat. The achievements that they obtained in intelligence gave us certain indications as to its effectiveness.

A careful analysis of events revealed that the Communist hands had been reinforced by certain external supports that facilitated to a great extent their intelligence collection effort. A high-ranking rallier who used to be responsible for cultural affairs and history and had served as personal secretary to another high-ranking cadre in the Saigon Military Command told us a revealing story that shed some light on this external support.

Everyday at 1700 hours, he recalled, Communist messengers were ready at pick-up points in Cu Chi (Hau Nghia province), Trang Bang (Tay Ninh province), Ben Cat (Binh Duong province) to take delivery of newspapers from Saigon. (As a matter of fact, all Saigon newspapers were published in the afternoon in order to reach newsstands across the country the next day). The procurement and shipment of newspapers were performed by Communist agents in Saigon and intended for the Press Section of COSVN. By the evening, this Section had completed a press analysis report for the consumption of COSVN's Military Intelligence Agency. The reason for three separate pick-up points, the rallier said, was to make sure that newspapers reached the Press Section in time for its analysis work because newspapers were a major source that provided abundant information on the RVN military, political, economic and diplomatic activities. Should one messenger cell fail to deliver them, there were always two others. It was estimated that up to 80% of information gathered on the RVN were found in newspapers. Communist military specialists took particular interest in reports carried by the "Tien Tuyen" daily (a commercialized Government Political Warfare Department publication) because these provided accurate and timely information. Political and economic specialists favored the "Chinh Luan" daily for its professionally written articles on political and economic affairs.

Even the tabloids of dubious quality could furnish some information of interest to COSVN and help it take timely and appropriate actions. Through press reports, for example, the rallier revealed, COSVN learned that Mr. Nguyen Van Bong, Chairman of the "Radical Movement," was being consulted for the post of Prime Minister and this probability was near certain. As a result, COSVN promptly decided to get rid of him the rallier concluded.

The press as well as other news media in South Vietnam such as radio and television constituted perhaps the wealthiest and quickest source of information. Saigon newspapers were usually censored by the GVN but in most cases, the censored reports just contained controversial information on internal politics. The reader was always able to get vital military information with relative ease. In a press interview he gave in February 1975, for example, the commander of II Corps withheld nothing from what he knew about the enemy's goals and future actions in his MR and even outlined his operational plans in no uncertain terms. There was once an article written by a VNAF officer who took pride in listing everything he knew about the VNAF organization, and the number and types of aircraft. Every morning, the Military Broadcasting Service gave a detailed account of recent battles, complete with live coverage and interviews with participants who reported in vivid and accurate details the battle progress, its objectives, the friendly tactic and, of course, their identities and position.

What made these things happen the way they did? Was it because the GVN wanted to prove some point or just because it wanted to get rid of an inferiority complex? The point to be proved was clear enough. We were a free and democratic society. Our life quality was improving and catching up with other advanced countries in the world. Thus, the GVN felt compelled to duplicate the Western democratic way of life in national affairs, even its errors and weaknesses. It seemed to be oblivious to the fact that South Vietnam was just an underdeveloped country that a vicious war was tearing apart.

Every year, budget projects prepared in detail by each ministry of the GVN were submitted to the Senate and Lower House for approval. The procedures for reviewing and hearings were as open as in any democratic country. Defense budget committees of both houses of the General Assembly naturally had the right to ask detailed questions about proposed expenditure and the Ministry of Defense was required to present justifications. Questions and answers resulted in the revelation of all defense secrets, for example, how many general reserve brigades, how many armor squadrons would be activated next year, or how would the GVN go about upgrading Regional Forces into regular forces, how many troops would be involved in the process, etc. All these were sensitive defense secrets which, after going through the legislative machinery, ceased altogether to be secrets. Each year, the Prime Minister's Office published a roster of key officials of the GVN, to include those of the Ministry of Defense, the Joint General Staff and the Services and Arms of the RVNAF, complete with position titles, dates of appointment, personal addresses, and home and office telephone numbers. This roster alone was apt to give the enemy a detailed knowledge about our governmental structure, its subordinate agencies and its responsible leaders, all for free. On the civilian side, it was known that government agencies were generally careless and peremptory in safeguarding classified papers and documents. A crypto clerk in the Ministry of Foreign Affairs was once found working on his encrypted messages in an open office in the presence of visitors. The loss or pilferage of documents, therefore, usually went unnoticed and even if it was discovered, there were chances it would not be reported. A utility man might by chance obtain old files and documents and sell them for a profit. In one instance it was discovered, also by chance, that classified papers by stacks were used by street vendors to wrap foods and sandwiches.

The kind of inferiority complex that obsessed the GVN was apparently its feeling of being the underdog in political struggle and propaganda effectiveness vis-a-vis the Communists. This explained why the GVN always went all out to regain an equal status. Intelligence was sometimes employed toward this purpose, unfortunately, without reservations or respect for the safeguarding of secrets. During a meeting of the Two-Party Joint Military Commission, a RVN delegate did not hesitate to quote the content of COSVN Directive No. 3/73, a recently captured document, to prove his point that the other side made a mockery of the Paris Agreement. The unfortunate result was that he had helped the enemy to learn that the RVN did not possess the complete text of the document. As a consequence, the enemy ordered all his cadres to destroy it. To prove that the enemy constantly violated the Paris Agreement, our information and propaganda agencies found it expedient to divulge intelligence data on his infiltrations of men and weapons, his scheme of attack, etc., and even disclosed the sources of these data. This either helped the enemy know to what extent our intelligence effort had succeeded or prompted him to take steps to counter it. Either way, it was the war effort that suffered the most.

The compromise of tactical operations was sometimes attributed to enemy penetration or monitoring feats. The general impression was that no matter how secret an operational plan was kept, the enemy would learn about it sooner or later. The Lam Son 719 operation in early 1971 was frequently cited to make this point on enemy forewarning. But the RVN-US strategic idea of striking into enemy-held sanctuaries and logistical bases across the border had already been exposed by the Cambodian incursion of the previous year. There were indications that Communist units operating in lower Laos had been warned to take precautionary measures against the probability of similar cross-border incursion in their area of operation by RVN-US forces. Thus, it was a matter of simple logic that the next target would be the logistical base complex in lower Laos and the time frame for a possible attack anywhere within the short dry season.

The amount of preparations and the delay in launching the attack could also have been elements that helped reinforce the enemy's reasoning and his alertness. While there was no proof that his intelligence actively sought to find out and know about Lam Son 719 while it was being planned, there were possible clues unconsciously given away by ARVN units getting prepared for the attack that any alert enemy agent could have picked up and reported.

Over the years, ARVN units were plagued by the impossibility to keep operational preparations under wraps. There were some reasons for

this. First, the unit's dependent quarter was always an abundant source
of information on the unit's activities. If the unit was preparing for
some action, the troops' dependents were bound to learn about it the
minute orders were given. Some units tried to offset this shortcoming
by confining troops to the barracks prior to an operation but even then,
the dependents always managed to learn about what their husbands and
fathers were up to. Second, it was a fact that small unit commanders
were extremely careless when talking over the radio despite warnings and
education. In addition to this deplorable habit, they also never bothered
to use voice codes which they considered cumbersome and inconvenient.
That explains why the enemy monitoring of ARVN low-powered FM networks
was so widespread and productive. Thus, to say that the RVN unconsciously gave Communist intelligence a helping hand is not an abusive statement.

In addition, North Vietnam must have received some intelligence
support from the Communist bloc and Soviet Russia in particular. This
support was evidenced by the supply of weather information and data
concerning B-52 flights. Weather information helped the enemy select
the more appropriate days to push their attacks without fear of our
tactical air. Data concerning B-52 flights such as take-off time, number
of aircraft, direction, speed, etc., certainly helped the enemy to anticipate the approximate time of strike and the general target areas.
At least, the kind of external support the enemy received from Russia
could be helpful in alleviating his constant fear of B-52 strikes and
comforting the morale of his troops. The common belief, instilled by
political commissars and held among enemy troops as true was that his
intelligence was infallible and knew everything. Enemy troops believed,
for example, that every B-52 overflight was known a few hours in advance
but never found out why. If this claim had been true, no one else could
have provided the forewarning but the Russians with their extensive,
sophisticated monitoring network. Other local indications could also
have forewarned the enemy about B-52 strikes, such as the suspension
of tactical air and reconnaissance flights over the target area, etc.
The ARVN could not possibly know about B-52 flights since no field commander had ever been notified in advance. Hence the contention that

leaks on the ARVN side which were picked up by agents within its ranks led to the enemy's advance knowledge on B-52 flights was unjustified. There was only once, an unique instance which was never repeated, that an ARVN corps commander was notified in advance of B-52 flights. The Corps commander felt it his duty to notify his division commanders who in turn notified their subordinates down the channels with the end result that at battalion level, notification was communicated among units by messages in clear. But that was the only time this ever happened. Moreover, the selection of B-52 targets was a MACV prerogative, based on recommendations by ARVN Corps commanders who always communicated directly with their US advisers or Field Force commanders in such matters by voice rather by correspondence. In strategic intelligence too, both Russia and Red China must have been of great help to North Vietnam by providing information concerning US policies, attitudes and probable courses of action for certain periods of time. But apart from this external help, conscious or unconscious, how in reality did Communist intelligence fare by itself?

As has been said earlier, the enemy succeeded reasonably in intercepting our communications through the use of his technical reconnaissance units. However, this effort was only of a small scale and his resources and techniques were rather rudimentary by US standards. The enemy communications intercept effort would have been less successful if on the RVN side, tighter countermeasures had been taken. A novel technique that the enemy introduced late in the war was air reconnaissance; first flights were recorded in late 1974. But the flights were few and their coverage, limited. The results must also have been marginal because sophisticated techniques such as SLAR and Red Haze were entirely beyond North Vietnam Air Force capabilities.

In technical intelligence, North Vietnam was in fact more concerned about finding out how US and RVN techniques worked than trying to employ these techniques. Since 1965, North Vietnam had been trying to learn about the capabilities and limitations of the EC-47, Mohawk, pilotless air reconnaissance, and sensors. Its interest focused particularly on ARDF methods. At first, it was evident that Communist intelligence was not familiar with this technique of intelligence collection. One of its reports in fact read: "Enemy intelligence has discovered the location of ...division headquarters at ... Please inform the division and apply strict security measures. Try to find out why information has been leaked." It certainly took the enemy a long time to find out. When the enemy began to know more about ARDF, he made a conscientious effort to shoot down what he called "electronic reconnaissance" aircraft whereever possible or took protective measures such as radio silence, or even radio deception as in the case of the NVA 320th Division which left behind its command radio station at Duc Co while slipping out surreptitiously toward Ban Me Thuot in February 1975.

By contrast, the enemy was more successful in people's intelligence. As has been said, the system was built on the base of "all-people" and "totality." Consequently, it provided the enemy with a considerable amount of sources in every locality, in every field, and at any time. The system was totally responsive to the enemy's intelligence requirements without creating incidental problems such as funds, recruiting, operational control, etc. which ordinarily plagued any human intelligence effort. Taking its roots from the people themselves, the Communist people's intelligence system was difficult to detect and destroy. Even if it could be detected, the leads would not help us go far or obtain information of any importance.

In addition to its contributions to intelligence on a professional point of view, the Communist people's intelligence system also played an important political role in the war. By actually participating in it, people felt they were truly involved and in fact behaved as though they held the initiative and actually directed the war effort themselves. This was a definite advantage over our side which was always hard put to elicit the people's participation.

It was however not the Communist intelligence agencies that actually organized the people's intelligence system and pushed it ahead. It was the party and its local committees that played a key role in pushing party policies and directives, enforcing and controlling them, and instituting appropriate sanctions. Even in regular meetings of local party committees, which were normally held once every week or bimonthly, the most important item of discussion was always a review of the enemy situation in every aspect. Local party committees, however, were active and effective only in Communists controlled areas. Their activities were severely restricted in contested areas.

For all its merits, the Communist people's intelligence system was plagued by a serious drawback: the non-professional or amateurish character of people's nets. Their reports were usually inaccurate, incomplete and confusing. But perhaps people's intelligence derived its merits more from quantity than quality, as Mao Tse Tung put it: "Quality could be replaced by quantity and morale."[4] Another deficiency of this system was that it worked more in theory than in practice. Although the basic motto prescribed that each citizen should be an informant, the passive and resilient nature of the Vietnamese common farmer or villager and his traditionally-ingrained aversion to authoritharian power would never make him a good one.

The extent of enemy penetration into GVN agencies and the RVNAF ranks, and the existence of turncoats among them, however, were not as ubiquitous and potentially serious as they appeared to be or as was generally surmised. If enemy penetration had been extensive and effective, what can explain then his dismal failure to incite disruptions or rebellious acts within the RVNAF ranks during his offensive campaigns of 1968 and 1975 which were, so to speak, go-for-broke affairs? The fact was, even during these extremely confusing times, not a single turncoat incident had been recorded save for the apparently enemy-induced bombing of the Independence Palace by a F-5 pilot in mid April 1975. An idea can be made, however, of the extent of enemy penetration as it existed in 1968, based on enemy documents. The enemy Saigon-Cholon

---

[4] Mao Tse Tung's Selected Works, opus cited.

Front Committee, in fact, disclosed in one of its documents captured during the Tet offensive that he had succeeded in enlisting the service of 112 sources in Saigon-Cholon—an open metropolitan area of over 2 million inhabitants. And this was at the height of his success in infrastructure activities.

A case study of Communist intelligence at work perhaps could give us a better idea as to its effectiveness. This is what a military intelligence cadre of Tay Ninh province told us about his provincial intelligence set up: The provincial military intelligence section has the mission to collect military as well as political intelligence in its area of responsibility (the province) and order of battle information such as unit designation, location, strength, biographies of military and civilian personalities of interest to the Party, defense plans and position of bases, outposts, reinforcement plans, and local terrain. This information is to be reported on a daily basis.

The Tay Ninh Military Intelligence Section was organized into five provincial collection teams under province control, eight district collection teams under respective district control, a number of people's collection nets, and most particularly, a technical reconnaissance team for the collection of communications intelligence. Four out of the five provincial MI teams were deployed around Tay Ninh city: Cau Sat, Cau Khoi, Giong Ca, Ho Don; the fifth one was Trang Bang district. Each team was controlled by from one to three cadres and its mission was to keep track of all ARVN troop movements.

For the dispatch of information, the Tay Ninh MI Section employed both "legal" messengers and radio. Messengers were responsible for dispatching routine or low precedence information between the Section and its teams or between the Section and infiltrated agents or regular agents. Radio was used only for transmitting important information to higher intelligence agencies. Among the teams, the technical reconnaissance team was regarded as the most effective, providing instant information through communications intercept. The Section's people's collection nets were not very active; they existed only in name.

The Tay Ninh MI Section was not successful in recruiting penetration

agents. So far, there were only two such agents known; one was a
member of the local Democratic Party (GVN-organized), the other was an
ARVN corporal working at Sector headquarters. The Cau Sat team had five
agents, none of them penetration. Other teams fared no better. "In
summary", the MI cadre concluded, "The Tay Ninh MI Section was not effective. Its activities were seriously curtailed by a shortage of MI
cadre, failure in agent recruiting and poor communications."

The status of enemy military intelligence in Tay Ninh of course
did not reflect the overall situation; it did, however, indicate that
the Communist intelligence system was plagued with many deficiencies
and difficulties. Still, it enjoyed some advantage over our own military
intelligence. For one thing, enemy intelligence plans were based on
and made up part of a national plan conceived by the Politbureau. For
another, the enemy intelligence effort was a unified effort, centrally
controlled and judiciously distributed to responsible agencies throughout the hierarchy. This feature could be observed through the enemy
general offensives of 1968 and 1975.

Regarding methods of collection, the Communists were more effective
in human intelligence than technological intelligence which was in effect one of its basic weaknesses. But they were apt to learn more about
it in time. What is more important to intelligence, however, lies not
in collection methods or the data gathered, but in the analysis and
synthesis of these data. This is something no intelligence specialist,
regardless of his ideological conviction, can deny. The problem is
always to arrive at an accurate estimate for every situation. But to
me this has always seemed to be one of the enemy's shortcomings.

His other shortcoming derives from his own shortsighted, subjective
view. By subordinating intelligence to politics, he has come up with
self-serving estimates just to keep in line with his ultimate goal. He
erred fatally in 1968 when surmising that the South Vietnamese population was ripe for an uprising. Only later was he able to find out why
it did not happen. In fact, the enemy intelligence establishment has
never been able to do a professional job just because it can never
bring itself to contradic the party line. To the Communists, facts

after all are not what actually happen but what they wish to happen. This has always been a major shortcoming.

CHAPTER VIII

Conclusions

Every qualified observer will agree that the RVN had too many intelligence agencies, civilian, para-military and military. These agencies were in different command channels and reported to different authorities. This gave rise to redundancies in tasks and objectives, dilution of effort and, worst of all, unhealthy competition. An effort was made to offset the handicaps of this situation by establishing intelligence coordination committees but this solution did not work out as expected. Effective coordination suffered from the fact that it depended upon the willingness to cooperate of the individual members involved. The members enjoyed equal status and enjoyed equal prerogatives; this statutory equality even existed among collection agencies and the command organization which directed the collection effort. The principal endeavors of these collection agencies usually tended toward gaining the trust and confidence of the high-ranking authorities to whom they were subordinate. Among the many ways they could achieve this approbation were by providing the kind of information that the authorities liked most to have and, by giving them raw information for the sole purpose of making them the first ones to know, regardless of the validity of the information which had yet to be analyzed, interpreted and evaluated. The lateral dissemination of such information to other interested intelligence agencies was relegated to secondary importance and sometimes withheld altogether; lateral dissemination was not mandatory.

The assignment of prerogatives and resources to intelligence agencies was based not on the mission, organization and performance of the agency concerned but on the relationship the agency enjoyed with the authority that employed it, and most particularly on the power of this authority.

South Vietnamese leaders were of course fully aware of the organizational complexity and multiplicity of the intelligence establishment and consequently, the need for streamlining, and unifying the intelligence effort. But the intricate interplay of political powers and interests prevented progress along these lines because it remained the basic desire of each executive authority to have under his personal control an intelligence agency that he could freely use for his own end. Moreover there was always the danger of creating a new kind of power rivalry if all intelligence agencies were placed under any one authority. No one really wanted an all-powerful intelligence authority.

Although there existed too many intelligence agencies, their efforts were nearly exclusively limited to in-country collection. Agencies such as the Intelligence Directorate of the Ministry of Foreign Affairs and the Research and Documentation Office of the Ministry of Defense, and its military attache offices overseas, were ineffective organizations which contributed very little in terms of collection effort in support of the intelligence requirements of the war.

Within South Vietnam, the primary interests in information and the objectives of intelligence activities focused mostly on the military situation and internal politics. Economic intelligence was largely neglected. The lack of good economic intelligence led to ineffective resource control programs. Rice, the most important national resource which directly affected the lives of the populace, was not subject to effective control. Production, distribution and trade in this vital commodity were manipulated by profiteering middlemen who always managed to divert large quantities into enemy-controlled areas. In addition to speculation and pilferage of rice, the RVN Government was also plagued by a proliferation of counterfeited banknotes. There were many reasons to believe that the enemy was behind this sabotage of the currency but this suspicion was never confirmed by hard intelligence.

Despite the emphasis on tactical intelligence, and some considered this emphasis excessive—the resources allotted for tactical intelligence collection were far below requirements. The RVN defense expenditures

represented the greatest share of the national budget but most of the
defense budget was earmarked for what were considered priority needs
"to move, to shoot and to communicate." Very little was spent "to see;"
the leadership failed to realize that it made little sense to have
mobility and firepower if the enemy could not be found and his activities anticipated.

Not only did the RVN political and defense leadership show little
interest in military intelligence, field commanders in general did not
regard military intelligence as a command responsibility such as operations, logistics and training. Strange as it may seem, military intelligence was considered a staff responsibility, an activity for which
intelligence specialists were primarily responsible. With this attitude,
it is not surprising that military intelligence was frequently made the
scapegoat for tactical failures while victories invariable appeared the
result of good tactical operation. Although the RVN military doctrine
defined command responsibilities as encompassing all tactical aspects
—including intelligence—the concept seemed to be lost on our commanders. The training of cadets in the military schools was heavily oriented
toward tactics. Future commanders were trained to maneuver troops but
learned little of other command responsibilities. As a result, thoughout their careers as commanders, they held the notion that tactics was
the only command responsibility.

Because most commanders had inadequate knowledge of the art of
tactical intelligence and consequently little confidence in the ability
of intelligence professionals to furnish competent evaluations, they
were not satisfied with the traditional method used to denote the readability and accuracy of intelligence information. For example, a piece
of information evaluated as B-2, should be considered reliable and of
high value. In South Vietnam, however, commanders usually did not consider B-2 information reliable enough to warrant action. Information
whose evaluation stood below A2 or A3 was generally regarded as inconsequential and ignored. In an effort to convince commanders of the
true validity of certain important information, and also to tactfully
defer to their intractable disposition toward the evaluation system,
eventually, all pieces of information were clearly identified as

to their specific source such as aerial photo, communications intelligence, prisoner of war or agents, etc. This disclosure of the nature of the source of course ran afoul of intelligence security principles which were established to protect the source, but it effectively served the purpose of convincing commanders as to the validity of the information. There were instances of course in which the source had to be protected at all costs. In those cases, the information was only described as "special" and "of high value."

Sometimes—and unfortunately with disastrous results—senior commanders were unable to understand the implications of critical intelligence information furnished them. It was not enough for the intelligence officer to gather and analyze accurate, timely information concerning enemy capabilities and intentions and furnish the commander a finished intelligence estimate. Unless the intelligence officer had the time, and opportunity to explain its importance and make sure that the commander fully understood, there was a fair chance that the estimate would be misunderstood and perhaps disregarded.

"Know thyself and know the enemy" is a recognized universal precept. But knowledge about the enemy, as far as intelligence is concerned, was limited to commanders only. Rarely did commanders take the trouble to inform or indoctrinate their troops concerning upcoming operations. A unit going into battles stands a better chance of success if each of its men knows something about the enemy he is likely to confront, such as his identity, type, size, capabilities and vulnerabilities. If such knowledge had been provided before each battle, each soldier would have felt more confident and would have performed his duties with greater spirit.

Intelligence on the enemy in South Vietnam derived from both political and military sources. A problem arose when they flatly contradicted each other. If such was the case, which source should be given more weight and used as the basis for a correct estimate? Civilian intelligence agencies tended to trust information obtained from political sources because they were usually connected with higher enemy echelons. In contrast, military intelligence organizations usually considered information derived from military sources more reliable even though the information was sometimes just the interrrogation of an enemy soldier. The rationale supporting the military intelligence viewpoint proved to be correct on many occasions. In contrast to the South Vietnamese and American practice of not informing lower echelons concerning strategic concepts, at places political indoctrination was the Communist normal way of life and an important part of basic military education. Communist soldiers were constantly updated on the latest Party line, political objectives, the demands placed on military units, and the specific tasks they had to carry out. As a result, strange as it may seem, even a Communist cadre of the lowest echelon possessed a surprisingly good knowledge about strategy and more specifically what his unit was about to do. Although there was always the risk that information could be planted by the enemy for deception. By and large, enemy tactical commanders did not often go to the extreme of deceiving their own units, neither were they permitted to alter plans once issued by higher authority. Thus information obtained from military sources was usually more reliable and more accurate than that from political sources. Information derived from political sources was frequently deceptive and misleading. As preludes to their offensives of 1968 and 1975 for example, the Communists implemented elaborate and detailed plans aimed at leaking political information designed to conceal military moves and degrade the importance of military intelligence gathered by the RVNAF.

In general, knowledge about major enemy offensive campaigns, and general offensives in particular, was predicated upon the following indicators listed in their usual order of appearance in intelligence reports.

1. Latest resolution adopted by the Politbureau of the Labor (Communist) Party.
2. Official trips overseas by key governmental or Party officials to seek aid and resulting increases in aid from the Communist Bloc.
3. Appearance of modern weapons.
4. Reorganization or activation of command and control systems.

5. Advance test of a certain form of tactical maneuver to be employed in the offensive campaign.
6. Intensive indoctrination or special study sessions held in units.
7. Visits made by high ranking military delegations from countries giving aid.
8. Decreasing rate of returnees (ralliers).
9. Movement of reserve units into the battlefield.

There were other indicators such as logistic preparations, replacements and replenishment of unit strength, but these are not listed because they were perennial activities applicable to campaigns of short duration as well.

Despite their relatively clear significance, indicators such as those listed above sometimes led to diverging assessments and different opinions as to the enemy design. This was chiefly due to the fact that military commanders and intelligence officers were usually interested only in enemy capabilities and totally overlooked enemy intentions. As a matter of fact this was exactly the way they had been trained to think; military intelligence doctrine always emphasized capabilities and gauged predictions based on intentions. The reason was simple; capabilities could be pretty well measured, qualified and described while intentions were often obscure, vague, and highly contentious. In the Vietnam war, with its strong ideological context enemy capabilities more often than not did not indicate the probability of attack and therefore did not protect against surprise. Political dictates usually overrode military common sense and Communists units were often tasked to launch attacks for political gain without having the required capabilities to execute such attacks successfully. "Suicide" was the usual term used to describe surprise attacks; we learned that suicide was one of the enemy's capabilities. It was apparent that intelligence estimates had to take into account both enemy capabilities and intention no matter how farfetched his intentions might be.

Intelligence estimates were sometimes erroneous because the analyst tended to see the enemy through the lens of his own culture and experience and judged the enemy's actions and behavior as if the enemy would react as he would given certain stimuli. This was a common shortcoming. Intelligence analysts were rare who could reason the way the enemy did. This at least in part accounted for the fact that RVN military intelligence establishment failed to predict the enemy attack across the DMZ in the 1972 Summer Offensive. Such an action, it was thought, would constitute such a blatant violation of the 1954 Geneva Accords that the enemy would certainly never do it, given his usually reverent remarks about the inviolability of the Accords. Similarly, few military commanders expressed concern when enemy tanks appeared in large numbers on South Vietnamese battlefields since the US and the Vietnamese Air Forces had absolute superiority in airpower and could easily cope with the new threat.

In fact, it was not easy to place ourselves in the enemy's position because our imagination, albeit aided by a thorough knowledge of the enemy, usually fell short of reality. For example, although it was common knowledge that the enemy attached importance to the defense of his bases and rural areas, we only discovered how important they were when he resolved to attack our cities at great cost, just to loosen our grip on the rural areas. To most of us it was a sobering experience that helped us learn more about the enemy.

Operational experience in South Vietnam showed that there were discrepancies between intelligence theory and practice. The discrepancy stemmed from two facts. First, Vietnamese military intelligence did not have a theory of its own. Like military doctrine in general, it was largely based on American combat intelligence theory which had been conceived for conventional war in which the enemy was always somewhere in front of us and reacted in generally predictable patterns. Vietnamese students attending intelligence courses found out that what they were taught could not be applied in totality to the local environment and the conditions of the war. Our tactical commanders acquired the practice of responding only to simplified, condensed pieces of intelligence. They were interested only in short, clear-cut answers to their queries about the enemy for example, what was he going to do, when and where? Seldom did they ask for more, such as how and why? It was almost a certainty that any intelligence estimate that was written according to prescribed staff procedures and format would be automatically disregarded for the simple reason that it was too long to read. Vietnamese tactical commanders rarely took any interest in documents having more than two pages. The gap between intelligence theory and practice, therefore, should have been reduced in the sense that for any theory to be useful, it should reflect realities and be more realistically adaptable to practice.

Intelligence in Vietnam was truly a complex business because the war itself was complex. It was at the same time a war of ideologies, a civil war between the North and the South, and a war that was half conventional, half unconventional, and finally totally conventional at the end. Furthermore it was a proving ground for strategies, tactics, and the modern weapon systems of two great contending world blocs.

Intelligence in Vietnam had its share of failures and successes. During the early period of the war, it was plagued by instability, dilution of effort and a lack of professionalism. With the advent of cooperation and coordination with US forces, however, it gradually improved and really attained solid ground after 1968. From that time on, its activities were crowned with successes on a professional point of view. But its successes could have been more substantial if intelligence had been given its justified status and most importantly, if its capabilities had been employed more impartially, objectively, and in a more disinterested manner. Intelligence could have reaped more successes if the political system to which it responded could have rallied more popular support and consequently obtained more contributions towards intelligence activities from people in all walks of life. Such assistance to one's own armed forces after all, was nothing more than a civil obligation which, like paying taxes, was perhaps not pleasant, but nonetheless was vital to the existence of the nation.

These conclusions on intelligence in Vietnam are not intended to advance any innovative ideas. They are rather an attempt to summarize what actually took place in intelligence activities there during the war. What we experienced there and the lessons we learned from our experiences, although set in perhaps the most complex environment in which any war was ever fought, were not greatly different from what others have experienced and learned in other conflicts. In fact, throughout there was a thread of sameness, of timelessness in the fundamental principles that have for ages been the foundation of successful intelligence practice. There needs to be simplicity of organization; unity of effort; careful delineation of interests and authority; free lateral exchange of information among agencies; comprehensive coverage of all categories of useful information and sources; clear definition of intelligence priorities; unity of command and recognition that intelligence is a command responsibility; finished intelligence rather than raw information flowing to the decision makers; appropriate high status accorded to intelligence among the other military arts and activities, and this high status must be recognized in the military budget; specific efforts to pass essential information about the enemy to the troops who do the fighting; an appreciation of the importance of learning the enemy's intention and of correctly interpreting intelligence concerning them; a theory of intelligence that fits the situation faced by the commanders and intelligence professionals who use it; and finally, any nation fighting for its existence must make every effort to mobilize its entire population in support of its armed forces, and this support must include intelligence. If it does, the reward could be immeasurable in terms of frustrating the enemy's intelligence and tactical operations as well as providing to the nation's armed forces a vast resource of information concerning enemy activities.

Glossary

ACOFS	Assistant Chief of Staff
AK-47	Russian designed assault rifle, 7.62-mm
ARDF	Airborne radar detection finding
ASA	Army Security Agency
A-2	Assistant chief of staff for military intelligence Air Force
BDA	Bomb damage assessment
CDEC	Combined Document Exploitation Center
CI	Counter Intelligence
CICV	Combined Intelligence Center Vietnam
CIO	Central Intelligence Office
CINCPAC	Commander in Chief Pacific
CMEC	Combined Materiel Exploitation Center
CMIC	Combined Military Interrogation Center
COMINT	Communication Intelligence
COSVN	Central Office of South Vietnam
CRA	Central Research Agency
DAO	Defense Attache Office
DAME	Defense against Method of Entry
DASE	Defense against Sound Equipment
DIA	Defense Intelligence Agency
DIOCC	District Intelligence Operation Coordination Center
DMZ	Demilitarized Zone
EEI	Essential Elements of Information
FFP	Field Force Police

FWMAF	Free World Military Assistance Forces
G-2	Assistant Chief of Staff for Military Intelligence Corps and Division level
HOPIRS	Hot and Immediate Photo Interpretation Reports
HUMINT	Human Intelligence
ICD	Imitation Communication Deceptive
IDHS	Intelligence Data Handling System
II	Imagery Interpretation
IIR	Intelligence Information Report
IPIRS	Immediate Photo Interpretation Read Out
JGS	Joint General Staff
J-2	Assistant Chief of Staff for Military Intelligence
J-7	Assistant Chief of Staff for Signal Intelligence
LOB	Lines of Bearing
MACV	Military Assistance Command Vietnam
MAP	Military Assistance Program
MI	Military Intelligence
MIA	Military Intelligence Agency
MIBARS	Military Intelligence Battalion
MID	Military Intelligence Detachment
MPD	Man Pack Personnel Detectors
MSD	Military Security Department (also MSS)
NICC	National Intelligence Coordination Committee
NILOS	Naval Intelligence Liaison Officer
NOFORN	No Foreign
NP	National Police
NSA	National Security Agency
NVA	North Vietnamese Army
N-2	Assistant Chief of Staff for Military Intelligence Navy
OB	Order of Battle
OSA	Office of the Special Assistant to the Ambassador
PF	Popular Forces

PHOTINT	Photo Intelligence
PIOCC	Province Intelligence Operation Coordination Center
POW	Prisoner of War
PRU	Provincial Reconnaissance Unit
PSDF	People Self Defense Forces
RF	Regional Forces
RVN	Republic of Vietnam
RVNAF	Republic of Vietnam Armed Forces
SA-7	Russian Heat-Seeking Rocket
SIGINT	Signal Intelligence
SLAR	Side Looking Airborne Radar
SPARS	Significant Problem Areas Report
STRATDET	Strategic Technical Detachment
SUPIR	Supplemental Photo Interpretation Report
S-2	Officer in charge of the Military Intelligence Section of Regiment or smaller unit, Sector and Sub-Sector level
TR	Technical Reconnaissance
TRAC	Target Research and Analysis Center
TRIM	Training Relation and Instruction Mission
T-34	Russian tank
T-54	Russian tank
T-59	Chinese copied T-54 Russian tank
T-60	Russian medium tank
USAAG	United States Army Support Activities Group
VC	Viet Cong
VCI	Viet Cong Infrastructure
VNSF	Vietnam Special Forces